THE THEATER OF HIS GLORY

Jon Balserak

THE THEATER OF HIS GLORY

Nature and the Natural Order in the Thought of John Calvin

SUSAN E. SCHREINER

Foreword by Richard A. Muller

BakerBooks

A Division of Baker Book House Co
Grand Rapids, Michigan 49516

Allan + Pior
Christa
Princeton
Jo
candles

Clothbound edition published 1991 by The Labyrinth Press

Paperback edition published 1995 by Baker Books
a division of Baker Book House Company
P.O. Box 6287, Grand Rapids, Michigan 49516-6287

Printed in the United States of America

Library of Congress Cataloging-in-Publication Data on file in Washington D.C. under the original publisher.

ISBN 0-8010-2004-2 (pbk.)

To my Mother and Father

TABLE OF CONTENTS

FOREWORD

With the exception of Richard Stauffer's *Dieu, la création et la Providence dans la prédication de Calvin* (1978) Calvin's thoughts on the natural order have not been the subject of an extended study until the appearance of Schreiner's *Theater of His Glory*. Moreover, Professor Schreiner's work examines not only the important discussions of creation and providence in Calvin's sermons but also the numerous passages in Calvin's commentaries that touch on these topics, together with the relevant sections of the *Institutes*. Her work evidences a sound understanding of the history of doctrine, a clear grasp of the medieval and the sixteenth-century background of Calvin's thought, and a refined approach to the issue of Calvin's place in the history of doctrine and exegesis.

In her first chapter, Schreiner offers a carefully balanced analysis of the relationship between Calvin's emphasis on the immediate and sovereign activity of God and his view of secondary causality, against the historical background and "polemical context" (p. 16) of Calvin's thought. It is, of course, an example of what one might call the residual Aristotelianism in Calvin's thought that, despite his stated distaste for Aristotle, he frequently had recourse to the concept of a fourfold (i.e., first, formal, material, and final) causality. Schreiner makes clear that Calvin developed his view of providence in such a way as to deemphasize the formal and material, or secondary, causality without undercutting his own insistence against the Libertines that nature and human beings have a certain independence and, in the case of the latter, responsibility. In this chapter Schreiner also offers a finely nuanced reading of Calvin's admiration for certain aspects of Stoicism, in the context of his debate with the naturalistic Stoicism of the sixteenth century.

The next three chapters present a view of Calvin's approach to spiritual beings in the natural order—angels and humans. It must be noted that virtually no previous work on Calvin has offered an extended discussion of his views on angels. Schreiner provides an entire chapter and, contrary to what might have been expected given the silence of the previous scholarship, shows that Calvin had a significant, albeit characteristically nonspeculative, doctrine of the function of angels in the providential protection of God's people. In her chapter on human nature, Schreiner sheds the dubious legacy of the Barth-Brunner debate and judiciously places Calvin's thought in the context of late medieval and early

Reformation theology. She indicates Calvin's adherence to a profoundly Augustinian sense of human fallenness and inability in sin, but recognizes his commitment to a view of fallen human beings as capable of reasoning, as capable of learning from "the common light of nature," and even of aspiring toward the truth, however haltingly and faultily (p. 71). By extension, in contrast to the claims of Barthian scholarship, Schreiner's understanding of Calvin's approach to the natural order, human nature, and "natural" knowledge points toward a logical as well as temporal priority of nature over grace. Nature is the theater of divine activity, created good and indicative of divinely given order over both the problematic character of fallen nature and over the divine regenerative work.

A subsequent chapter builds on these findings in a discussion of human beings in society. Both here and in her final chapter on the restoration of creation, Schreiner convincingly demonstrates not only the positive relation of natural law theory to Calvin's thought but also, and perhaps more significantly, the emphasis placed by Calvin both on the problem of sin and its resultant disorder and on the divine solution and the reestablishment of order in the world. This ordering activity is seen in the restraining of wild beasts by a fear of human beings and in the parallel restraining of human beings by a fear of rulers. It is also seen in the restoration of human nature and of the created order through the redemptive process. Indeed, as Schreiner demonstrates, Calvin's assumption that the world order will be renewed and reconstituted rather than annihilated and replaced parallels his approach to the redemption of human beings. Calvin speaks frequently of the growth and advance of humans in their relationship to God in Christ. But he also indicates that the course of history bears witness to the reestablishment of order in society through the work of Christ, and that the natural order also experienced a reordering in Christ, though in individual people and in society it is incomplete prior to the second coming.

In sum, this is a very significant work that carefully assesses the contributions and the deficiencies of previous scholarship and that offers a little-seen portrait of Calvin's thoughts on the natural order and its operation. In particular, by examining Calvin's views on nature and the natural order—from creation, through history, to the eschaton—Schreiner sheds new light on a positive approach to nature that may well pervade Calvin's thought. The underlying theme, reflected in the title, that the natural order is the "theater" of God's glory is played out in a detailed examination of Calvin's works accompanied by a firm grasp both of the classical and medieval background and of sixteenth-century debate.

Richard A. Muller
Calvin Theological Seminary

ACKNOWLEDGMENTS

This book is a revised version of my dissertation directed by Dr. David C. Steinmetz at Duke University. Several areas have been expanded and reworked. Historical background has been added, not to establish historical influence but to provide comparison between Calvin and the preceding Christian tradition. The chapter on providence now includes an extended discussion of the history of cosmology. The chapter on angels now recognizes more clearly the importance of angels in Calvin's understanding of providence and history. And finally, the polemical aspects of Calvin's various discussions about the created order are explained more fully.

Since this work grew out of my dissertation, I owe a primary debt of gratitude to my doctoral committee: Drs. David Steinmetz, Edward Mahoney, Robert Gregg, Kalman Bland, and Arthur Ferguson. Donn Michael Farris, head librarian at Duke Divinity School, generously made the resources of that excellent library available to me. I would also like to thank several friends and readers who offered support and made critical suggestions: Richard Muller, Patricia Poteat, Gregory Robbins, Conrad Fulkerson, and Rick and Jill Edens. I am also indebted to Debra Weiner for her careful and thoughtful editorial suggestions and to J. Samuel Hammond for preparation of the index. The remaining weaknesses and errors in this volume are, of course, my own.

INTRODUCTION

According to the "orthodox" Christian tradition, God brought into being an "order of creation." Encompassed in this created order were the angels, the human soul and body, the cosmos, and natural law. All of these orders or natures stood under the guidance of God's sustaining and directing providence. In their interpretations of Genesis and Romans, Christian exegetes explained that some parts of this natural order were corrupted in the fall. Some of the angelic creation followed the fallen angel Lucifer. Adam's sin destroyed the supernatural gifts and corrupted the natural gifts of the soul. The cosmos now suffers decay and groans under the burden of corruption. In the Augustinian tradition, government was instituted by God after the fall to restrain sin and to govern fallen human relations. It then, however, became a part of that created order maintained by God. Nonetheless, the order of creation survived. It was of theological significance that the sun still shone, the stars revolved, and the crops still grew. The unfallen angels continued to sing God's praises and to help govern a now fallen and blood-ridden history. The human conscience still distinguished right from wrong and recognized the necessity for law. The angels, the elect, and the cosmos now await redemption. The creation, therefore, remained intact and continued to be the object of God's care.

Consequently, the subject of creation has been an enduring theological locus throughout the tradition of the church. Often it was a polemical one. The early Fathers defended the doctrine of *creatio ex nihilo* against the Greek doctrines of emanationism and the eternity of the world. Against the dualism of the Gnostics they identified the Creator of the Old Testament with the Redeemer. In opposition to the dualism of the Manichees, Augustine sought a literal interpretation of Genesis that protected God from change, affirmed the reality of creation and of biblical history, and defined a proper love of the created realm. Despite the appeal of asceticism within early Christianity, in these arguments the church defended the fundamental goodness of creation. Dualistic heresies, however, did not cease to trouble the church. In the twelfth century Innocent III combated the heresy of the Cathari that relegated the material world to Satan. The thirteenth century confronted new problems as theologians defended the orthodox views of creation, immortality, and providence against the inroads of radical Aristotelianism. In these and many other disputes the church repeatedly maintained the doctrines of *creatio ex nihilo*, the immortality of the soul, God's knowledge of singulars, the goodness of creation, and the reality of providence in the sublunar realm.

In the sixteenth century the doctrine of creation was not the point of controversy between Catholics and Protestants. Their central debates concerned justification, the Eucharist, authority, the interpretation of Scripture, and the certainty of salvation. Presuppositions about creation emerge more clearly, however, in debates among Lutheran, Calvinist, Zwinglian, and Radical Reformers. Assumptions about the mode of the divine presence in the world, the nature of the soul, and the character of God's providence can be detected in discussions about the Eucharist, the accessibility of God in the natural order,[1] immortality, and the relationship between the church and the world.

Moreover, the subject of creation remained a theological locus of discussion independent of debate and polemic. Sixteenth-century theologians inherited long traditions about the created order and articulated theological views of creation. Therefore, exegetical and systematic writings include discussions about angels, providence, nature, government, the soul, natural reason, and natural law. The views of creation in the sixteenth century and their influence in Catholic and Protestant doctrines are beyond the scope of this work but such a book needs to be written.

Perspective of This Study

This book attempts to make a contribution to the study of creation in the sixteenth century by examining Calvin's understanding of nature and the natural order. In so doing I will deal with several issues which have been studied independently in Calvin's thought, including debates about natural theology, natural law, and common grace. While treating these and other topics, I will seek to articulate Calvin's overall view of creation and to determine the fundamental recurring themes that continually resurface in his writings and make his understanding of creation a coherent whole.

It is customary for scholars to study Calvin's thought in comparison to his fellow reformers. This useful pursuit is not, however, the main focus of this work. Although relevant comparisons with other reformers are presented, I have approached Calvin's treatment of creation themes primarily from the perspective of the ancient and medieval traditions. The first four chapters begin with brief, and no doubt oversimplified, sketches that illustrate the ways in which previous thinkers discussed these subjects. In some cases, such as the subjects of immortality and providence, earlier debates are reflected in Calvin's polemics. However, my main concern is not to draw lines of influence or to argue that Calvin derived a particular argument from a certain author. The purpose of these historical contexts is to determine which traditional questions and positions Calvin repeated, discussed, ignored, or rejected.

Such a general comparison will show that Calvin stood in a line of continuity with the past teachings of the church. He too taught the doctrines of *creatio ex nihilo*, the direct and mediate providence of God over nature and history, the goodness of creation, the revelatory function of nature, and the redemption of the cosmos. As Richard Stauffer's important work has demonstrated, many of these doctrines find expression in Calvin's sermons.[2] Often he discussed these teachings in a polemical context. In Calvin's view, many of the traditional doctrines of creation were threatened in the sixteenth century by the Anabaptists, the Libertines, and the Italian and French rationalists.

While he presupposed and used traditional Christian doctrines, Calvin's thought is characterized by his own particular emphases. Central to all his discussions about creation is the concept of order. Ever since the work of Joseph Bohatec, Calvin scholars have recognized the "passion for order" in the Reformer's thought. Bohatec concentrated on Calvin's "Pathos der Ordnung" in his treatment of law, society, and the state. According to Bohatec, organic thinking was fundamental to Calvin's thought. As a result, his discussions of society, natural law, and the state reflected his desire for unity, harmony, and order as well as his fear of disorder.[3] Scholars such as Wallace and Richard have analyzed the concept of order in Calvin's spirituality: the renewal of the *imago Dei* is the restoration of order in the human soul.[4] According to Milner, the idea of order governed Calvin's ecclesiology. Milner argued that the unifying principle of Calvin's thought is the "absolute correlation between the Spirit and the Word and the contingent correlation of the Spirit and the diverse manifestations of the Word."[5] These manifestations are the *ordinationes Dei*, including the church which works to restore order in the historical realm.

This study argues that the motivating principle of this quest for order is to be discerned in Calvin's view of providence. Calvin sensed that the foundations of the late "medieval" world had crumbled. The portals of change had been opened and threatened to sweep everything away. In the face of such chaos, Calvin encouraged his audience to hold to the Word of God. That Word, which had caused the morning stars to sing together and the sons of God to shout for joy (Job 38:7) was, he believed, able to call light out of the darkness that was the sixteenth century; hence his interest in grounding the events of his age in a doctrine of God's providence active in the created order.

Armed with his belief in providence, Calvin interpreted the cosmic and societal realms. He assumed that these spheres of reality did not contain within themselves an inherent element of stability or order. Their continued ordered existence, especially after the fall, depends on the constant sustaining and restraining providence of God which prevents them from falling into chaos. Related to this central subject of order in Calvin's doctrine of creation are several recurring themes: the faithfulness of God to creation, the belief that creation is the stage for God's activity, the revelatory function of nature, the survival of human nature after the fall, the preservation of societal life, and the redemption of the cosmos.

In the course of his exegetical and polemical writings, Calvin's treatment of these themes underwent considerable development. This is clear from the fact that creation themes gained increased attention in his commentaries and the different editions of the *Institutes*. To my knowledge, however, Calvin's development did not cause him to recant earlier statements on creation but, rather, to emphasize the instability of nature, the immortality of the soul, the role of the conscience and natural reason, the function of natural law, the instrumentality of angels, and the necessity for a strong doctrine of providence. We can illustrate this increase in emphasis by tracing the references in Calvin's writings to creation themes in three areas: the cosmos as a reflection of God's glory; the discussions of natural law and society; and the belief in God's active providence.

Descriptions of the cosmos as a reflection of God's wisdom, power, goodness, and providence date from Calvin's early thought. The preface to Olivétan's translation of the Bible, published in 1535, describes his belief that all the beauties of creation are a divine revelation of the nature of God.[6] Descriptions of nature reappear in the 1539 edition of the *Institutes*, where Calvin explained that the thunder, lightning, sea, and earth cannot profit us without the instruction of Scripture.[7] Calvin continued to discuss the nature imagery of the Bible in his commentaries and sermons on Job, Isaiah, and the Psalms. His reflections on the creation themes found in these books bore fruit in the 1559 *Institutes*. Repeatedly he drew upon Psalm 104 to show that the world reflected God's glory. Both the Psalms and Isaiah were cited to show that divine providence directed all particular natural and historical events. Finally, his interpretation of Job, namely, that God's will and providence often transcends reason and empirical evidence, recurs in his 1559 exposition on providence.[8]

The continual restatement of an earlier belief can also be discerned in Calvin's discussions of natural law and societal life. The commentary on Seneca's *De clementia* included several discussions in which Calvin described man as a social animal, defined the state as an assembly of men associated by law, appealed to natural equity and those natural properties which are "according to nature."[9] The 1536 edition of the *Institutes* contained extensive discussions of the necessity for government and laws, as well as the assumption that dictates of the conscience and natural law were impressed in the hearts of all people.[10] In both the 1536 and 1539 editions Calvin expressed the traditional principle that the written law teaches what is now obscure in the conscience or the natural law.[11] This principle passed unchanged into the later editions of the *Institutes* as well as into his commentaries on Romans and the Pentateuch.[12] The latter, as well as the sermons on Deuteronomy, show that Calvin frequently drew on the "dictates of nature" to present his views on property, law, government, and morality.

A third example of the unfolding of a principle can be seen in Calvin's statements about providence. Calvin's concern to defend God's direct providence was expressed in his commentary on Seneca's *De clementia*, where he attacked the Epicurean philosophy which portrayed God as idle and unconcerned about human affairs.[13] This concern appears in succinct form in the 1536 *Institutes* where he attacked the "Sophists" against whom he argued: "But when we call him [God] almighty and the creator of all things, we must ponder such omnipotence whereby he works all things in all and such providence whereby he regulates all things—not the sort the Sophists fancy: empty, separate, and idle."[14] The 1539 edition contains a continuation and enlargement of this same principle. Here Calvin directed his polemic against the "Epicureans" who claimed that God was idle and the "Stoics" who believed in fate.[15] Finally, the 1559 edition of the *Institutes* included the fullest exposition on providence and the most extended polemics against these misconceptions.[16]

To a large extent, the insertion of creation themes into later editions of the *Institutes* reflects Calvin's controversies with various groups. In his battle against resurgent Epicureanism, Stoicism, and Aristotelianism, Calvin clarified his views on providence and secondary causality. In his opposition to the Anabaptists, Libertines, and rationalists,[17] Calvin defended the Christian belief in immortality and distinguished it from a false view of deification. In the 1543 edition of the *Institutes* Calvin added a section on the angels and demons and defended their existence with arguments he was soon to elaborate in his tract against the Libertines. His controversy with the Anabaptists forced Calvin to articulate further his own view of God's revelation in history and the relationship of the church to the world. Throughout these debates his exegetical work was crucial, especially his commentaries and sermons on Genesis, Isaiah, Job, and the Psalms. The creation passages in these books led him to expound both providential and cosmological themes. Throughout his writings, therefore, Calvin fleshed out his understanding of creation. Although his thought did not change in any radical way, it deepened.

In all of these writings Calvin taught that God's glory extended beyond the fate of the individual soul and encompassed the whole of creation: "For our salvation was a matter of concern to God in such a way that, not forgetful of himself, he kept his glory primarily in view, and therefore, created the whole world for this end, that it may be a theater of his glory."[18] In Calvin's understanding, sin neither annihilated the natural realm nor thwarted God's purpose in creation. Divine immutability guarantees that the original purpose of creation is irrevocable; the natural order remains the subject of God's preservation, a reflection of his glory, and the object of restoration. According to Calvin the immutability of election finds its parallel in God's faithfulness toward the preservation and restoration of creation. Therefore, not only does God save the elect but he maintains the integrity of nature, governs the cosmos and history, and reclaims the "works of his hands." For Calvin, believers are actively involved in God's purpose for creation; they too govern society, build up the church, contemplate nature, and restore societal order. All of these activities take place under the direct guidance of divine providence, the subject to which we turn first.

I

PROVIDENCE: THE PROSCENIUM ARCH

Scholars have long recognized the importance of Calvin's doctrine of providence. However, prior to Bohatec's essay, "Calvins Vorsehungslehre," historians such as Schweizer, Scheibe, Ritschl, and Seeberg had analyzed the idea of providence primarily in terms of its place in Calvin's system.[1] Bohatec approached providence independently of Calvin's other doctrines. His essay examines the sources, background, and "character" of providence, especially in terms of issues such as determinism and the purposefulness of God's governance. In the end, however, Bohatec concluded that predestination was in fact Calvin's central doctrine but not as a dogmatic starting point. Providence, he argued, is the foundational or "root doctrine," [*Stammlehre*] because in it one finds the presuppositions of predestination, Law, the work of Christ, and the means of grace.[2]

Today Calvin scholars are more wary about identifying the "central doctrine" in Calvin's theology. Nonetheless, in the course of this study we will see that providence is indeed a *Stammlehre* or, rather, a "proscenium arch." But we will examine providence as a foundational doctrine not in terms of predestination or the work of Christ, but in terms of creation. The created order functions in Calvin's thought as the theater of God's glory, the arena of divine reflection and action. Providence frames that stage. Articulated in Calvin's doctrine of providence are all those themes that govern his view of creation: the passion for order, the horror of chaos, the power and sovereignty of God, and the faithfulness of God to his creation.

The idea of providence gained increasing importance in the Reformer's thought. We find its earliest expression in the *Commentary on Seneca's "De clementia."* The 1536 *Institutes* mentions providence only sporadically and combines it with the doctrine of predestination. Between 1539 and 1559 Calvin developed his understanding of divine governance in nature and history. As the following analysis will show, Calvin developed his view of providence in a polemical context: against the Libertines, astrologers, Stoics, and Epicureans. Two exegetical works were also crucial; namely, the Commentary on the Psalms and the sermons on Job. Finally, in the 1559 *Institutes* providence is separated from predestination and finds full expression as a part of the knowlege of God the Creator.

As a sixteenth-century theologian, Calvin inherited a long tradition regarding the doctrines of creation and providence. In the early church these were not controversial beliefs. However, they were gradually defined and defended in reaction to challenges posed by non-Christian philosophies, primarily the Greek doctrines of eternity of the world, the dualism of Gnosticism, and the later reintroduction of Aristotelianism into the West by the Averroists. We will discuss briefly the main developments of these disputes in order to see which elements Calvin reflected. We limit ourselves primarily to Irenaeus, Chrysostom, Augustine, Thomas Aquinas, and the reaction of the Nominalists.

1. HISTORICAL BACKGROUND

In his attempts to establish the superiority of the Christian doctrine of creation over the myths of the Olympian tradition, Theophilus of Antioch was one of the first church fathers to argue clearly that creation was *ex nihilo*.[3] Opposing Greek ideas about the eternity of the world, he used the idea of *creatio ex nihilo* as proof for the dependency of the world on God. Arguments against Greek beliefs in the eternity of the world became a common part of the patristic apologetic tradition, as can be seen in the writings of Origen, Diodore of Tarsus, Lactantius, and Basil.[4]

However, early Christian thinkers established not only the reality of creation against Greek arguments for the eternity of the world, but also combated the Gnostic belief that the created order was the work of an evil or ignorant Demiurge who stood in opposition to the God of Light. In combating Gnosticism, theologians such as Irenaeus defended the unity of God, the goodness of creation, and the full reality of God's historical providence.

Against the Gnostic separation of the Creator from the Redeemer, Irenaeus argued for the unity of the one God who both creates and redeems. Basing his arguments on the Prologue to John's Gospel, Irenaeus insisted that "there is only one God who made all things by his Word."[5] The phrase "all things" in John 1:4, Irenaeus contended, refers not to the Gnostic Pleroma but to the physical, temporal, or historical realm.[6] This world, Irenaeus maintained, is good and the work of the good Creator God.

Irenaeus' emphasis on the unity of God and the goodness of creation led him to depict salvation as God's reclaiming or redeeming of creation. Having lost the *imago Dei*, the human being (who stands at the head of creation) now lies under Satan's unjust tyranny. Through the blood of Christ, God is now reclaiming the image and bestowing the gifts of incorruption on the human race.[7]

According to Irenaeus, however, God reclaims not only the human being but all of creation. In order to maintain this all-encompassing nature of God's salvation, he defended the Old Testament against Gnostic attacks that it referred only to the lower Creator god. In his defense of the Old Testament, Irenaeus employed traditional arguments of typology and prophecy: figures and events of the Old Covenant prophesied and were providentially guided by God as they pointed to the New Testament.[8] The only difference between the Testaments was based on different dispensations, established by God. In his view of the Old Testament as the realm of God's creative and salvific work, Irenaeus depicted the vast, all-encompassing unity of the divine plan which extended from creation to the second coming. He therefore articulated a view of providence which depended on the continuity between creation and redemption.

Irenaeus' doctrine of recapitulation most forcefully expressed this belief in the historical continuity of God's work. In Irenaeus' theology, God came not to an "alien" world in order to rescue elect souls; rather, the Lord came to redeem his own creation.[9] God's intervention in history reversed the fall and renewed the original creation. Irenaeus believed that both human and cosmic realms would be restored to their pristine state: "Neither the substance nor the essence of the created order vanishes, for he is true and faithful who establishes it. But the pattern of this world passes away, that is, the things in which the transgressions took place, since in them man has grown old."[10] For Irenaeus, the physical restoration of the cosmos in the millennium functioned as a vindication of the temporal-material creation. Although the church became wary of the millenarianism advocated by Irenaeus, nonetheless, his defense of creation and providence became an integral part of the Christian tradition. In the course of this study we will see that Calvin's theology distinctly echoes the thinking of Irenaeus.

After Irenaeus, the most extensive treatment of providence was by John Chrysostom. Chrysostom was primarily interested in defending providence in the face of suffering, particularly the suffering of the church. Although his views of providence and suffering are found throughout his writings, we limit our analysis to two treatises, "Ad eos qui scandalizati sunt" and "Ad Stagirium a daemone vexatum."[11]

In his letter "To those who are scandalized," Chrysostom argued that the wonders of nature proved the existence of divine providence. He never tired of extolling the order, harmony, beauty, and usefulness of nature as proof that it was governed by the hand of God. The stars amazed him; their clarity, diversity, and usefulness in guiding sailors prove that they stand under the providence of God.[12] The revolutions of the seasons and the rotation of the heavens reflect God's glory. For Chrysostom, the winds, sea, plants, herbs, animals, mountains, valleys, and trees all mirror the goodness and the "infinite providence" of their Creator.[13] In Chrysostom's view, God governs each individual creature; the world could not exist for a moment without God's continual sustaining and directing providence. To Chrysostom, then, the world evidences not only God's general care but the continuity of God's creative action in providence.[14]

Although the harmonious and beautiful order of nature reflects divine providence, nonetheless, Chrysostom warned, the historical order does not so easily prove the reality of God's governance.[15] When one looks out at historical events some people are "scandalized." The just suffer tribulations and injustices while the wicked often prosper. It was the scandalous nature of history that caused Chrysostom to defend providence to Stagirius and to those disturbed by the sufferings endured by believers, both throughout the Bible and at the present time.

Chrysostom offered basically two arguments in defense of providence. The first might be called his "theology of suffering." Repeatedly he insisted on the moral usefulness of suffering and temptation. He explained to Stagirius that even the assaults of demons could be the occasion for spiritual progress.[16] Abraham, Joseph, St. Paul, and above all, Job are all examples of men who made spiritual progress by means of suffering.[17] According to Chrysostom, the suffering of the church paralleled the suffering of these men.[18] Through suffering Christians render glory to God, discern true from false believers, and attain to eternal life. Finally, Chrysostom also argued that the just will be rewarded in the afterlife and the wicked, who fail to use suffering as a means of conversion, will be punished in the life to come.

Chrysostom further defended providence by his insistence on the incomprehensibility of God. We are incapable of understanding God's particular purposes or designs within the historical realm.[19] God, Chrysostom wrote, is too high, too distant, too infinite, and his purposes are impenetrable to human reason.[20] Even the angels cannot penetrate the "ineffable providence of God which is without limit and is unfathomable."[21] Before the inscrutability of divine providence, all beings must restrain themselves from curious questions and from trying to find the causes of human events. Chrysostom believed that such restraint would preserve believers in faith and trust so that they would respect the infinite distance between God and creation. As Chrysostom argued, we see now only in a mirror dimly and from a distance; in the afterlife we will finally understand God's ways and see "face to face."[22] Therefore, Chrysostom explained, "it is necessary to believe that the revelation which comes from God is more trustworthy than that which one sees with his eyes."[23] In Chrysostom's theology the proper response to the "scandal of history" is Romans 11:33: "Oh the depths and the riches of the wisdom and knowledge of God. How unsearchable are his judgments and how inscrutable are his ways!"[24]

St. Augustine also struggled to give full expression to the Christian doctrines of creation and providence. Throughout his life, he tried to find a literal interpretation of Genesis 1–3 which would protect the immutable nature of God and the reality and goodness of creation. He succeeded with his treatise *De Genesis ad litteram*.[25]

From his earliest commentary on Genesis, *De Genesi contra Manichaeos*, Augustine had to confront that age-old question, posed now by the Manichees: "What was God doing before he created the world?" In the Literal Commentary Augustine answered this taunt by combining three biblical passages: (1) Genesis 1:1–2:3 which implied temporal succession; (2) Ecclesiasticus 18:1, which, on the basis of the Old Latin Text, Augustine read as "God who lives forever created all things at one and the same time," and (3) Genesis 2:4, "This is the book of heaven and earth. When day was made, God made heaven and earth and every green thing."

St. Augustine resolved the contradictions in these texts by distinguishing two "moments" or "aspects" of creation.[26] Genesis 1:1–2:3 describes the first aspect of creation which, according to Ecclesiasticus 18:1, was simultaneous and, therefore, nontemporal. In this "moment" of creation, God brought all things into being through the Word (identified with the phrase "in principio" of Genesis 1:1).[27] The simultaneity of this creation is also signified by the single "day" of Genesis 2:4.[28] Augustine can therefore argue, as he did in the *Confessions* and again in the *City of God*, that since time and change were created simultaneously with the world, there was no "time" before creation.[29] With his metaphysic of Being, Augustine explained that God alone truly "Is" and stands immutable above a temporal and changing universe.[30] God "preceded" creation not by time but by an eternity beyond the temporal process. The order related in Genesis 1:1–2:3 is not, according to Augustine, a temporal succession but a *connexio causarum*.[31] The "six days" were not temporal intervals but a description of angelic knowledge: "morning" refers to the knowledge of created things in the Word while "evening" signifies the knowledge of created things in themselves.[32]

According to Augustine, all plants, animals, and vegetation described in Genesis were also created simultaneously in their "causal" or "seminal reasons" that were inserted into the primal elements of the world.[33] The causal reasons, in which all things potentially existed, contained within themselves the force and laws of each creature as it would develop in its future temporal succession.[34] The theory of seminal reasons played a twofold mediatory role in Augustine's doctrine of creation: the causal reasons united the two creation stories in Genesis and connected the transcendent and natural realms of existence.

Since Augustine believed that nothing in Scripture can be superfluous or erroneous, he argued that the two creation stories taught different truths about creation. The first story, he argued, depicts the simultaneous nontemporal creation while the second story narrates the beginning of real temporal development governed by God's *administratio* or providence. Augustine also used the causal reasons to reconcile exegetically the "rest" described in Genesis 2:2–3 with the statement about God's unceasing activity in John 5:17: the former verse refers to the simultaneous creation which is now complete, while the latter describes the providence that continually rules over the development of the causal reasons in the temporal realm.[35] This exegetical maneuver allowed Augustine to move from the nontemporal to the temporal plane.[36]

With this move to the temporal realm, Augustine affirmed the contact between the transcendent and the natural. But while he zealously restricted the activity of creation to God alone, he allowed a miminal level of mediation and causality to exist between God and the world of nature and history. In Augustine's understanding of natural causality, the causal reasons play an active role, though not one independent of God. The "reasons" possess a principle of activity or dynamism so that they now develop or unfold according to their "numbers" or "laws" which were inserted into them at the beginning. In Augustine's view, the causal reasons account for the activity, rationality, stability, or order in nature.[37] Nonetheless, the creation remains continually dependent on God at every moment:

> The power, omnipotence, and all-sustaining strength of the Creator is the cause of the subsistence of every creature. And if this power were ever to cease ruling created things, their species would at once cease to be and all of nature would collapse. . . . For if God were to withdraw his rule from it, the world could not stand, even for the blink of an eye.[38]

Augustine insisted on both God's continual governance and the mediatory role of the angels when he discussed God's temporal providence. In the *De Genesi ad litteram* Augustine argued that the angels carry out God's commands in the course of history.[39] Therefore, without positing Plotinian mediators between God and the world, Augustine believed that God created and continually sustains all substances in being. However, God governs creation through the activity of creatures, the unfolding of the causes, and the ministry of the angels. With this theory, Augustine established a divine providence which operates in a linear irreversible time beginning with God's act of creation.[40] In the *City of God* Augustine, of course, traced this providence in the course of the two cities. There, as in the Literal Commentary, Augustine's God remains immutable and Genesis 1–3 becomes the literal beginning of God's providential plan in human history.

These fundamental doctrines of creation and providence were again challenged in the thirteenth century by the reintroduction of beliefs in the eternity of the world and the restriction of providence. The Averroist controversy and the rediscovery of Aristotle's writings on nature forced the Christian West to define and defend God's creation and providence over the world.

Between 1260 and 1265 a new movement developed in the Faculty of Arts at the University of Paris known today as "Latin Averroism" or "Radical Aristotelianism."[41] Siger of Brabant and Boethius of Dacia were among its leading exponents. From the commentaries by Averroes on Aristotle, the Latin Averroists derived such critical doctrines as the unicity of the intellect, the eternity of the world, the denial of free will, and the restriction of divine providence. They defended the autonomy of philosophy and argued that it was unnecessary to reconcile such beliefs with the Christian faith.

Among those who refuted these Averroistic theories were St. Bonaventure and St. Thomas Aquinas. In 1267 and 1268, Bonaventure warned against several philosophical errors.[42] According to Bonaventure the central errors were: the eternity of the world, the belief that God cannot create *ex nihilo*, the unicity of the intellect, the denial of immortality, and belief in the determination of the will by the heavenly bodies.[43] In his series of conferences known as the *Collationes in Hexaemeron* (1273) Bonaventure argued that the "errors of the philosophers" resulted from the belief that God knows only himself. According to Bonaventure, Aristotle's denial that the divine exemplars were in the First Cause led to the subsequent error that God had no knowledge of particulars. This rejection of the divine ideas resulted in a denial of divine providence over singulars since God "does not have within himself the intelligibilities of things through which he might know them."[44]

Thomas Aquinas, of course, also refuted Averroism and defended the Christian doctrines of creation and providence. In the *Summa Theologiae* Thomas argued for the Christian doctrine of *creatio ex nihilo*.[45] Thomas further argued that the creation of the world cannot be demonstrated; *creatio ex nihilo* can only be affirmed on the basis of revelation.[46]

Thomas also argued that divine providence is necessary in order to preserve the world in existence: "For the *esse* of all creaturely beings so depend upon God that they could not continue to exist even for a moment, but would fall away into nothingness unless they were sustained in existence by his power."[47] In order to explain the dependency of creation on God, Aquinas articulated the doctrine of participation and the distinction between essence and existence. Creatures, he explained, do not contain within themselves the necessary reason for their existence and, therefore, must participate in their First Cause. In his earlier work, *De potentia Dei* (1265–1266), Aquinas had written that "from that one being all other beings must necessarily proceed that are not their own being, but have being by participation." Creatures, then, possess being "from that first agent by a certain participation." That which belongs to a thing by participation, however, is not that thing's substance.[48] In his treatise *De substantiis separatis* (1271–1273) Thomas maintained that the existence of providence can be argued on the basis of this participation of being. Just as every being is derived from the first being which is its own being, so too every good is derived from the first good, which is its own goodness.[49] Consequently, the orders of individuals must be derived from the first absolute truth. Thomas concluded that since providence is the order instituted by God, divine providence must rule over all things.[50]

In the *Summa Theologiae* Thomas again demonstrated that the ontological contingency of creation required the continual providence of God in order to be upheld in being, ". . . every creature stands in relation to God as the air to the light of the sun. For as the sun is light by giving its own nature, while the air comes to be lighted by sharing in the sun's nature, so too God alone is being by his essence which is his *esse*, while every creature is being by participation, i.e. its essence is not its *esse*. This is why Augustine writes 'were God's power at any moment to leave the being he created to be ruled by it, their species would at once cease to be, and their nature would collapse . . .' "[51] Against Maimonides and the Averroists Thomas further argued that God's knowledge and providence extended to the singulars of the corruptible, sublunary realm.[52] He insisted that all things are subject to divine providence, not only in their general species but also individually: "Now the causality of God, who is the first efficient cause, covers all existing things, incorruptible and corruptible, not only their specific principles but also the source of their singularity. Hence everything that exists in any way whatsoever is bound to be directed by God to an end."[53]

Thomas also established that God has both immediate providence over all things and that God makes use of secondary causes. According to Thomas, God exercises immediate providence over all things because "his mind holds the reason for each of them, even the very least, and whatsoever causes he appoints for effects, it is he who gives them the power to produce those effects. Consequently, the whole of their design, down to every detail is anticipated in his mind."[54] By working through these causes Aquinas' God governs through intermediaries. "For God governs the lower through the higher, not from any defect of his power but from the abundance of his goodness so that the dignity of causality is communicated even to creatures."[55] Among the secondary causes which God uses in his divine providence are the human will, the celestial bodies, and the angels.

The view of the Radical Aristotelians was condemned in the Parisian condemnations of 1270 and 1277.[56] Among the propositions that were condemned, several regarded the Averroistic denial of providence. In 1270 Stephen Tempier censured the following theses: (4) that all that happens here below is subject to the necessity of the heavenly bodies; (10) that God does not know singulars; (11) that God does not know things other than himself; (12) that human acts are not governed by divine providence. Errors concerning creation *ex nihilo*, God's knowledge of particulars, and divine providence were again condemned in 1277.

In reaction to theories of determinism, late medieval nominalist thought further emphasized the contingent and dependent character of creation. Employing the common medieval distinction between the *potentia absoluta* and the *potentia ordinata*, late medieval nominalist thought stressed the freedom and omnipotence of God and the contingency of creation.[57] These terms expressed the distinction between what God could do by means of his completely sovereign and omnipotent power and what he has actually chosen to do within his creation and according to his purposes. God's absolute power is limited only to the principle of non-contradiction and not by anything external to his will. The fact that God's will is free and omnipotent renders the entire created order radically contingent; there is nothing inherently necessary about the ordained process of justification or the secondary causality found in creation. The miraculous survival of the three youths who were placed in the fire by King Nebuchadnezzar demonstrated to Pierre d'Ailly that heat does not follow from fire by any inherent necessity but by God's concurring will.[58] So too, a created habit of grace is no more inherently necessary for salvation *de potentia absoluta* than the fact that water runs downhill or that spring follows winter.[59]

However, God's freedom from and transcendence over created structures did not cause the nominalists to doubt the stability and reliability of the created ordained order. Nominalist thinkers stressed that God has promised to act in accordance with those structures established *de potentia ordinata*. According to nominalist theology, God has limited himself in his *pactum* or covenant to justify sinners in the way he has promised, and for this reason alone all sinners must be infused with the habit of grace. Although neither the natural order nor the ordained process of salvation contains any inherent necessity, God has limited himself by his commitment to these ecclesiological and natural structures. Because of God's fidelity to his covenants, nominalist theology concluded that the created order was both radically contingent and ultimately reliable.[60]

2. CALVIN ON CREATION

As did his predecessors, Calvin affirmed God's creation of the world *ex nihilo*. Calvin repeated the traditional teaching that God created the world through the Word who was begotten of the Father before all time. The world was made through the Son who upholds all things by his power.[61] According to Calvin the entire Trinity, of course, was active in the creation. In Calvin's exegesis, Genesis 1:2 means that the Spirit was necessary to sustain the undigested or unformed mass out of which God created the world. "For this doubt might occur," Calvin wrote, "how such a disorderly heap could stand, seeing that we now behold the world preserved in such order. He [Moses], therefore, asserts that this mass, however confused it might be, was rendered stable for the time by the secret efficacy of the Spirit."[62] Although he did not engage in philosophical proofs against the eternity of the world, Calvin did affirm the *creatio ex nihilo* in the context of Augustine's earlier debates. In his opening to the Genesis Commentary, Calvin defended the biblical account of creation against those who jeered at the idea that God suddenly decided to create the world after having remained inactive in heaven. Against such scoffers he cited with approval Augustine's statement that God had been preparing hell for the curious. He also generally repeated Augustine's anti-Manichaean argument that if one disputes about the time the world was created, he might as well also dispute about the particular space in which God placed the earth.[63]

But Calvin was critical of Augustine's interpretation of Genesis 1-3. He argued that Augustine mistranslated Ecclesiasticus 18:1; the Greek text cannot be used to mean "He who lived forever created all things at one and the same time."[64] Calvin saw no need to insist that the creation of the world was free of temporality; Gen. 1:5 shows "the error of those is clearly refuted who maintain that the world was made in a moment."[65] According to Calvin, God took six days to create the world because he accommodated his works to human capacity. God distributed the creation into successive portions in order to "fix our attention" and to compel us to pause and reflect on the infinite glory of God, "in order that our minds might the more easily be retained in the meditation of God's works."[66] Moreover, the fact that God created man on the "sixth day" shows his solicitude and fatherly favor "in that before he fashioned man, he prepared everything he foresaw would be useful and salutary for him."[67]

3. CALVIN'S DOCTRINE OF PROVIDENCE: THE POLEMICAL CONTEXT

When Calvin discussed the continuing *administratio* or providence of God, he confronted contemporary opponents. Crucial to understanding Calvin's view of providence is the fact that he perceived providence to be under attack in the sixteenth century. As a result, he placed his discussions in a polemical context. Since Calvin rarely mentioned any opponent by name and did not distinguish carefully among the scholastic theologians or the various strands of the Radical Reformation, attempts at identifying his opponents are often like entering a labyrinth. The following efforts to identify and characterize the objects of his attacks can rarely transcend the level of informed suggestions. Calvin's failure to identify carefully his opponent was due not only to his polemical style but also to his conviction that the various groups were guilty of common errors. In Calvin's view, both the Libertines and Stoics were guilty of tying God too close-ly to the world and they fell, therefore, into determinism. The Epicureans and the "Sophists" shared the guilt of separating God too far from his creation. However, these distinctions were fluid in Calvin's thought. For example, the atomism of Epicureanism also made nature into a god while the alleged im-moralities of the Libertines caused Calvin to label them as Epicureans. The following sections are divided, then, only according to the two general views that Calvin opposed: that which would imprison God within creation and that which would remove God from the world and place him idly in heaven.

4. THE STOIC, PANTHEISTIC, AND NATURALISTIC ERRORS

Calvin's early commentary on Seneca may be seen as part of the revival of Stoicism in the fifteenth and sixteenth centuries. The popularity of Stoicism was reflected in the wide circulation of Stoic texts and other writings citing Stoic arguments. Leontine Zanta's *La Renaissance du Stoïcisme au seizième siècle* re-mains one of the most comprehensive studies of this Stoic revival. According to Zanta, Stoicism was sympathetic to the prevailing spirit of individualism, was a reaction against Aristotle and the Scholastics, and served as a check against resurgent Epicureanism.[68] Humanist scholars were attracted to certain themes of Stoicism: the importance of man *qua* man, the love of truth, and the freedom of inquiry.[69] Moreover, the belief of such thinkers as Budé and Erasmus that profane studies were a preparation for "Christian philosophy" provided a receptivity for the Stoic views on providence and morality.[70]

The reformers also found elements of Stoicism appealing and often developed their positions in conscious recognition of certain Stoic doctrines. Zanta argued that the reformers defined their views on providence, fate, predestination, evil, and morality in explicit recognition of Stoic beliefs. On the basis of their studies of Calvin, Nuovo, Partee, and Ganoczy have supported this claim. Although the reformers were discriminating in their appropriation of Stoicism, they did appreciate its emphasis on providence and some of its teachings on morality.[71]

Calvin's relationship to the Stoics was complex; he found much to admire in their thinking, but denied their pantheism and the virtue of passionlessness.[72] However, because Stoicism affirmed the reality of providence, he recognized its philosophy to be superior to Epicureanism. "Yet those philosophers who assign the supreme authority to nature are much sounder than those who place fortune in the highest rank."[73] Nonetheless, Calvin repudiated all forms of naturalism, whether they were inspired by Stoicism or the atomism of Epicurus and Lucretius. Combating the views of such men as Dolet and Rabelais, Calvin opposed the deification of nature as an independent source of life and power. Therefore, neither Stoic nor Epicurean naturalism, popular in sixteenth-century humanism, found any support in Calvin.[74]

Moreover, although Calvin was drawn to the Stoic recognition that nature was orderly and to their belief in some all-encompassing providence, Calvin was careful to distinguish his idea of providence from Stoic determinism or fate.[75] He argued that the "Stoic" error was to substitute nature for God. The Stoics, Calvin argued, tied God too closely to the world and enclosed him within the stream of nature. They thereby confused God and nature and failed to recognize divine independence over creation. The will of God which governed all things was thereby lost in the concentration on the perpetual connection of secondary causes in the natural order.[76] Calvin argued that, unlike the Stoics, he did not "contrive a necessity out of the perpetual connection and intimately related series of causes which are contained in nature; but we make God the ruler and governor of all things."[77] Consequently, in his defense against the charge of fate or determinism, Calvin stressed God's transcendence over nature and over the realm of secondary causality.

Calvin's polemics against a determinism that failed to disassociate properly God from creation is most clear in the 1545 treatise against the Libertines.[78] The object of Calvin's attack was the Quintinist movement which was represented in France by Quintin of Hainaut whom Calvin had known in Paris. George Williams has argued that the exact relationship between the Loists and Libertines cannot be defined but that it is clear that there were similarities between the two groups. Williams has explained that the "Libertine" doctrine of the one universal spirit may stem indirectly from the Averroist view of a universal Intellect.[79] Calvin portrayed the Quintinists as holding a pantheistic view of the one divine spirit that permeates all things. This belief, he thought, led them to a deterministic understanding of divine omnipotence and providence, the result of which was to make God the author of sin and to relieve human beings of all responsibility.[80]

The treatise against the Libertines contains Calvin's strongest rebuttal of determinism and his most vigorous defense of secondary causality. In order properly to evaluate his understanding of God's providential governance of creation, we must note the context in which these statements were made. Calvin opened the discussions about providence by charging the Libertines with the belief that a single Spirit did all things in the world.[81] The implications of this view are that the human being would have no more will than a stone and that God would be the author of sin. If the divine Spirit did everything, there would be no difference between God and the devil; and, consequently, people would not try to avoid evil but like brutes would indulge their sensual appetites without discretion.[82]

Within the context of these moral concerns, Calvin defended the "fitting" consideration of divine providence. In his eyes, a proper view of divine providence acknowledges the universal operation through which God directs all creatures "according to the condition and property which he [God] gave them in forming them."[83] Calvin identified this divine direction with the "order of nature." In a statement reminiscent of his polemics against Stoicism, Calvin argued that nature was not a goddess who ruled over all things, for this governance must be reserved only to the will of God.[84] In Calvin's interpretation, Acts 17:28 must not be interpreted in a pantheistic or deterministic manner because it really means that God gives all creatures their ability and power. "Nevertheless, the universal operation does not at all hinder each creature in heaven or on earth, from having and retaining its own quality and nature, or from following its own inclination."[85]

Following this affirmation of the integrity of natural or secondary causality, Calvin returned to his main concern in this treatise: the problem of sin and moral responsibility. According to Calvin, Satan and the wicked are executors of the divine will and carry out God's purpose. But God does not use creatures in such a way that "the creatures, therefore, do nothing at all." Human beings are not rendered passive simply because they are instruments of the divine will. ". . . Satan and the wicked are not instruments of God in such a way that they do not act for themselves as well. One must not imagine that God works through an iniquitous man in the same way that he works through a stone or a tree trunk. Rather, according to the quality of nature he has given them, God makes use of them as rational creatures. When we say, therefore, that God works through the wicked this does not deny that the wicked work at the same time in their own right."[86] In the *Institutes* Calvin repeated this same argument against the Libertines. God's providence does not relieve human beings from responsibility nor does it exculpate wickedness. Here Calvin reconfirmed that divine providence employs secondary causality and that godly people must not overlook intermediary or secondary causality, for "God's providence does not always meet us in its naked form, but God in a sense, clothes it with the means employed."[87]

Against both the Stoics and the Libertines Calvin defended God's transcendence over the realm of creation and insisted that God must not be entangled in the inferior course of his works. In Calvin's view, providence must not be identified with the "stream of nature" nor with a single divine Spirit which works in all things.[88] Basically pantheistic, both groups fell into a false determinism which resulted in the doctrine of fate and the idea that human beings are not responsible for evil, since nature, God, or the Spirit effected all things. When confronted by the implications of such determinism, Calvin defended the integrity and activity of the created order which included the human will as well as the operation of secondary causes. Calvin works here with the idea of *concursus*; in his polemics against the Libertines he claimed the activity of the finite agent but insisted on the positive presence of the divine willing in all acts or events. Bohatec, Doumergue, and Strohl have all relied on such passages to refute the charge that Calvin's thought was fatalistic.[89] Their conclusions are valid insofar as they analyze the passages in which Calvin defended himself against the implications of determinism. Any acquittal of the charge of fatalism in the Reformer's thought, however, must take seriously the discussions found in the following arguments directed against the "Epicurean" error.

5. THE EPICUREAN ERROR: THE DISTANT GOD

Calvin was primarily concerned with the error of those who distanced God from the world; he referred to two types of thinkers who reflected this basic view. One group was the "Sophists" and the "Philosophers" who attributed an omnipotence to God which made him only a "general principle of confused motion." In the *Institutes* Calvin inserted an attack on the idea of God as *primum agens* who was the cause and origin of motion but that left creation to the perpetual laws of nature.[90] Such a theory posited a God who allowed all things to be borne along according to the universal law of nature. Calvin repeatedly associated this view with the identification of God as the cause of motion. "Such thinkers," he said, "attribute a governance to God, but a confused and mixed sort, as I have said, namely, one that by a general motion revolves and drives the system of the universe with its several parts but which does not specifically direct the actions of all individual creatures."[91] For Calvin, the notion of a "general" or "universal" providence led to the further error of allowing the creature to be moved contingently or of allowing human beings by free will to turn themselves in any direction.[92]

It cannot be determined exactly to whom Calvin was referring in Book

I.15.1–4 of the *Institutes*. However, Calvin scholars have made several suggestions, all of which point to late-medieval and sixteenth-century Aristotelianism.
Barth and Niesel direct the reader to several works, including Pomponazzi's
arguments and refutations in *De fato* while Partee has noted Calvin's references
to Aristotle.[93] Partee points to the commentary on Ps. 107:43 where Calvin
identified Aristotle as the head of those who tried to conceal the providence of
God by ascribing all things to secondary causality.[94]

In his research into the background of Calvin's doctrine of providence,
Bohatec argued that Calvin's statements must in part be seen against the
background of the Aristotelian influence on discussions of providence in the
Scholastic tradition.[95] Bohatec demonstrated that for the Scholastics,
providence had been a part of an Aristotelian natural philosophy and had been
concerned with the relationship between the divine regulation of the world and
the great system of cause and effect. The concept of providence had served to
explain how God as First Cause moved and influenced lower, mediate causes.

Both Bohatec and Busson have also identified the threat posed to faith by
the influence of Italian and French rationalism.[96] In his detailed analysis of this
movement in France, Busson showed that between 1529 and 1539 all of Aristotle
was published in Lyon or Paris with commentaries by Averroists from the
Paduan school. Calvin directly opposed the teachings of these Averroistic
Italians, especially with regard to the immortality of the soul and providence.[97]

Calvin's polemics against the identification of God as a source of movement, then, may be directed against the rationalist movement influenced by
Averroes. The belief that God's immediate creative and causal activity was
restricted to the production of the first separate intelligence resulted in the denial
that God knew or governed singulars and specific human action. As noted
above, the latter two propositions were condemned in 1270 and 1277.[98]

Against this equation of God and the principle of motion and the belief in
a "universal providence," Calvin argued that providence was lodged in the divine
act and due not merely to God's might but to his determination. In Calvin's
exegesis, Psalm 115:3 referred not to some general motion but to a "certain and
deliberate will."[99] Calvin emphasized the ceaseless activity of God: the Lord
does not merely watch over the order of nature which he has set in motion but
also exercises special care over each of his works.

Intimately related to Calvin's attacks on "Averroism" or Aristotelianism were
his attacks on the "Epicureans." The phenomenon of sixteenth-century Epicureanism is a complex and elusive one. Nonetheless, scholars such as Busson,
Bohatec, Lienhard, and Wirth have analyzed this complex group of dissidents.[100]

Ever since the work of Lucien Febvre, it is clear that the terms "atheist"
and "Epicurean" were polemical ones and must be understood in terms of their
sixteenth-century polemical context.[101] Rationalists who allegedly denied the
immortality of the soul were often called Epicureans. Rabelais and Dolet were
only two such targets.[102] In his treatise *De scandalis*, Calvin attacked Agrippa,

Villanovanus, Dolet, Rabelais, Deperius (Des Périers), and Antoine Govéan for their skepticism, satires, and denials of immortality.[103] Bucer referred to a "crowd of Epicureans" that plagued the city of Strassburg. In his study of Strassburg Epicureanism, Lienhard identified two general groups: those humanists who were resolutely individualistic on the religious plane and those cultivated men who rebelled against the moral rigorism imposed by Bucer. These people displayed a common mentality characterized by reserve toward dogmatic questions, opposition to civil restraint in matters of faith, and an emphasis on interior, spiritualized religion.[104]

As is evident in the publication of ancient texts about or by Epicureans, a philosophical Epicureanism also surfaced in the Reformation era. Writings by Diogenes Laertius, Cicero, and Lucretius were all published in the fifteenth and sixteenth centuries. Readers also had available patristic texts which presented and combated ancient Epicureanism, including the *Divinae Institutiones* of Lactantius. And finally, Epicureanism found expression in the attempts by Valla and Erasmus to reconcile Christianity with Epicurus.[105]

This philosophical Epicureanism was combated by the reformers. Luther, Zwingli, and Bucer all warned against the "godless" teaching of this philosophy.[106] Philosophical Epicureanism was also central to Calvin's doctrine of providence. Unlike his references to the "Sophists," at least one of Calvin's sources is easily identified as the portrayal of Epicureanism found in Cicero's *De natura deorum*. According to Cicero, the Epicureans believed that although the gods existed and were blessed, they did not create the world and they were free from the affairs of this earthly sphere. Cicero's Velleius argued that "there is no happiness save in repose. If, on the other hand, god dwells in the universe as its ruler and governor and rules the stars in their courses and the changing seasons, and all the varying sequences of nature, looking down on earth and sea and protecting the life and goods of men, then he must be involved in all kinds of troublesome and laborious affairs. But we define the happy life as peace of mind and freedom from all care."[107]

In his defense of the doctrine of creation, Calvin combated these views that depicted God as unconcerned with creation. Both the "Averroistic" identification of God with motion and the "Epicurean" denial of God's intervention in history portrayed a God who was distant from the created order. Therefore, while Calvin struggled against the Stoics to remove God from the interconnection of causes, he did not allow God to be separated from creation so that the universe was left to the rule of chance. According to Calvin, underlying the idea that God was unconcerned with creation and that nature flowed on independently of divine guidance, was a misunderstanding of both the nature of God and of creation. Calvin's preoccupation with Epicureanism reflected more than the existence of "Epicurean" groups in cities such as Strassburg. Central to Calvin's attacks is a fundamentally different view not only of providence but of the cosmos and of God. We turn first to an analysis of Calvin's cosmology.

6. THE FRAGILE AND PRECARIOUS NATURE OF THE CREATED ORDER

In agreement with the tradition of the church, Calvin argued that without the constant activity of divine providence, nature would cease to exist or, what is more uniquely Calvin's view, would disintegrate in complete "disorder" and "chaos." He also interpreted Psalm 104:29 to show that any withdrawal of God from nature would reduce the latter to nothing. From the time of its formation, creation required the power of God to uphold it in being. Such sustenance was required not only of that original chaos created by God but also of the order that the Lord established in the six days of creation. In Calvin's view, the order that God gradually brought into being out of chaos was not a stabilizing force which made nature more independent but, on the contrary, that order itself was dependent, requiring the direct, specific, and powerful providence of God.

> But if that chaos required the hidden inspiration of God lest it suddenly dissolve; how could this order, so fair and distinct, subsist by itself unless it derived strength from elsewhere? Therefore, let the Scriptures be fulfilled, "Send forth Thy Spirit, and they shall be created and Thou shalt renew the face of the earth," [Ps. 104:30] and, on the other hand, as soon as the Lord takes away his Spirit all things return to their dust and vanish away.[108]

The concept of order was central to Calvin's cosmology and, like Melanchthon, he frequently called attention to the order in creation as proof of God, creation, and providence.[109] Unlike his patristic and medieval predecessors, however, Calvin did not rely on hierarchical schemes in his understanding of order. To this writer's knowledge, Calvin did not depict God as the measure of all being, nor did he describe the natural order as a detailed hierarchical chain of being.[110] Except in his rejection of the Dionysian scheme of angelic natures, we do not even find any explicit rejection of a hierarchically ordered universe. The "ordre de nature," i.e., that order found throughout the cosmos and society, revealed to Calvin not a hierarchy but the stability, regularity, and continuity of creation.

Calvin always placed his emphasis on the inherent instability of this order. One of his recurring cosmological themes was that only a great and divine power could be responsible for the order found in nature. In passages reminiscent of Cicero, Seneca, and Chrysostom, Calvin called attention to the orderly course of the stars and heavens in order to demonstrate the presence of divine power.[111] Calvin presupposed a geocentric world view and regardless of the heated debate between Edward Rosen and Joseph Ratner, there is no real evidence that Calvin ever read Copernicus.[112] For our purpose, however, the important point is how Calvin used the traditional cosmology that he inherited to prove the necessity of providence in a dangerous universe. For example, the fact that the stars did not collide in their vast and winding courses absolutely fascinated Calvin and produced in him a spirit of awe and wonder. His descriptions of the orderly heavens presupposed that, by nature, the stars and planets would collide and create confusion; and, therefore, only God's presence could account for their regularity and harmony. The following passage is one example of Calvin's emphasis on the direct governing presence of God discerned in this preservation of order throughout the revolving heavens.

> The first part of this rule is exemplified when we reflect upon the greatness of the artificer who stationed, ordered, and put together this multitude of stars (and nothing more beautiful in appearance can be imagined), who so set and fixed some in their stations so they cannot move; who granted to others a freer course, but so they could not by straying, wander into a further space; who so adjusted the motion of all things so that the days and nights, months, years, and seasons of the year could be measured off; who also so proportioned the inequality of days which we daily observe, that no confusion occurs. It is so, too, when we observe his power in sustaining so great a mass, in governing the swiftly revolving heavenly system and the like. For these few examples make it sufficiently clear what it is to recognize God's power in the creation of the world. [113]

With these words Calvin praised the power and wisdom of God, evidenced by the fact that the great mass of the heavens is upheld by God in continual order. Commenting on Isaiah 48:13 ("And my right hand has measured [or upheld] the heavens)," Calvin wrote:

> By the word "measure" is denoted God's amazing wisdom in having equalized on all sides with exact proportion the vast extent of the heavens, so that it is neither nearer to the earth nor farther from it than is useful for preserving order, and that in this great expanse there is nothing unconnected or disfigured. If we prefer the world "upheld" this is also no uncommon praise of the wisdom and power of God, that he upholds the huge mass of the heavens in continual motion so that it neither totters nor leans more to one side than another. [114]

Calvin's discussions presupposed the fragile and insufficient character of nature. In Calvin's interpretation, Psalm 104 teaches that order is not self-subsistent but requires the immediate, continual, and powerful presence of God. However, in Calvin's thought nature was more than merely contingent and dependent; it was also precarious. By paying careful attention to his use of water imagery, the descriptions about the position of the earth, and the effect of the fall, we can see clearly the precarious aspect of creation.

Calvin drew on traditional cosmological beliefs to express God's preservation of a precarious and fragile creation. In agreement with the traditional exegesis of Genesis 1:9, Calvin argues that water is a circular element, lighter than the earth and heavier than the air. As did former exegetes, [115] Calvin then asked why the waters do not overflow and cover the earth.

Although writers offered different solutions to this problem, Calvin's answer was reminiscent of thinkers such as William of Auvergne who, in his interpretation of Genesis, argued that the commandment or word of God keeps the waters in their place. By nature, he insisted, the waters should cover the earth. The existence of dry land is evidence of a permanent miracle by God.[116] Throughout his commentary on Job, Thomas Aquinas also argued that the waters, according to nature, ought to cover the earth. The fact that some land is dry is due to the power of God and to his plan to make room for plants, animals, and humans.[117] To thinkers such as Giles of Rome, this appeal to the miracle or power of God was insufficient. Nonetheless, it continued, in various forms, to find support. Nicholas of Lyra, for example, argued that by his power God hollowed out the earth so that its concavities would receive parts of the water in order that human and animals might have a place to live.[118]

Calvin too relied on the miraculous power of God to explain why the waters do not cover the earth. He also believed that in order to make room for animals and human society, God's power must keep the waters from overflowing the earth. Calvin emphasized the divine restraint imposed by God to keep the waters in their bounds. The following quotation from his commentary on Jeremiah 5:22 recalls the turbulent sea of Genesis 1:2, the belief that creation came about in the midst of a chaotic sea and was therefore surrounded by water (Gen. 1:6–7; Prov. 8:27–29), as well as the belief that the sea must obey the Lord (Psalm 65:7, 89:9, 114:3). Combining the biblical imagery with his cosmology, Calvin explained that, by nature, water should overwhelm the earth, making the planet uninhabitable by the human race.

> . . . for there is nothing more terrible than a tempestuous sea. It appears as if it would overwhelm the whole world when its waves swell with so much violence. . . . But the sea itself, which strikes terror into all, even the most constant, quietly obeys God, for however furious may be its tossings, they are yet restrained. Now if anyone inquires how this is, it must be a miracle for no reason can explain this. For we know that the sea, as other elements, is spherical. As the earth is round, so also is the element of water, as well as air and fire. Since, then, the form of this element is spherical, we must know that it is not lower than the earth, but being lighter shows that it stands above it [the earth]. How is it then that the sea does not immediately overflow the whole earth for it is liquid and cannot stand in one place except restrained by some secret power and impulse of God? Now the word of God, though not heard by us, nor resounding in the air, is yet heard by the sea, for it is confined within its own limits.[119]

Not only did the waters once cover the earth, but also, in creation, God suspended some waters in the heavens, placing the human being in the midst of this threatening element. The belief in supracelestial waters stems from Genesis 1:6: "Let there be a firmament in the midst of the waters and let it separate the waters from the waters."[120] Pagan philosophers were quick to point out that these waters could not exist above the last celestial sphere. Basil cited their objection: "They ask us how, if the body of the firmament is spherical, as sight shows it to be, and if waters flow off high spots, it would be possible for the water to lie on the convex circumference of the firmament."[121] Basil answered that it is not necessary that the outer surface of the firmament be completely spherical. Caves, for example, have a semicircular form according to their inner appearance but a flat surface on top.[122] John Chrysostom met the philosophers' objection by arguing that Christians must humbly accept the teaching of Scripture.[123] Augustine struggled with this verse throughout his commentaries on Genesis. In *De Genesi ad litteram* he finally insisted on a literal interpretation. According to Augustine, the weight of water does not prevent the presence of water above the highest heaven, if it is in the form of minute particles for "water in a vaporous state is not prevented by its weight from being above the air."[124]

Calvin used this traditional theory of lower and supracelestial waters to stress the dangerous and threatened position of the human being in the world. The human race, he argued, was surrounded by the waters below and the celestial waters above because "God has purposely placed us between two graves lest in fancied security, we should despise that kindness on which our life depends. For the element of water which the philosophers consider one of the principles of life, threatens us with death from above and below except insofar as it is restrained by the hand of God."[125] Interpreting Genesis 1:9 ("Let the waters be gathered together"), Calvin relied on the traditional argument that by his power God made room for human beings:

> This also is an illustrious miracle, that the waters by their departure have given a dwelling place to men. For even philosophers concede that the natural position of the waters was to cover the whole earth, as Moses explains that they did at the beginning; first, because being an element, it must be circular and because this element is heavier than the air and lighter than the earth, it ought to cover the latter in its whole circumference. But that the seas, being gathered together as on heaps, should yield to man, is seemingly against [*praeter*] nature. . . . Let us know, therefore, that we are dwelling on dry ground because by his command God has removed the waters so that they should not submerge the earth.[126]

Throughout his descriptions of nature Calvin dramatically portrayed the threat that water continually poses to the human race. He constantly reminded his readers that "if we behold the waves which are elevated it seems that the world should be engulfed." In Calvin's view, only God's immediate power keeps the waters from passing beyond their appointed limits. The fact that the waters stay within their bounds is "beyond nature" and demonstrated to Calvin that the natural order was continually threatened by a force which could, in a moment, destroy creation if God loosened the barriers. Calvin repeatedly depicted the raging sea, the violent tempests, and the billowing waves to remind his readers of the precarious nature of their own existence; if the waters were left to themselves, they would "rush forth and overwhelm the whole earth." The great flood that God sent to destroy the earth was, for Calvin, a sign of that continual threat of the waters that surround us on all sides. During the flood, God "let loose the barriers" of the supracelestial and the lower waters, allowing them to overflow the earth.[127] For Calvin, Psalm 33:7, Jeremiah 5:22, and Job 38:11 depict this threat of the waters which daily confronts us.

The position of the earth also demonstrated to Calvin this same precarious character of the cosmos. We have seen how Calvin used the "motion" of the stars and the "restraint" of the waters to prove the power and providence of God. So too, the position of the earth further demonstrated the necessity for this providence. Calvin was acutely aware that the earth is a mass which is heavier than the surrounding elements upon which it appears to rest. Just as Calvin wondered why the stars do not collide, why the waters stay in their bounds, so too he asked why the earth does not fall down, for there is nothing inherent in the earth that would secure its floating position.

This was an ancient cosmological question. In his treatise *De caelo*, Aristotle listed the various solutions offered by different thinkers to this problem. To Anaximenes, Anaxagoras, and Democritus, he attributed the belief that the flatness of the earth caused it immobility. According to Aristotle, the theory that the earth rests upon water dates back to Thales of Miletus, who argued that the earth can float like wood upon the waters. And Xenophanes of Colophon is believed to have said that the earth is "infinite in its roots" and thus extends downwards indefinitely. And, finally, Aristotle reported that Anaximander argued that the earth keeps its place because of an "indifference"; all motion is inappropriate to that which is set at the center and indifferently related to every extreme point.[128]

Aristotle disagreed. Against the theory that the earth rests upon the waters, he argued that "as air is lighter than water, so is water lighter than the earth. How can they think that the naturally lighter substance lies below the heavier?" In Aristotle's view, all objects move downwards toward their "natural place." The "indifference" theory cannot be true because the movement to the center is peculiar to the earth. Aristotle argued instead that the weight of each part of the (spherical) earth bears it toward the center of the world. He then concluded that the earth, with all its parts, found its "natural place," namely, at the center of the universe.[129]

Basil warned Christians not to be too preoccupied with this question. However, in his warning he analyzed the problem and concluded, as would later Calvin, that the *hand of God* keeps the earth in its place.

> If you say that air is spread under the surface of the earth, you will be at a loss as to how its soft and porous nature pressed down under such a weight, endures and does not slip through in all directions. . . . Again, if you suppose that water is the substance placed under the earth, even so you will inquire how it is that the heavenly and dense body does not pass through the water but instead, although greater in weight, is supported by the weaker nature . . . if you suggest that there is another body heavier than the earth to prevent the earth from going downward, you will notice that, that too, needs some like support to keep it from falling

down. . . . We shall go on endlessly always inventing another basis in turn for the bases found. . . . Moreover, we must, even if we grant that the earth stands by its own power and if we say it rides at anchor on the water, depart in no way from the thought of true religion, but admit that things are kept under control by the power of the Creator. . . . In the hand of God are all the ends of the earth.[130]

More so than Basil, Calvin was willing to specify the elements upon which the earth rested, namely, on air and water. In his interpretation of Psalm 104:5 Calvin granted limited validity to Aristotle's reasoning, but then, in a manner reminiscent of Basil, quickly turned his attention to the power of God.

> The stability of the earth proclaims the glory of God, for how does it hold its place unmoved when it hangs in the midst of the air and is supported only by water? This indeed can be explained on natural principles for the earth, as it occupies the lowest place, being the center of the world, naturally settles down there. But even in this contrivance the wonderful power of God shines forth. Again, if the waters rise above the earth, because they are lighter, why do they not encircle and cover the whole earth? Certainly the philosophers have no answer for this except that the providence of God has counteracted [*correctum*] the order of nature so that a dwelling place may be found for man . . . nothing in the world is stable except as it is sustained by the hand of God.[131]

In his sermons, however, Calvin was not so respectful of philosophical or Aristotelian solutions. Instead, the position of the earth becomes proof of the constant necessity of God's sustaining and restraining power:

> Behold a terrible mass; this is not just a great castle or house to which there is no approach. But we see what weight there is there. It seems impossible to find a foundation sufficient to sustain it. And on what does it rest? Upon water. It is necessary that the earth is hanging in the air (as is the truth) and that there is water all around it. True, the philosophers who have not considered that is it God who created it, have indeed found reasons for how the waters surround the earth and how the whole thing is hung in the air. They have indeed disputed subtly about this and have deduced some reasons for it. Nevertheless, they are constrained despite themselves to confess that this is beyond nature, that is, that the waters are held back in order that man would have some place to live. By nature that cannot be. It is necessary, therefore, that there be some divine providence at work here.[132]

One last quotation suffices to show how Calvin used this traditional cosmological theory as proof of divine providence:

> If we regard the earth, I beg you, upon what is it founded? It is founded upon water and air; behold its foundation. We cannot possibly build a house fifteen feet high on firm ground without having to lay a foundation. But look at the whole earth founded upon trembling, indeed poised above such bottomless depths that it might be turned upside down at any moment and become disordered. Hence, there must be a wonderful power of God to keep it in its condition.[133]

Here again, then, nature bore an inherently precarious aspect for Calvin.

The continual wonder that he expressed about the beauties of nature was rooted in his belief that God's presence was seen there, upholding, restraining, ordering, and directing creation. The joy Calvin took in the wonders of nature has been well documented by Calvin scholars, but it is necessary to remember that this joy presupposed the inherent fragility of creation; nature does not, in Calvin's view, remain ordered in and of itself. To Calvin, the inherent character of creation was not conducive to order; only a great divine power could preserve the grand orderliness we perceive in the universe. The stability of nature depends on "the continual rejoicing of God in his works."[134] If God ceased to rejoice therein, if he ceased to give vigor to the earth or if he looked upon creation with wrath, the sphere of nature would collapse into disorder. Therefore, Calvin believed that behind the beauty of nature lay its fragility, dependence, and precarious nature which required the continual preservation of God, for without his providence the stars would collide, the earth would fall down, and the waters would gush forth and engulf the earth.

7. THE FALL AND THE THREATENING CHARACTER OF CREATION

The precarious nature of the cosmos took on a positively threatening aspect with the fall because at that time the forces of disorder actually invaded the world. Although the original harmonious creation contained the ever-present possibility of disorder and chaos, actual disorder entered only at the fall. Calvin's identification of the fall with disorder is clear in his commentary on Genesis where he defined Adam's rebellion as "the subversion of all equity and well-constituted order."[135] Calvin imagined a prefallen world where all creatures had assigned places: Adam commanded Eve and humans governed animals. The serpent "overstepped his bounds" when he tempted Eve and the fall of Adam revealed his "violation of all order," because now humans had been led into rebellion by one "lower than themselves."

The act of unbelief was, then, an act of disorder among the creatures, which unleashed disorder into God's fragile but ordered world. The oneness of the human being with creation is seen in the fact that the fall affected all of nature. In agreement with the exegetical tradition of the church, Calvin argued that nature itself was changed in the fall: the earth was no longer as fertile and such things as briars and locusts came into being.[136] In Calvin's interpretation, nature was not just weakened in the fall; it had actively rebelled against the human race. The elements are now in disorder and threaten human existence. The animals, which were originally endowed with a submissive spirit, are now wild, savage, and dangerous to man. Originally the world had been created for the comfort and service of humans but now it has risen up and rebelled. Scorching heat, the deluge of rains, earthquakes, noxious and savage animals, and terrible winds are all evidence that our sin has overturned the order in nature:[137]

> In a word nothing is certain, but all things are in a state of disorder. . . . We throw heaven and earth into disorder by our sins. For if we were in right order as to our obedience to God, doubtless all the elements would be conformable [i.e. "sing"] to us and we should thus observe in the world, as it were, an angelic harmony.[138]

With the fall this beautiful and fragile creation took on a threatening countenance; consequently, the forces of disorder are lapping at our heels just as Calvin's oceans threaten us from their shores. After the fall, the forces of disorder became so threatening that creation required even more the immediate restraining providence of God lest it collapse into complete chaos. In his commentary on Romans, Calvin wrote that the whole machinery of the world would "dissolve at almost every moment and all its parts fail in the sorrowful confusion which followed the fall of Adam, were they not borne up from elsewhere by some hidden stability."[139]

Not only has disorder penetrated the physical elements of creation, but the historical sphere is now also characterized by moral disorder. The threatening image of water recurs when Calvin described this dangerous confusion in history. The world, he said, is engulfed by a "flood of iniquity" which must be continually restrained by God lest it rush forth and engulf the earth.[140] Just as the devil subverted legitimate order in the fall, so now the wicked are always trying to create disorder in society. In Calvin's view, the fall of governments and the subsequent confusion and chaos in society are to be traced back to the wrath of God evident in societal confusion.[141] For Calvin, the continual wars, injustices, revolutions, and changes in society are evidences of the moral disorder which invaded the world after the fall and have since then permeated the historical sphere.

To Calvin's mind, the disorders in nature and in history are real; they are not due merely to the perceptual or noetic effects of sin.[142] Calvin knew that when Job or David lamented the evils of society they actually saw the good suffering and the wicked revelling in evil. When one looks out on history and society, as Calvin frequently did, one must admit " . . . that everything is mixed up such that one can say nothing except that things are confused in this world . . . that everything goes into confusion, that there is disorder so great that we are astonished."[143]

But Calvin also knew that events are not fortuitous or outside of divine control. God still holds the reins over the real forces of disorder, although we cannot at the present time understand the reasons for his actions. Calvin interpreted the book of Job to mean that while nature reflects God's glory, history is a period in which "God still allows things to be confused in the world."[144] Nonetheless, he insisted, above the "clouds" of this disorder stands the rule of God which governs all events and brings order out of chaos.

Calvin's view of the sinister and threatening aspect of creation is also demonstrated in his reliance on the image of a bridle which reins in those forces that would obliterate nature and society. We have seen that God must restrain and bridle the waters in order to keep them in their appointed bounds. So too, the Lord must bridle the animals lest they come forth and devour people and he must bridle people lest they devour each other.[145] For Calvin, the "bridle of divine providence" curbs the wicked and the devil lest they completely overturn all order and make life unlivable. The fact that Satan had to present himself to God in Job 1:6 proved to Calvin that God was always in sovereign control, bridling the wicked "because with the bridle of his power, God holds him [Satan] bound and restrained."[146] Calvin's refusal to rely on the concept of a permissive will in God, in order to keep God from being the author of evil, also demonstrates his emphasis on the need for the active, ceaseless, and immediate power of divine providence. Calvin would not stand for a "watchtower" divinity; God never "indolently permits" nature, history, or people to take their course: Calvin's God exercises his supreme will and determines all events.[147]

8. PROVIDENCE AND SECONDARY CAUSALITY

Calvin's emphasis on the need for God's immediate and active providence again raises the issue of secondary causality. Does nature really have any integrity or independence? Does Calvin contradict his affirmation of secondary causality which we noted above in his treatise against the Libertines? Throughout his polemics against the Epicureans Calvin tried to define the idea of a "general providence" without either denying the integrity of nature or granting nature too much independence.

Frankly, Calvin was ambivalent about the role of secondary causes. As we saw above in his treatise against the Libertines, Calvin could speak of the laws of nature and grant that each element has its own particular property. In the 1559 *Institutes* he explained that "the several kinds of things are moved by the secret impulse of nature, as if they obeyed God's eternal command, and what God has once determined flows on by itself."[148] In both his treatise against the Libertines and in the *Institutes* he argued that God works through the evil intent of the wicked and that providence does not excuse us from taking precautions.[149] A godly man, he said, "will not overlook the secondary causes." And finally, when describing God's guidance of the world and especially of the church, Calvin explained that providence "is the determinative principle of all things in such a way that sometimes it works through intermediary, sometimes without an intermediary, sometimes contrary to every intermediary."[150]

So too, in his treatise against astrology Calvin conceded limited causality to the stars. In his attempt to distinguish true from false astrology, Calvin granted that the stars, planets, and the moon exercise influence on the qualities of earthly bodies. By means of "true astrology," doctors can decide which remedies to administer at certain times. Because of the sympathy [*convenance*] between the stars and human bodies, the former influences the "complexion" of people "et sur tout aux affections qui participent aux qualitez de leurs corps, qu'elles dependent en partie des astres, ou pour le moins y ont quelque correspondance. Comme de dire qu'un homme soit plus enclin à colere qu'à flegme ou au contraire."[151]

However, Calvin's warning against false astrology also reveals his hesitation about secondary causality. Calvin directed his treatise against a book on astrology by Mellin de Saint-Gelays and, in general, against the increased interest in astrology in his age, particularly by Renaissance thinkers.[152] In opposition to this prevailing spirit, Calvin argued that it was a blasphemy to remove from God the rule of the universe. God, he insisted, governs human events and directs human wills.[153] To deny God such rule would overturn all morality and societal order.[154] According to Calvin, believers in astrology, including Melanchthon, imprisoned God within the prison of nature or of alleged secondary causes.[155]

Therefore, when Calvin spoke of nature independently of the problem of evil and the responsibility for sin, he often mitigated the affirmations noted above. He feared that a full and unqualified recognition of secondary causality would be interpreted as a "blind instinct" by means of which nature could operate independently of God. Such a view would render God distant and idle. Although Calvin never denied secondary causes, he insisted that the sun does not rise nor the rain fall "by a blind instinct of nature"; bread does not nourish by its own strength and thunder does not proceed merely from the collision of cold and humid vapors with dry air.[156] Calvin was acquainted with the scientific explanations of his day but insisted that they not be allowed to create the illusion that nature is a self-contained totality, thereby taking on the independence assigned to it by the "depraved opinion" of "carnal reason."[157] Instead Calvin talked of a "secret influence" or "secret infusion" by which God governs and regulates all things so that no movement can take place among the elements without his previous decree.[158] He maintained that nature is an instrument to which God directly imparts effectiveness. Referring to the fecundity of nature Calvin argued that "all this wonderful operation, co-operation, and continuance, can certainly never be thought to proceed from any other cause than the directing hand of God."[159] The general or universal providence which Calvin grudgingly admitted was never an independent effectiveness of nature or an interconnected series of causes.[160] In Calvin's exegesis, John 5:17, Acts 17:28, and Hebrews 1:3 all testify to God's continual special providence over all of creation.

This is also true in history. All events take place by God's regulation. Nothing is due to chance "but we make God the ruler and governor of all things who in accordance with his wisdom has from the farthest limit of eternity decreed what he was going to do, and now by his might carries out what he has decreed. From this we declare that not only heaven and earth and the inanimate creatures, but also the plans and intentions of men are governed by his providence that they are borne by it straight to their appointed end."[161] Although Calvin granted that events look fortuitous to us, nonetheless, by the "bridle of his providence he [God] turns every event whatsoever way he wills."[162]

Calvin's inclination to mitigate secondary causes resulted from his understanding of nature and of history. Order and harmony are not, in his view, "natural" to creation. After the fall, disorder further upset a previously beautiful but precarious harmony. And history is always awash in blood. Calvin's world was simply too dangerous a place to leave it to the realm of secondary causation. It needed God.

9. CALVIN'S ARGUMENTS FOR THE PROVIDENCE OF GOD

The dark and threatening aspect of creation surfaces repeatedly in those texts where Calvin defended divine providence against empirical evidence. Like Chrysostom, Calvin was acutely aware that nature and history did not equally reflect the providence of God. Calvin believed that although history *can* reflect the providence of God, he also knew that the disorders in history often cast a "cloud" between human perception and God's providential rule.[163] Believers can now only "see though a mirror dimly" and "only in part," because they cannot perceive God's providence at work or comprehend the rational governance of the world.[164] It is not always evident that God is at work restraining the wicked and the forces of societal chaos. No wonder, Calvin said, there exists an almost universal belief that all things are governed by chance and that the world is aimlessly tossed about by the blind impulse of fortune.[165] The dramatic passage in Book I.17.10 of the *Institutes* represents the perspective Calvin adopted about the need for providence in a dangerous world:

> Innumerable are the evils that beset human life; innumerable too the deaths that threaten it. We need not go beyond ourselves since our body is the receptacle of a thousand diseases—in fact holds within itself and fosters the causes of diseases—a man cannot go about unburdened by many forms of his own destruction. . . . Embark upon a ship, you are one step away from death. Mount a horse, if one foot slips, your life is imperiled. Go through the city streets, you are subject to as many dangers as there are tiles on the roofs. If there is a weapon in your hand or a friend's, harm awaits. All the fierce animals you see are armed for your destruction. But if you try to shut yourself up in a walled garden, seemingly delightful, there a serpent sometimes lies hidden. Your house, continually in danger of fire, threatens in the daytime to impoverish you, at night even to collapse upon you. Your field, since it is exposed to hail, frost, drought, and other calamities, threatens you with barrenness and hence, famine. I pass over poisonings, ambushes, robberies, open violence, which in part besiege us at home, in part dog us abroad. Amid these tribulations must not man be most miserable since, but half alive in life, he weakly draws his anxious and languid breath, as if he had a sword perpetually hanging over his neck?[166]

Because it is not always evident that God is controlling the world, condemning the wicked, and rewarding the good, Calvin refused to say that providence is an empirical doctrine.[167] Precisely on this point, Calvin believed the views of Eliphaz, Bildad, and Zophar in the book of Job were condemned: it is not true that the judgments of God are known and obvious, "for in this world the wicked abound in riches and power and this confusion, which is, as it were, a dark night, will continue until God shall raise the dead."[168] Calvin's recognition of the disordered nature of history prevented him from arguing for the reality of providence on the basis of experience. Although nature continues to reveal the glory of God (even while subject to corruption), history is often marked by blood and confusion so that "it is necessary that we wait in patience until our Lord puts things back into order, which will not be done in this age."[169]

Therefore, Calvin took on the burden of showing that in spite of natural and historical disorders, providence is real. His main arguments for providence are found in the commentaries on the Psalms, the sermons on Job, and the 1559 *Institutes*, all of which give evidence that the doctrine of providence gained increasing importance in his thought. All of his arguments show the same overriding concern: the attempt to find an indisputable foundation upon which to affirm that a reliable God controls a rational universe.

The argument to which Calvin returned most frequently was based on the unchangeable nature of God's attributes. The divine attributes become the starting point which, if acknowledged, forces one to conclude that God must continue to care for and govern his creation. According to Calvin, God's very nature is to be providential; and, therefore, the present empirical disorders notwithstanding, the Christian can believe that God is actively governing the world. This argumentation recurs throughout the commentary on the Psalms in which Calvin emphasized that God "cannot deny himself," that is, God cannot contradict his nature or act other than he is. Calvin believed that regardless of the empirical evidence of disorder, we cannot conclude that God has ceased to care for his creation. The following passage is typical of the many found in the commentary on the Psalms:

> The consideration that although God, who by his very nature is merciful, may for a time withdraw his hand, yet he cannot deny himself or divest himself of the feeling of mercy which is his by nature and which can no more cease than his eternal essence. . . . We must not imagine that he can be unlike himself or that he has changed his purpose.[170]

Repeatedly Calvin stated that God "cannot forget his office"; that is, God cannot forget that he is governor and judge of the world. "Although God may seem for a time to take no notice of what his creatures do, yet he never forgets his office. Since God is Governor of the world, it is utterly impossible for him to abdicate his office as it is for him to deny himself."[171] God's mercy and power guarantee that God cannot withdraw from nor abandon his creation, leaving human beings to the forces of disorder "without derogating from his honor." To abandon creation to the forces of sin and confusion would be to deny the very character of God which brought creation into being in the first place. In Calvin's view, trust in God is that assurance which arises from "a recognition of his attributes."[172]

Among the most important attributes that Calvin used to guarantee providence was the power of God. Divine power sustains and upholds the earth, governs nature and history, and shines forth in the conservation of creation as much as in its original formation.[173] In view of the disorder ushered in by the fall, and because God's power secured his control over those hostile forces which threaten creatures, the importance of this attribute took on increased significance. For Calvin, divine power maintains order, restrains the waters, and curbs or bridles both the savage beasts and the wicked will. To posit a permissive will in God was, in Calvin's view, to cast doubt on this powerful control that God exercised over creation.[174]

Calvin was eager, however, to define this power as reliable rather than as an ungoverned, cruel, or tyrannical will. His rejection of the distinction between the *potentia absoluta* and the *potentia ordinata* demonstrates this concern.[175] Ignoring the nominalist emphasis on God's reliable commitments to his ordained *pactum*, Calvin angrily rejected this "blasphemous" separation of God's power from his justice. Such an (alleged) separation of God's attributes, he feared, would make God into a tyrant who could *de potentia absoluta* act according to a tyrannical and absolute will and could "toss men about like balls." Calvin feared that this distinction would tempt Christians to suspect that God's power was "disordered," "unregulated," and "tyrannical," all of which would mean that neither rationality nor order nor justice would underlie the seemingly fortuitous appearances in the world.[176] Beause Calvin wanted to preserve a divine omnipotence that would not be confused with an unbridled tyrannical power, he insisted that God's power must be called "infinite" but not "absolute."[177]

To this purpose, Calvin repeatedly insisted that the divine attributes may not be separated from one another. Although the inseparability of God's attributes was certainly not a new theological principle, Calvin's emphasis again demonstrates his concern to find a reliable God on whom to base providence. Hence, he insisted, God's providence cannot be disassociated from his wisdom, goodness, or justice. Believers need not fear that God will act according to whim because power, goodness, wisdom, and justice are not separated in his essence.[178]

Such discussions presuppose that we are often unable to see this wisdom, goodness, and justice of God in the world. Statements regarding the absolute and ordained powers of God and the inseparability of the divine attributes were means by which Calvin assured his readers of providence in a world that often appeared chaotic, irrational, and unjust. Like Job, we may not be able to understand the reasons behind God's rule; yet because his will is inherently wise, just, and good, we can trust him. Calvin counseled believers that if this rationality and justice escape human perception, they must not posit some absolute power but must rely on the unity of God's will and justice.

All of Calvin's attempts to tie providence to the divine attributes presuppose that God was unchangeable; only his immutability could guarantee that he could not abdicate his office nor abandon his creation, acts which would be contrary to his nature. Consequently, except by way of theological accommodation, the term "repentance" is not properly applied to God.[179] In Calvin's interpretation, I Samuel 15:29 and Numbers 23:19 testify to the immutability of God, securing his providence over creation and offering certainty and comfort to the believer. In short, the concept of God's immutability, which has given rise to the fear that Calvin's thought was fatalistic or deterministic, was the only sure guarantee of the reliability of God in the sphere of creation.

For Calvin, divine immutability and power made the doctrine of providence a source of comfort for the believer. To leave human beings exposed to the forces of a dangerous universe was intolerable in his eyes. The idea that we are tossed and whirled about by the blind impulse of fortune made life unlivable.[180] While it may seem harsh to allow for no contingency in the world or to say that the tree that falls on one's head is divinely willed, that was the price Calvin was willing to pay in order to remove humanity from an unpredictable universe.[181] He did not fear evil in itself so much as an evil that was irrational, uncontrolled, and without purpose. Consequently, he thought it better for God to decree the "evils" that beset us than to make human beings the victims of a blind fortune or chance under the control of no divine power. The nearness of God to the world, his preservation and restraint of nature, his continual control and guidance of each event provided the Christian with "abundant comfort" and "never-failing assurance" that when the world appears to be aimlessly tossed about, the Lord is everywhere at work in control of all the forces that would harm people or threaten creation. Waters stay in their bounds, the earth hangs in the air, the stars stay in their courses, and the moral disorder of history is curbed by the "bridle of God's providence." Depending on the immutable nature of God's commitment to his creation, Calvin can conclude that "the ignorance of providence is the ultimate of miseries, the highest blessedness lies in the knowledge of it."[182]

10. CONCLUSIONS

1. In his discussions about providence, Calvin relied, to a large extent, on the tradition. In agreement with past theologians, Calvin argued that God created the world *ex nihilo*, sustains it by his power, and governs each creature. As did patristic and medieval thinkers, Calvin repudiated an "Aristotelian" view of creation and providence. According to Calvin, sixteenth-century "Averroism" or "Epicureanism" rendered God distant and nature independent. As he

repeatedly insisted, God is not a "momentary Creator who once and for all finished his work." Instead, Calvin argued, God's creation and providence are inseparably joined.

2. In his desire to combat the Epicurean error, Calvin displayed ambivalence toward secondary causality. Augustine had granted reality to secondary causes through his theory of seminal reasons. Thomas Aquinas had perceived that the fullness of divine perfection was clear in the communication of causality to lower agents and had argued that all created beings imitated divine goodness by imitating God's causality.

Calvin, however, reflected the late medieval or "nominalist" emphasis on God's independence over mediate causes, a view that gained increasing support after the Parisian condemnations. References to God as First Cause or Prime Mover unnerved Calvin because such phrases seemed to make God distant and to deprive him of power. Therefore, in comparison to thinkers such as Augustine and Aquinas, Calvin strove to tie God's ever-present hand to each secondary cause and created movement.

3. Underlying Calvin's ambivalence toward secondary causality was his view of cosmology and of history. Calvin drew on traditional cosmological views as well as traditional hexameral exegesis in order to describe what was for him two faces of creation. In his hands, these traditional views served to demonstrate both the beautiful but precarious nature of creation as well as its dangerous and threatening character.[183] The order and harmony in creation was precarious and needed God to hold it constantly in existence. After the fall, nature took on a threatening aspect which required God to restrain the forces of chaos or disorder. One might say that in the prefallen creation disorder was in potency rather than in act but that after the fall disorder was in act rather than in potency. For Calvin, the fallen creation is characterized by rebellion and confusion in nature and moral disorder in history. Therefore, he believed that the created order could not be granted any real independence because to do so would cause all of creation to collapse. Calvin's concern was not simply the freedom of God or the contingency of creation; rather, his interest was in the precarious, threatening aspect of nature, resulting both from the fall and from the fact that creation did not inherently contain order.

Therefore, the active, immediate will of God served not only to explain to Calvin the bestowal of existence on the world, but also to describe the restraint of disorder. Although his doctrine of providence explained the sustenance of creation, his primary interest was in the "bridle" of divine providence. God's bridle restrained the wicked and held nature in check so that the earth did not plummet into disorder, the stars collide, or the waters rush forth to engulf the earth.

4. But Calvin never denied secondary causality. He did believe that God worked immediately and mediately in nature and history. Although he tied God as closely as possible to these secondary means or instruments, Calvin knew

that God guided history through natural law, chosen leaders, governments, the human will, and the angels. By these means, as well as by direct intervention, God preserves the world's beauty, stability, regularity, and order. Like Chrysostom, Calvin was acutely aware that God's governance in history was often not as clear as his providence over creation. History does not usually present us with wonders as clear as the stars that revolve without colliding or an earth that rests upon the waters. Calvin reminded his readers that in the historical sphere we see only dimly and "in part." Nonetheless, we will see that in a very Irenaean sense Calvin argued that God was actively preserving and reclaiming his creation. The natural order belongs to God, is the work of his hands, and the arena of both human and divine activity. As such, creation is not to be shunned by the believer. We turn now to the various aspects of this divinely preserved creation which are the objects of God's continuing care, guidance, and redemption. We begin with the angels.

II

THE ANGELS WHO DO HIS BIDDING

Calvin's world was not limited to the visible realm. He recognized that God's creation extended beyond the earthly sphere to the world of purely spiritual beings, namely, the angels and demons. He even called upon believers to contemplate the angels ". . . for if we desire to recognize God from his works, by no means ought we to overlook such an illustrious and noble example."[1] Warfield argued correctly that a concern with angels was a characteristic both Luther and Calvin shared with their age. "Perhaps," Warfield wrote, "what strikes the reader most forcibly upon the surface of the discussion is the completeness of the faith which it exhibits in the real existence of angelic beings and the concernment of man with them. . . . The supernaturalistic tone of the conception of the Reformers is in nothing more visible than their vital sense of the spiritual environment in which human life is cast."[2]

Nonetheless, the subject of angels has not been the most popular aspect of Calvin's theology. Secondary scholarship has been largely silent about their role in the thought of the Reformer. Niesel passed over them in a sentence, Doumergue gave them a page, and Wendel was surprised by the length of the exposition on angels in the 1559 *Institutes*.[3] Despite their analysis of Calvin's understanding of demonology and spiritual warfare, Fröhlich, Kolfhaus, and Hall hardly mention the role of angels in Calvin's thought.[4] Warfield and Stauffer have studied Calvin's angelology most extensively. Warfield stressed the biblical and antispeculative character of Calvin's statements about angels in the *Institutes* and the problem posed by angelic mediators for the belief in divine immanence.[5] Stauffer demonstrated that the nature and function of angels is a subject recurring throughout Calvin's sermons.[6]

As these latter scholars have shown, the subject of angels does recur in Calvin's writings. Repeatedly angels dart in and out of his commentaries, polemical treatises, and the *Institutes*. This chapter will demonstrate that Calvin's angelology is characterized by both an attitude of reserve and a belief in the protection and assistance of angels. He tried to restrict angelic speculation to the information found in the Bible, to abolish all idolatrous worship of angels, and to assure his readers that God had placed the care and protection of the church in the hands of the angels. In these discussions Calvin had an eye to the teachings about the angels found in the Christian tradition as well as to the "denial" of angels by such groups as the Libertines.

1. BACKGROUND: ANCIENT AND MEDIEVAL ANGELOLOGY

In 325 the Council of Nicea declared that "We believe in one God, the
Father Almighty, Creator of heaven and earth, of all things visible and invisible."
Very early in the tradition of the church, Christians developed the Judaic belief
in angels and discussed the nature of this "invisible" or angelic world. In so
doing they formulated questions which were transmitted to the Middle Ages and
became the basis for fully developed angelologies.[7]

Every conceivable question was asked regarding the nature, creation, and
function of angels. When were they created? Are they corporeal or incorporeal?
Why did angels fall? Are good angels still able to sin? How and what do the
angels know? How many angels are there? What is the nature of the angelic
hierarchy? May we properly adore the angels? Early Christian writers offered
varying and often unsystematic answers to these questions. Nonetheless, as
Daniélou has shown, the belief in angels formed an important element of early
Christian theology and worship. This section surveys only the main lines of
discussion found in Patristic and Scholastic authors—portions of which Calvin
adopted, ignored, or vigorously denied.

Many of the Fathers, including Justin, Clement, Origen, Basil, and
Ambrose, believed that angels possessed ethereal bodies.[8] The possession of
this spiritual body placed angels between God and the human race; they were
of a more spiritual nature than human beings but less spiritual than God. This
opinion continued to find advocates in the Middle Ages, including Peter
Lombard and Bernard of Clairvaux.[9] The Pseudo-Dionysius, however, affirmed
an unqualified or absolute spirituality of the angels and this latter doctrine was
confirmed by the Fourth Lateran Council in 1215.[10] Against such Franciscan
thinkers as Bonaventure, St. Thomas rejected the idea of spiritual matter and
argued for the absolute spirituality or incorporeality of angels.[11]

Christians all agreed that all angels originally were created good by God.
But the time of their creation and the cause of the devil's fall were disputed.
Before Augustine, Christian writers often assumed that the angels were created
before the visible world. But taking his cue from the Old Latin translation of
Ecclesiasticus 18:1 ("All things were created at one and the same time"),
Augustine argued that the angels were created simultaneously with all of creation. According to Augustine, the angels were in an "unformed" or potential
state until (without any lapse of time) God illumined them and formed them
through the Word.[12] Thomas agreed that Augustine's opinion was more
probable. Thomas argued that since the angels were a part of the universe, their
creation was included in the opening statement of Genesis, "In the beginning
God created heaven and earth."[13]

Christian thinkers also believed that some angels fell while others
persevered in their original creation. But interpretations of the angelic fall
varied. Danielou points to a very early tradition according to which the angels

were jealous of the honor bestowed on Adam when he was made in the divine image.[14] Equally important was the belief that the devil fell through pride which caused him to try to be like God. Augustine argued that the devil immediately turned away from God because he was "swollen with pride and corrupted by delight in his own powers."[15] The devil, Augustine believed, never experienced the blessed life of the good angels because ". . . unwilling to receive this blessedness, he forsook and lost it." Furthermore, Augustine explained, the devil and his fallen angels were driven from paradise and now live in the misty air surrounding the earth.[16]

Thomas also argued that the devil fell by trying to be like God. Satan did not, Thomas specified, try to be like God through equality but through likeness. The devil desired to be like God ". . . as something to which he had a claim in justice as by his own power and not from the power of God." This meant, according to Thomas, "that he placed his ultimate beatitude in an objective to be obtained by the force of his own nature alone, rejecting the supernatural beatitude which depends on the grace of God." The devil, Thomas said in agreement with Anselm, ". . . sought to obtain final beatitude by his own power, whereas this is proper to God alone."[17]

The present state of the angels was also debated throughout the tradition. Clement of Alexandria argued that the good angels must pray that they will persevere in God.[18] Tertullian implied that the good angels could repent[19] and Basil explained that the angels remain united with God through the power of the Holy Spirit.[20] Ambrose also taught that in order not to sin, angels need grace.[21] Augustine, however, insisted that the unfallen angels were immutably confirmed in the good. The good angels, he argued, possess that "secure" or "certain" happiness which no cyclical theory of souls can offer.[22] Aquinas agreed that the good angels were permanently confirmed in their beatitude and assured of the vision of God.[23]

The nature and present state of the angels also led to questions about angelic knowledge. Early church Fathers were of the general opinion that the angels were not omniscient. Angels knew God but did not "comprehend" the divine nature. Nor did the angels know the future or the secrets of the human heart. As Tertullian and Cassian assumed, these areas of knowledge were characteristic of divinity.[24] Many Fathers also believed that the angels were instructed about divine mysteries through the teaching of the church. As Chrysostom argued, the angels learned of the incarnation only through the teaching of the church.[25] The angels, according to Chrysostom, were astonished and rejoiced at the ascension of Christ and their reconciliation with the human race.[26]

With Augustine we receive the first extended discussion of angelic knowledge, some of which contradicted earlier teachings. In his comments on Ps. 7:9, Augustine also argued that angels cannot know our innermost thoughts.[27] But in the De Genesi ad litteram Augustine held that both good and bad angels can read the thoughts of human beings.[28] Augustine also suggested that angels and demons know the future. Demons can see some of the things that may occur in time, but are often deceived. Unfallen angels, however, are able "to foresee the changes of times in the eternal and immutable laws of God. . . ."[29]

Augustine also discussed the manner or nature of angelic knowledge by distinguishing between a morning and an evening knowledge. According to Augustine, "morning knowledge" is that by which the angels know themselves and all created things in the Word who is the reason and cause of all that exists. "Evening knowledge" is the direct vision that the angel has of the created thing in itself.[30]

The question of angelic knowledge became increasingly important in the Middle Ages. The Pseudo-Dionysius believed that angelic knowledge was immaterial or purely intelligible. The knowledge of angels transcends the exteriority and fragmentation inherent in the temporal-spatial realm of human existence, ". . . but rather, being free from all taint of matter and multiplicity, they [angels] perceive the spiritual truths of divine things in a single immaterial and spiritual intuition."[31] Dionysius also portrayed a progressive illumination on the part of the angels: the higher orders of angelic beings illumine or initiate the lower orders regarding the divine mysteries.[32] It was, however, with Thomas Aquinas that the question of angelic knowledge became central.

According to the Angelic Doctor, angels are subsisting beings, not composed of form and matter.[33] Since they do not possess bodily senses, Thomas explained their purely intellectual knowledge by distinguishing between human and angelic intellection. Human understanding differs from angelic knowledge in terms of its proper object. The proper object of angelic knowledge is an intelligible substance through which it knows material things.[34] Since the angels do not derive knowledge from the sensible world, the angelic intellect cannot be distinguished into an agent and possible intellect.[35] The "intelligible species" known by the angels come directly from God who placed them in the angelic mind at creation.[36] Therefore, St. Thomas concluded, angels know the essence of material things through inborn intelligible species which are simple and immaterial.[37] Furthermore, against Maimonides, Aquinas argued that through these species angels know things both according to their universal nature and according to their singularity. According to Thomas, it is necessary that angels know singular or particular beings in order that they may administer divine providence in obedience to the divine will.[38]

The knowledge of angels as well as their providential missions were crucial elements of the hierarchical formulations in the Middle Ages. The number or hierarchy of angels played a central role in medieval angelology and hierarchical speculation.[39] The Pseudo-Dionysius formulated a complete theory of angelic hierarchy according to which there are nine levels of angels: three hierarchical orders with each consisting of three levels. In this vast descending hierarchy, the orders perform the spiritual functions of purgation, illumination, and unification with God.[40]

> The higher order, which is composed of Cherubim, Seraphim, and the Thrones and which is closest of all, by reason of its dignity to the secret sanctuary, mysteriously initiates the second order, composed of Dominations, Virtues, and Powers. This order, in turn, reveals the mysteries to the Principalities, the Archangels, and the Angels who are set in charge of the human hierarchy.[41]

This hierarchical scheme, which became standard in the Middle Ages, formed the basis for discussions about the angelic missions in the human realm. As the Pseudo-Dionysius stated, the lower order of angels are in charge of human affairs. Even before the elaboration of this hierarchy, early Christians believed that there were different angelic orders and that angels intervened in human affairs.[42] Based on Acts 7:53 and Galatians 3:19, they believed that angels delivered the law to the Jews. They also maintained that angels were present to Jesus throughout his earthly life, especially at the nativity and the ascension.[43] In early Christian thought, angels governed nations as well as churches and were present as intercessors at the Eucharist and for prayers.[44] On the basis of Tobit 3:25, Matthew 18:10, and Acts 12:15, Christians taught that guardian angels stand over each soul as protector, teacher, and guide.[45]

These beliefs about the intercession and nature of the angels passed into the Middle Ages. The Pseudo-Dionysius relegated the angelic missions in the world to the last order, primarily to the "Angels."[46] This lower order gave the Law to Moses, stood at the head of nations, and led people in their return or ascent to God. Thomas both adopted Dionysius' formulation of the angelic hierarchy and taught that angels ministered to the corporeal realm. The higher angels, he thought, perceive the secrets of the divine mysteries in the divine nature and announce or explain these works of God to the lower orders.[47] In distinction from the Pseudo-Dionysius, however, Thomas granted the external ministry of angels to the lower five levels of the hierarchy whose names indicated some kind of adminstration, namely, the Virtues, Powers, Principalities, Archangels, and Angels.[48] Also, while the Pseudo-Dionysius was silent about guardian angels, Thomas affirmed their existence and assigned the task of individual guardianship to the lowest level of the angelic hierarchy.[49]

Discussions about angelic knowledge of and care for the individual soon gave rise to the cult of angels which developed very early in the church.[50] Statements by Justin, Origen, Eusebius, and Theodoret testify to the rise of the angelic cult. As early as St. Paul, however, church leaders battled the idolatrous worship of angels. The fourth-century Council of Laodicea condemned Christians who abandoned the church in order to invoke angels, and repeatedly Christians writers warned against the idolatrous worship of celestial spirits. Finally, Augustine, who was reserved toward angelic devotion, formulated a distinction which became authoritative in the church. According to Augustine believers must distinguish between the love due to angels and the adoration due to God:

"Honoramus eos [angels] charitate, non servitute."[51] Angels, Augustine explained, do not wish us to sacrifice to them, but to God alone. Christ alone,
not the angels, can mediate between fallen mortals and God. While Christians,
therefore, may love and honor the angels, *latria* [*servitute*] is due to God only.

While the Scholastics were not primarily interested in angelic devotion, the
cult of angels did grow throughout the Middle Ages. St. Benedict told his monks
that they celebrated the holy office in the presence of angels who reported on
their life to God.[52] St. Bernard taught that angels are our friends, our fathers,
our confidants. They burn with love and good will towards us. In return, we are
to love and honor them: "When he [God] uses the ministry of angels for the
salvation of the human race, is it not so that the angels may be loved by men?
For it is clear that men are loved by the angels because they are not unaware
that the losses in their ranks will be made up by men. Indeed it would not be
right that the kingdom of charity, which men and angels are to rule together,
should be governed by other laws than those of mutual love and pure affection
for each other and for God."[53] As we progress in holiness and virtue, the
angels rejoice until we are finally worthy of joining their company.

Especially important to ancient and medieval devotion was the Archangel
Michael. Constantinople devoted about fifteen churches and oratories to
St. Michael and from Constantinople his veneration passed to Italy. Before
the ninth century, at least seven churches in Rome were dedicated to the
Archangel. In the Leonine Sacramentary, St. Michael is mentioned in four
masses for September 30th for a dedication festival of a basilica erected in
his honor on the Via Salaria. His cult had grown originally as a result of an
apparition on Mt. Garganus during the pontificate of Pope Gelasius (492–6).
Throughout the Middle Ages kings invoked his name, monasteries were devoted
to him, and St. Bernard extolled his feastday.[54]

In the later Middle Ages, several teachers and writers continued the devotion to angels. Among the most important were St. Gertrude, St. Mechtilde,
Jean Gerson, John Tauler, and Dionysius the Carthusian. Dionysius wrote both
a commentary on the *Celestial Hierarchy* and delivered a series of seven sermons on St. Michael and all the angels, in which he urged the religious to love,
honor, invoke, imitate, and cooperate with the angelic hosts. Nor did angelic
devotion wane in the sixteenth century. Ignatius of Loyola and the teachers of
the Society of Jesus called on Christians to imitate the purity of angels, to
discern the spirits, and to fight the demons under the banner of Christ.[55] And
finally, the fifteenth and sixteenth centuries were the ages of the confraternities,
many of which were devoted to guardian angels.[56]

Calvin would only address those questions about angels that he considered biblical. Consequently, in comparison to the tradition sketched above,
he is reserved and sometimes critical. He categorically rejected all curiosity into
"obscure questions" about the time of the creation of angels or the nature of the
angelic hierarchy. He expressly denied Augustine's theory of a simultaneous

creation[57] but refused to speculate about which day the angels were created: ". . . is it not evidence of stubbornness rather than of diligence to raise strife over the time and order in which they were created? Moses tells us that the earth was finished and that all the heavens with their hosts were finished. What point, then, is there in anxiously investigating on what day, apart from the stars and the planets, the other, more remote heavenly hosts also began to exist?"[58]

As did Luther and other sixteenth-century Protestants, Calvin rejected the attempts of the Pseudo-Dionysius to order the angels hierarchically.[59] According to Calvin, Pseudo-Dionysius ("whoever he might be") represented that inveterate tendency among theologians to succumb to wild and curious speculations which are of no use to Christians and which stray beyond the bounds of Scripture. After all, Calvin argued, St. Paul was raised to the third heaven and he never described such an elaborate hierarchy.[60] As did the early Christians, however, Calvin did grant that the diversity of angelic names found in Scripture indicates the existence of various angelic orders.[61] However, Calvin added, "to attempt to settle these with exactness and to fix their number or determine their ranks would not merely be foolish curiosity, but would be rash, wicked, and dangerous."[62]

Calvin also disliked the notion of guardian angels. In the *Institutes* he was somewhat circumspect: "But whether individual angels have been assigned to individual believers for their protection, I dare not affirm with confidence."[63] In his commentaries, however, Calvin was more forceful. Commenting on the traditional proof-text for guardian angels, Matt. 18:10, Calvin wrote "For the words of Christ do not mean that a single angel is occupied continually with this or that person; such an idea is inconsistent with the whole doctrine of Scripture which declares that the angels encamp around (Ps. 34:7) the godly, and that not one angel only but many, have been commissioned to guard every one of the faithful."[64] In place of one angel, Calvin wanted hosts of angels available to individual believers and churches.

Despite his rejection of these teachings, Calvin did affirm many traditional beliefs about angels. Throughout his discussions Calvin was concerned to affirm their creation, define their nature, explain their providential mission, and abolish all idolatrous worship and angelic cults.

2. THE EXISTENCE AND NATURE OF ANGELS

In his commentary on Daniel 3:28 Calvin stated that even the heathen knew something about angels. This knowledge was "a kind of anticipation and early persuasion, since all people are persuaded that angels exist, so that they [the pagans] had some idea of angels, although only a partial one."[65] Nonetheless, in the 1543 edition of the *Institutes* and again in the treatises written in 1545 Calvin had found it necessary to defend the existence of angels against the

Libertines, who, as we saw in Chapter I, were also accused of misunderstanding the nature of providence. The problem was pantheism. According to Calvin the Libertine belief that only one spirit extended throughout the universe denied the essence of both human and angelic natures. Consequently he accused the Libertines of believing that the angels were "only inspirations or movements and not creatures possessing an essence." Against this error Calvin argued that angels possess "subsisting natures"; they are not merely impulses which God inspired in the soul or simply examples of divine power.[66] On the contrary, Calvin maintained, angels are incorporeal, created beings. Calvin also reaffirmed the traditional belief that all angels were created good. He attacked the "Manichaean error" by arguing that no evil nature can exist in the universe, "for the depravity and malice of both man and the devil or the sins that arise therefrom, do not spring from nature but rather from the corruption of nature."[67] Accordingly, Calvin concluded that angels are created, spiritual beings, all of whom were originally created good by God.[68]

Some, however, revolted against God. Calvin insisted that Scripture does not clearly and systematically explain the cause, manner, time, and character of this fall. As a result he warned that Christians must be satisfied with the information supplied by Scripture: ". . . they were, when first created, angels of God, but by degeneration they ruined themselves and became the instruments for the ruin of others. Because this is profitable to know it is plainly taught in Peter and Jude. God did not spare those angels who sinned and kept not their original nature but left their abode."[69] With this statement Calvin affirmed what he believed to be the biblical teaching but dismissed any further "speculation" about the fall of the devils.

The elect angels, Calvin explained, are a part of that unfallen creation which retained its original integrity. These celestial spirits did not revolt against their Creator and consequently underwent neither sin nor separation. According to Calvin, these "eminent," "noble," and "excellent" creatures were not tempted by evil affections and therefore there was neither defection nor sin among them.[70] They remain before God, contemplate his face, and render unto him praise. Even when executing divine commands, Calvin argued, these unfallen angels are never separated from God.[71]

3. THE FUNCTION OF UNFALLEN ANGELS

Throughout his discussion about angels Calvin's main purpose was to define—and limit—their function in the world. Repeatedly Calvin stated that God entrusts the earth and human beings to the care of angels. According to Calvin, angels are "celestial spirits whose ministry and service God uses to carry out the things he has decreed."[72] Several of Calvin's most extensive comments are found in his interpretation of Ezekiel 1:11–24. For Calvin, the living creatures in Ezekiel's vision were angels whom God inspired by a secret power so that he could work by means of their "hands." Just as wheels were drawn along by the living creatures, so too the angels ". . . are discharging their office and by their motion and inspiration things in themselves motionless are carried along."[73] Heaven and earth, Calvin believed, are "quickened by angelic motion."[74]

> Neither air nor sea nor earth, have any vigor by themselves, unless so far as God by his angels directs the earth to this use, or while he bends the purposes of men in one direction or another, to either war or peace. Now, therefore, we see clearly the meaning of "the spirit of the living creatures being in the wheels," namely, that God transfuses his power through the angels so that not even a sparrow falls to the earth without his foresight [*providentia*], as Christ says.[75]

In Calvin's view, God presides over angels so that through them he protects, defends, and comforts the church. In Calvin's view, the main function of angels is the protection of the faithful, especially in their battle against demons. Calvin saw history as that arena in which God and his angels do battle against Satan and his forces.[76] An enemy, Calvin warned, "relentlessly threatens us, an enemy who is the very embodiment of rash boldness, of military prowess, and crafty wiles. . . ." Calvin never tired of reminding his readers that, as I Peter 5:8 states, "Your enemy, the devil, prowls around like a roaring lion, seeking someone to devour." Calvin also believed that the devil "rules in the air and holds the world in subjection under his feet."[77]

Against this enemy, Calvin taught, Christians must always be on guard. They cannot allow themselves to be overcome by faintness or carelessness: "since military service ends only with death, let us urge ourselves to perseverance."[78] Calvin believed that the church is engaged in constant battle against those who "assail God's glory and man's salvation." Through his attacks on the church, Satan attacks God's glory and, therefore, believers must battle against him: "If we are concerned to affirm Christ's kingdom as we ought, we must wage irreconcilable war with him who is plotting its ruin."[79] But, Calvin explained, believers are too frail to undertake this warfare alone. Therefore, in the midst of a dangerous and demonic world, God commissions angels to protect the safety of the church.

Despite his thorough analysis of Calvin's concept of spiritual warfare, Charles Hall devotes only several sentences to the assistance rendered by angels. But Calvin defined the angelic mission in the world precisely in terms of this assistance against the threats to the church waged by Satan and the wicked. He delighted in describing the armies of angels who surround and protect the faithful. Commenting on Daniel 10:13, Calvin interpreted the Archangel Michael in terms of the angelic defense of the church:

> From this passage we may clearly deduce the following conclusion: angels fight for the church of God both generally and for single members, as their help may be needed. Therefore in these respects we know that angels are employed

in protecting the faithful by Christ's help, and, as it is said in Psalm 34, they fix their camp in a circle around them [believers]. God, therefore, plants his angels against all endeavors of Satan, and all the fury of the impious who desire to destroy us and are ever plotting for our complete ruin. If God were not to protect us in this way, we should be completely undone. . . . What prevents Satan from daily absorbing us a hundred times over, that is, the whole church both collectively and individually? It clearly becomes necessary for God to oppose his fury and he does this by angels.[80]

Interpreting Zechariah 2:3, Calvin again described angelic protection of the church:

Therefore it appears from the whole context of what the prophet says, how carefully God provides for the safety of his church; for he always has angels as his emissaries who hasten at his nod, and aid the church in its necessities. Since then, the angels unite to secure the safety of the church, we perceive how dear to God are the faithful in whose favor he employs all his angels.[81]

And in his commentary on Isaiah 37:36 Calvin wrote:

Nor is it a new thing for the Lord to make use of the ministry of angels, to promote the safety of believers, for whose benefit he has appointed all the armies of heaven and it tends greatly to confirm our faith when we learn that an infinite number of guardians watch over us.[82]

Rather than positing individual guardian angels, Calvin insisted that God put armies of angels at the service of the church. According to Calvin, God uses these angelic armies as a way of comforting believers and of accommodating his majesty and power to their weakness:

It serves not a little as confirmation of our faith to know that God has innumerable legions [of angels] always ready for his service as often as he pleases to aid us; nay, more, that those too, who are called celestial principalities and powers, are always intent upon the protection of our life . . . but as a help for our present state, according to the extent of our ignorance, he, [God] manifests himself in his angels.[83]

Despite the fierceness of this spiritual warfare, however, Calvin believed that God's omnipotence had already secured final victory for the church. God's immutability, faithfulness to his promises, and invincible power guarantee Satan's defeat.[84] Calvin's emphasis on God's sovereignty and control over creation resurface in his descriptions of spiritual warfare. Continually Calvin insisted that God was in control of evil; unless he directed the devils according to his infallible purposes, evil would be outside the divine will. Job 1:6 teaches, according to Calvin, that the devil always stands under the command of God and acts only insofar as God wills.[85] Throughout his sermons on Job, Calvin reminded his hearers that unless God bridled the demons they would "overflow" the earth and crush believers.[86] Just as Calvin's God bridles the threats of nature, so too he restrains the fury of Satan: "But because with the bridle of his power God holds him [Satan] bound and restrained, he carries out only those things which have been divinely permitted to him; and so he obeys his creator, whether he wills or not, because he is compelled to yield him service wherever God impels him."[87]

Precisely because the devils can only serve God's purposes, their final defeat has been secured. Although the unclean spirits exercise believers in temptation and combat, ". . . yet they never vanquish or crush them."[88] Interpreting Genesis 3:15 Calvin argued that the church cannot be conquered by Satan.[89] According to Calvin, although the spiritual battle has already been won by Christ, the victory appears on earth "only in part." Nonetheless, God, who is beyond all repentance, firmly executes his plan and consequently the warfare against the demons has been ordained, permitted, and executed by God – but the outcome has already been determined.[90]

4. LIMITATION OF ANGELS

Although modern readers are often surprised by the extent to which Calvin discusses the angels, Calvin himself was, in many ways, reserved and uneasy about angelic beings and tried to limit their adoration and their role in the church. He continually warned that the angelic creation must not become an object of worship or devotion. Emphasizing Pauline warnings against such adoration, Calvin attacked the idolatrous transfer of divine glory and honor to angels.[91] In these attacks, which repeat his criticisms of the cult of saints,[92] Calvin opposed the medieval cult of angelic devotion which had grown steadily in the church. In the devotion to angels Calvin saw the ever-recurring phenomenon of idolatry. For Calvin, the veneration of the saints and the glorification of angels were both examples of that idolatrous drive by the fallen mind to create idols by attributing divinity to creatures.[93] Calvin's attempt to abolish this idolatrous worship of angels focused on the dependent, subservient nature of angels. The angels, he argued, are creaturely, possess only partial knowledge, cannot act as mediators, and are below and in need of Christ. Angels, he warned, are only creatures and, like the human soul, they are by nature mortal and of a finite essence.[94] Angels possess neither constancy nor firmness in and of themselves and, like all creatures, must continuously derive their being from God.[95]

The creaturely and dependent status of angels is clear, according to Calvin, in their role as servants. Since angels only carry out divine commands ". . . there should be no question but they are also his creatures."[96] Commenting on Hebrews 1:14 Calvin admitted that since angels are spirits they are "superior" to corporeal creatures. But, he added, their office "reduces them to their own rank since it is the opposite of dominion; and this he [Paul] more distinctly states when he says that they are sent to minister." Calvin concluded that "the service which God allots to angels is indeed honorable but the very fact that they serve shows that they are far inferior to Christ, who is the Lord of all."[97] In their service to God angels never act independently. The governance of the universe, Calvin insisted, is never transferred to angels. After describing the "angelic motions" which quicken the universe, Calvin hastened to add to his comments on Ezekiel 1:22:

> But when Ezekiel places God on his throne, we understand that angels who inspire motion in other things, have neither vigor nor motion in themselves. Generally the prophet teaches that angels so move all things that are done under heaven that nothing ought to be ascribed to them as their own. Why? Because God presides over them and governs their actions.[98]

Angels, then, are "so subject to God that they always depend upon his nod and are borne wherever he commands them."[99] In Calvin's view, the wings of the angels described in Ezekiel 10:8 testify that angels have no independent motion but are governed by God's "secret instinct."[100] Interpreting Isaiah 63:9 Calvin wrote that angels do nothing by themselves but only under God's command: "Let us not fix our whole attention on them, for they lead us straight to God."[101] Calvin also praised Daniel for seeing that despite angelic assistance, all praise was due to God alone: "He [Daniel] prominently puts forward the unity of God and then adds the presence of angels as God's assisting servants, showing how they perform whatever they are commanded. Thus the whole praise of their salvation remains with the one God, since angels do not assist whomsoever they please and are not moved by their own will, but only in obedience to God's commands." Nor, Calvin argued, is God under any necessity to use angels. ". . . for as often as he pleases, he disregards them and carries out his own work through his will alone."[102]

This subservient nature of angels is also clear from their relationship to Christ. Calvin never tired of arguing that Christ excels all angels. Passages such as Hebrews 1:13–14 supported Calvin's contention that Christ stands at the head of the angelic creation.[103] But it is in his exegesis of several passages crucial to angelology (Colossians 1:20, Ephesians 1:10, and Job 4:18) that one sees Calvin's emphasis on this point and his distinction from the exegetical tradition. Here we see Calvin's attempt to keep the angels in their created rank. Interpreting Ephesians 1:10, Calvin wrote:

> So far as they are creatures, had it not been for the benefit they derived from Christ, they would have been liable to change, to rebellion, and to punishment and consequently their happiness would not have been eternal. Who then will deny that both angels and men have been brought back to a fixed order by the grace of Christ? Men had been lost and angels were not beyond the reach of danger.[104]

Commenting on Colossians 1:20, Calvin explained:

> Between God and angels there is a far different reason [for reconciliation], for there was with them no revolt, no sin, and consequently no separation. Nevertheless,

there are two reasons why angels must be made at peace with God, for being creatures they were not beyond the risk of falling had they not been confirmed by the grace of Christ. . . . Furthermore, in that very obedience which they render to God, there is not such absolute perfection which would give satisfaction to God in every respect and without need for pardon. And without doubt this is what is meant by that statement in Job 4:18 "He will find iniquity in his angels." . . . But the Spirit declares here that the greatest purity is vile if examined before the righteousness of God. We must, therefore, conclude that there is not on the part of angels so much righteousness as would suffice for their being fully joined to God.[105]

Calvin differed from traditional interpretations of these passages on several points. Instead of applying Job 4:18 to the fallen angels, Calvin insisted that before God even the good angels could be found unclean.[106] In his sermons on Job Calvin developed the idea of God's secret justice to interpret this verse; according to the hidden justice of God even the unfallen angels could be condemned.[107] In his explanations of Colossians 1:20 and Ephesians 1:10 Calvin denied that the reconciliation "of things in heaven and on earth" referred *only* to the reconciliation between the human race and the unfallen angels.[108] Instead he argued that these verses mean that the angels themselves were reconciled to God through the redemptive work of Christ.[109] This interpretation of the unfallen angels reveals again Calvin's uneasiness before the elevation of angels and his attempt to confine them within the created realm.

This uneasiness resurfaces in his insistence that angels possess only partial knowledge. Although he indicated no interest in the way angels know things, Calvin was determined that angels know only "in part." Here Calvin used the traditional denial of omniscience to angels in order to combat idolatrous devotion. The Reformer argued that believers are not to be surprised that the Bible depicts the angels as inquiring into the future and wondering when the last day would come since they too are creatures "knowing only in part."[110] Like Chrysostom, Calvin believed that the means of human redemption had not been revealed to the angels before the incarnation: "Nor is it surprising that it was a new spectacle to the angels, who, though they know about the redemption of mankind, yet did not at first understand the means by which it should be accomplished, and from whom it must have been concealed, in order that this remarkable display of the goodness of God might be beheld by them with greater admiration."[111]

Nothing demonstrates Calvin's determined efforts to limit the adoration of angels more than his insistence that the angels cannot be mediators between God and human beings. This attempt to invoke angels as mediators, Calvin said, stems from the Platonic tradition; the "Popish" errors in this regard were all drawn from the writings of Plato.[112] The Reformer grudgingly admitted in Zechariah 1:12 that angels may offer prayers for believers but denied that we are to invoke them.[113] At every possible opportunity Calvin argued that angels cannot pacify God, cannot be invoked as mediators, and are not to obscure the divine glory.[114] In his exegesis of Genesis 28:12, Calvin reminded his readers that Jacob's ladder signified Christ, not the angels:

> Moreover the angels, to whom is committed the guardianship of the human race, while strenuously applying themselves to their office, yet do not communicate with us in such a way that we become familiar and, as it were, conscious of their presence. It is Christ alone, therefore, who connects heaven and earth. He is the only mediator who reaches from heaven down to earth; likewise it is he through whom the fulness of all celestial blessings flows down to us, and through whom we in turn ascend to God. . . . For the likeness of a ladder suits the Mediator well, through whom the ministry of angels, righteousness, life, and all the graces of the Holy Spirit, descend to us step by step.[115]

5. CONCLUSIONS

The foregoing discussion shows that the subject of angels frequently occupied Calvin. Certainly, angels appear in his writings far more frequently than much of the secondary literature indicates. The Reformer's angelology was characterized by a limited acceptance of traditional teachings about angels and a rejection of anything he considered nonbiblical or "speculative."

1. In his attempt to be purely biblical Calvin portrayed a world filled with angels and demons. With the tradition he agreed that all celestial spirits were originally created good by God and were of a purely incorporeal spirit. He agreed that some angels fell and that now these demons live in the air and take the impious captive. But that is as far as Calvin would go when it comes to the narration of the angelic creation and fall. He rejected all speculation about the time of their creation or the present nature of the angelic hierarchy.

2. Calvin's angelology focused on the providential mission of angels. Not surprisingly, therefore, his discussions about angels reflect those themes central to his doctrine of providence. Angels testify to God's presence in and care for the world, particularly the defense of the church. But even in those passages where Calvin vividly described the power, security, and comfort of angelic protection, Calvin was concerned not to attribute too much efficacy to angels. He continually qualified his statements by limiting their glory, forbidding speculation about them, insisting that they were only obedient servants, and restricting them to the level of creation. Christ, he said, is the head of angels and our only Mediator.

3. This limitation of angels was due to two factors. First, Calvin was attempting to abolish all idolatrous worship, which he saw personified in the cult of the saints as well as the cult of angels. If angels are only creatures, as Calvin asserted in agreement with the tradition, then to invoke them is simply idolatry. But Calvin's restriction of the power and authority of angels is also indicative of his doctrine of providence as a whole, which never allowed real independence

to secondary means. Typically Calvin placed God as close to his "secondary causality" as possible. Therefore, Calvin's God directly and continually commanded the angels, inspired them by a "secret instinct," and inclined them in the directions that he wished. Consequently, Calvin granted particular importance to the wings and the swiftness of angels; their prompt and instantaneous obedience exemplified their willingness to be servants and God's close and immediate control over their movements. For these two reasons, therefore, Calvin's remark that "one God is better than a universe of angels" characterized both his angelology and his doctrine of providence.

III

IMAGO DEI: THOU HAS MADE HIM
A LITTLE LOWER THAN THE ANGELS

Nowhere was Calvin's combative nature more evident than in his discussions of human nature; and, therefore, perhaps it is fitting that secondary scholarship on this subject has been characterized by controversy and heated debate. The central issue, growing out of the debate between Brunner and Barth, has been whether Calvin believed the image of God was lost in the fall. The answer has depended on the definition of the divine image. If one stresses the relational character of the *imago Dei*, namely, that one stands in the proper relationship to God, then the image was clearly lost in the fall. On this basis (early) Barth, Niesel, and Torrance have all insisted on the loss of the image.[1] According to these authors, Calvin believed that the sinful human being no longer retains the "right spiritual attitude," "gratitude," "reflection," or "mirroring" originally characteristic of the image of God.[2] Brunner, Gloede, and Stauffer, however, argued that in Calvin's view, a remnant of the divine image still belongs to the sinner: the image of God, they insisted, belongs in Calvin's thought to the order of creation and was "engraved" on the soul.[3] According to these scholars, Calvin saw the reason and will, and the capacity for language, knowledge, and culture as a remnant of the divine image still present in fallen human nature.

This debate has so governed contemporary scholarship that Calvin's use of the tradition, often polemical in nature, tends to fade from view. Calvin did not discuss the *imago Dei* only in terms of the possibility or impossibility of a natural theology. He also formulated his ideas about human nature in answer to the preceding tradition and sixteenth-century debates. His analysis presupposes knowledge of previous definitions of the divine image, late-medieval and sixteenth-century controversies about immortality, and the longstanding debate about free will.

1. HISTORICAL BACKGROUND

Genesis 1:26 ("Let us make man in our image and likeness") has long served the church in its analysis of prefallen, fallen, and restored human nature.[4] Irenaeus' famous distinction between the *imago* and the *similitudo* determined subsequent interpretation of this verse. According to Irenaeus, the *similitudo* or likeness was lost in the fall, while the *imago* or image remained.[5]

The likeness, Irenaeus explained, consisted of the spirit which is a supernatural gift of God. In the fall, human beings lost this supernatural element of their nature but remained human beings. For Irenaeus this meant that they retained the image, namely, rationality and freedom. In Irenaeus' view, these fundamental endowments, which make us human, could not be destroyed by sin. According to Brunner, this is a "two-story" anthropology which continued to dominate medieval exegesis and ultimately became the basis for the Scholastic distinction between natural and supernatural gifts.[6]

The second major contribution to the interpretation of Genesis 1:26 was that of St. Augustine. Augustine argued that since God is a Trinity, the image of God must be a trinitarian structure within the human being. Moreover, Augustine argued, this trinity must be located in that which is immortal.[7] Augustine began by locating this trinitarian image in the rational or intellectual soul and, finally, in "the noblest part of the mind, by which it knows or can know God. For although the human mind is not the same nature as God, yet the image of his nature, which is better than any other nature, ought to be sought for and found there in us, where there is also the best thing that our nature has."[8] Since nothing in the human being excels the rational nature, Augustine sought the *imago* in the mind.

After trying several trinitarian or threefold structures, Augustine concluded that the divine image consisted of the memory, understanding, and love: "Well then, the mind remembers, understands, and loves itself; if we discern this, we discern a trinity, not yet indeed God, but now at least an image of God."[9] Augustine added further, however, that these three functions of memory, understanding, and love are fully a reflection or image of God only because the mind which contains them can also remember, understand, and love "him by whom it was made."[10] With Augustine, therefore, the divine image is equated with the rational nature of the soul and defined in terms of a relationship between the soul and God.[11]

St. Thomas Aquinas also identified the divine image with rationality; only intellectual beings (angels and humans) are made in the image of God. Irrational creatures bear only a "trace" or an "approximate image" of the divine nature.[12] Thomas also cited the *De trinitate* approvingly and affirmed Augustine's location of the image in the trinitarian structure of the soul.[13] Thomas, however, also distinguished three degrees of the *imago*. On the lowest level, all people have the image because they possess a natural aptitude or capacity for understanding and loving God. On the second level, people "actually or habitually know and love God, though imperfectly." This is the image as it consists in the "conformity of grace." And, finally, when one knows and loves God perfectly: "this image consists in the likeness of glory."[14] In agreement with Augustine, Thomas defined the image in relational terms, i.e., the ability of the soul to know and love God: "Thus the image of God is found in the soul insofar as the soul turns to God or possesses a nature that enables it to turn to God."[15] In the final state, the blessed will see God in his essence.[16] And, finally, in agreement with the broad medieval tradition, Thomas argued that in the fall humanity retained the natural powers of the soul but lost the superadded gift of grace. The loss of this superadded divine gift caused the soul to become liable to punishment. Human nature, which was previously ordered and harmonious, became disordered by the fall into sin.[17]

In the later Middle Ages, the discussions central to our topic are the Aristotelian debates about the immortality of the soul; namely, the Averroist controversy, the condemnations of 1270 and 1277, and the reaction by such Renaissance Aristotelians as Pomponazzi.

We have already seen that Latin Averroism raised the controversy about God's knowledge of singulars and divine providence. Equally important was the issue of the soul's immortality. The debate centered on the interpretation of Aristotle's *De anima* III.5 where he speaks of the intellect as "separable," "impassible," and "eternal." Two interpretive traditions developed based on the exegesis of this passage. Alexander of Aphrodisias (c. A.D. 200) had argued that there are three kinds of intellects: the active intellect, identified with God; the material or potential intellect, which belongs to each human being and is corruptible at death; and an acquired intellect, which is the conjunction of the two in the knowing of eternal truths. Averroes, however, argued that the potential intellect is separate from all materiality, is one for all human beings, and is immortal. According to Averroes' exegesis of Aristotle, human knowledge and happiness consist in the union of the human *vis cogitativa* with the possible intellect by means of the illumination of the phantasms by the agent intellect.[18]

From Averroes' complex epistemology it follows that the human soul is neither immortal nor responsible for its actions since it is determined by the intellect. The intellectual power cannot be the "substantial form" by which the human being is constituted to be what he is; this function of the "substantial form" is fulfilled by the "human soul" which is corruptible with death. The individual human soul is not an immortal or spiritual substance which can outlast the body; the only "immortality" the individual mind can possess is its participation in the one Active Intellect. Consequently, there is no personal immortality and, of course, no rewards or death in the afterlife. On the basis of Aristotle's writings, Radical Aristotelians such as Siger of Brabant defended the doctrine of the unicity of the intellect which entailed a denial of personal immortality.[19]

In their battle against Radical Aristotelianism St. Bonaventure and St. Thomas opposed the doctrine of the unicity of the intellect. In December of 1270, Aquinas refuted the doctrines of Siger of Brabant in his treatise *De unitate intellectus*, and Bonaventure opposed this teaching in his treatises *Collationes de decem praeceptis* and *Collationes de septem donis Spiritus Sancti*.[20] Most importantly, the Parisian condemnations of 1270 condemned a list of propositions aimed at the Aristotelian view of immortality: (1) that the intellect of all men is one and the same; (2) that it is false or improper to say that "man understands"; (3) that the will of man wills or chooses necessarily; (7) that the soul, which is the form of man inasmuch as he is man, corrupts on the corruption of the body; (8) that the soul separated after death does not suffer from corporeal fire; (13) that God cannot grant immortality or incorruptibility to a corruptible or mortal thing.[21] Nonetheless, the 1270 condemnations did not stop the spread of Radical Aristotelianism. In 1277, the Radical Aristotelians on the Arts Faculty were still defending their views and John XXI warned against adherence to their teachings. Finally, in 1277 Stephen Tempier again issued a condemnation of 219 propositions, including articles on the unicity of the intellect and the denial of individual immortality.

Still the controversy over immortality was not over, as speculation continued about the afterlife, the soul's immortality, and the state of the soul after death. John XXII became embroiled in a dispute about the Beatific vision and denied that souls enjoy this vision before the last judgment. His opinion met with strong resistance from the Masters at the University of Paris. In the *Benedictus Deus* of 1336, Benedict XII censured the belief that death is a sleep that all souls must undergo until the last day. Speculation about the nature and state of the soul continued to flourish in the Renaissance. The orthodox position of the soul's immortality was again challenged by Renaissance Aristotelian thinkers such as Pomponazzi of Mantua (1462–1525) who taught at the Universities of Padua, Ferrara, and Bologna.[22] In his treatises *De immortalitate animae* (1516) and the *Apologia* (1518), Pomponazzi argued against both Thomistic and Averroistic interpretations of Aristotle. Pomponazzi, too, argued that the soul is essentially mortal.

Underlying Pomponazzi's analysis of the soul is his understanding of man's place in the hierarchy of being. According to Pomponazzi, the human being is midway between the angels and the animals.[23] The human intellect, therefore, functions at an intermediate level and shares in both the material and the immaterial. In Pomponazzi's view there are three modes of cognition corresponding to the three modes of separation from matter: "For there are things which are totally separated from matter and, therefore, in their knowing need neither a body as subject nor as object . . . and these are the separated substances which are called Intellects or Intelligences, in which there is neither discursive thought nor composition, nor any motion."[24] At the other extreme Pomponazzi posited sensitive powers which need a body both as subject and as object and whose knowledge is limited to particulars. Citing Psalm 8:5 ("Thou has made him a little lower than the angels"), Pomponazzi argued that the human intellect stands in the middle of the hierarchy: "Now since nature proceeds in an orderly fashion . . . between these two extremes of not needing a body as subject or as object and of needing a body as subject and object, there is a mean, which is neither totally abstracted nor totally immersed. . . . We shall place the human intellect above the cogitative and below material things, partaking of both, so that it clearly does not need the body as subject . . . and does need it as object. . . . Hence it [the soul] must be placed among material forms."[25]

Because the soul is a material form, Pomponazzi concluded that it is "unqualifiedly mortal and relatively immortal."[26] Since the soul is the highest material form "and lies at the boundary of immaterial things, it savors somewhat of immateriality but not in an unqualifed way."[27] Therefore, in Pomponazzi's thought, insofar as the intellect can grasp universals (in the singular object), it participates in a relative immateriality and immortality. However, he insisted that the soul is, of itself, mortal: "Whence it is truly a form beginning with and ceasing to be with the body, nor can it in any way operate or exist without the body."[28] As a safeguard, Pomponazzi added that his arguments were only deductions of philosophy or human reason; the immortality of the soul is an article of faith and should be proved by that which is proper to faith.[29]

At the Fifth Lateran Council in 1513, Pope Leo X condemned all "mortalist" heresies which denied the natural personal immortality of the soul:

> In these our days . . . the sower of tares, the ancient enemy of the human race, has dared to sow and foster in the field of our Lord certain very pernicious errors, always rejected by the faithful, especially as the nature of the rational soul, that it is mortal or one and the same in all men; and some rashly philosophizing, declare this to be true, at least according to philosophy. . . . We with the approbation of the Sacred Council, condemn and reprobate all those who assert that the intellectual soul is mortal, or one and the same in all men, and those who call these things in question, seeing that the soul is not only truly of itself and essentially the form of the body . . . but also is immortal and according to the number of bodies into which it is infused singularly multipliable, multiplied, and to be multiplied.[30]

Bohatec and Busson have shown that debates about immortality were frequent throughout the sixteenth century.[31] Undoubtedly, the translation and publication of Aristotle and Averroist commentaries helped to keep the controversy alive. Besides the work of Pomponazzi, we see disputes about immortality in the writings of men such as Dolet and Rabelais. Dolet appears to have equated immortality with the ancient concept of glory. The Averroistic denial of immortality also found expression in the writings of Rabelais. Not surprisingly, Calvin attacked both men as atheists and Epicureans since, he said, they denied eternal life and personal immortality.[32]

George Williams has argued that these debates about the soul's immortality influenced the sixteenth-century radical reformers. According to Williams, "the acceptance of the philosophical disproof of immortality combined with a vindication of life after death on the strength of revelation will be the mark of Italian Evangelicals. Within the philosophical framework of the two Paduan conceptions of the soul's mortality (Averroist absorption in the collective intellect and Pomponazzi's virtuous mortality), they will seek to rehabilitate the New Testament postulate (cf. I Thess. 4:13) of the death (thnetopsychism) or the unconscious sleep of the soul (psychosomnolence) in a lively expectation of the imminent resurrection of the virtuous, or, in other cases, the resurrection of both the virtuous and the wicked. . . ."[33] Calvin's opponents in his attack on the doctrines of soul-sleep and soul-death are hard to identify. Williams argues that in 1534 this was a Lutheran view and that Calvin's opponent in the original draft of *Psychopannychia* may have been Luther. Christian Neff denies that the sleep of the soul was ever a tenet of Anabaptism. Williams finds Neff's claim "curious." In his analysis of the *Brieve instruction*, Williams identifies Calvin's opponents as the French- and German-speaking Anabaptists. Battles judiciously notes that while the doctrine of soul-sleep or soul-death may not have been one widely held by the Anabaptists, the doctrine was more common in France and it is possible that the French-speaking Anabaptists did maintain some type of psychosomnolence.[34] In any event, Calvin simply lumped together and characterized as Anabaptist two groups with whom he had come into contact in Orleans: the psychosomnolents (who taught the unconscious sleep of the soul) and the thnetopsychists (who taught that the soul perishes and is resurrected with the body). He took up his defense of the soul's immortality against three opposing views: (1) alleged "Anabaptist" teachings, (2) the "pantheistic" error of the Libertines, Osiander, and Servetus, (3) the views of the philosophers and (4) the speculations and satires of men such as Rabelais.

2. NATURE OF THE SOUL

In the 1559 *Institutes* Calvin turned to his first detailed discussion of human nature as a continuation, in part, of his defense of the soul's immortality: "In short, the pre-eminent gifts with which the human mind is endowed proclaim that something divine has been engraved upon it; all these are testimonies of an immortal essence."[35] It was no accident that Calvin placed his analysis of the human soul in the context of such a defense. The frame of reference shows that Calvin undertook his description of human nature over and against what he perceived to be two fundamental errors: the denial of the soul's immortality and the denial of its created status. However indirect his knowledge may have been, Calvin's polemics were a continuation of those developments sketched above regarding late-medieval Aristotelianism and their impact on the sixteenth-century humanists and on the radical reformation.

Calvin's earliest analysis of the nature of the soul concerned the dispute about immortality. In his refutation of psychopannychism he argued both for the substantial existence of the soul and for its immortality. At the outset of the treatise he described two groups of opponents:

> Some while admitting it [the soul] to have a real existence, imagine that it sleeps, without memory, without understanding, and without sense from death to the day of judgment when it will awake from its sleep. Others will sooner admit anything

than its real existence, maintaining that it is merely the power of life which is derived from the arterial spirit or the action of the lungs and, being unable to exist without the body, perishes along with the body and becomes evanscent until the time when the whole man shall be raised again. We on the other hand, maintain that it is a substance and after the death of the body it truly lives, being endued with sense and understanding.[36]

According to Williams, the first group that Calvin described, namely, those who believed in the sleep of the soul, were French Paduans, Netherlandish Libertines, and perhaps Anabaptist refugees. Among the Radicals who held to psychopannychism, Williams lists Renato, Servetus, many of the Anabaptists, some of the Spiritualists (including the Libertines), and later the Socinians. On the basis of Calvin's reference to the physiological argument, Williams identifies the second group with Michael Servetus and his circle in Paris. It is necessary to note, however, that a physiological or materialistic conception of the soul is also described by Dolet and Rabelais. The latter places in the mouth of his characters the theory that life resides in the blood. Busson notes that this identification was common among the doctors and philosophers of the age. Rabelais could even find the identification of the vegetative soul with blood in Melanchthon. Busson cautions, however, against identifying such statements too quickly with a purely materialistic conception of the soul.[37]

Against those who argued that the soul was merely a vital power unable to subsist without a body, Calvin argued for the real and substantial existence of the soul distinct from the flesh. In this argument Calvin maintained that the image of God is *not* a part of the body and is not to be equated with the dominion that God gave humans over the beasts. The image, he said, is separate from the flesh and has its seat only in the spirit.[38] The *imago Dei*, he insisted, applies to the soul which dwells in the body as in a prison. But, Calvin explained, with the death of the body the war between the spirit and the flesh ceases and the soul is set free from impurities and is truly eternal.[39] Calvin admitted that the soul does, for a time, actuate and sustain the body but he argued that by virtue of its immortality the soul transcends the body: "let us hold fast the faith that our spirit is the image of God, like whom it lives, understands, and is eternal. As long as it is in the body it exerts its own powers, but when it quits this prison-house, it returns to God, whose presence it enjoys while it rests in the hope of a blessed immortality."[40] In this argument Calvin used the idea of the *imago Dei* to prove the immortality of the soul and thereby to refute at least one form of the "mortalist" heresy.

Against the view of soul-sleep, Calvin asserted that after the death of the body the soul exists in a watchful state, endowed with intellect, and awaits the resurrection. He argued that when Scripture says that the soul "rests," it means only the "tranquility and security of conscience."[41] Calvin further maintained that this "peace is increased and advanced by death, which freeing, and as it were discharging them from the warfare of this world, leads them to the place of peace, where, while wholly intent on beholding God, they have nothing better to which they can turn their eyes or direct their desire."[42] While Calvin admitted that this rest is complete only when souls see the glory of God perfectly, nonetheless he insisted that this interim state is a joyful one to the fully conscious soul.

Calvin repeated these arguments in *Brieve instruction pour armer tous bons fideles contre les erreurs de la secte commune des Anabaptistes*. In this reply to the *Schleitheim Confession* Calvin again identified two groups: those who hold that the soul is a substance but imagine that it sleeps until the resurrection and those who believe that the soul is merely a power animating the body so long as it is alive.[43] Against this latter position Calvin again argued that the soul has its own substantial essence. Since the soul possesses the image of God, he said, it is, by definition, an immortal spirit.[44] Following the death of the body, this immortal soul awaits the resurrection in a state of conscious joy and peace.

In his attack on the Libertines, however, Calvin confronted a different problem. Here he fought against the theory that the redeemed person is already in union with a single spiritual essence, Intellect, or Spirit which indwells all things.[45] This belief, which may reflect the influence of Averroism, failed, Calvin believed, to distinguish the Creator from the creature.[46] Describing what he believed was the "pantheistic" error of the Libertines, Calvin wrote: "From this they conclude that the spirit is reunited with the essence of God, so much so that only a single spirit remains."[47] Against this idea of a reabsorption into a single Intellect (*spiritus*), Calvin insisted that the resurrection has not yet occurred; presently our salvation is still hidden and our confidence is based on hope in that which is not yet fulfilled.[48] But he also combated briefly a view which recurs in various forms in the 1559 *Institutes*; that is, the identification of the soul with the divine essence. Disputing the proper interpretation of Ecclesiastes 12:7, Calvin asked, "but whom are they trying to persuade by such an interpretation that the human soul upon returning to God becomes God?"[49] Against an interpretation of this verse that would support deification, Calvin asserted that God receives human souls into his safekeeping and preserves them until they shall be reunited with their bodies.

In the 1559 *Institutes* Calvin again confronted the issue of the soul's nature and immortality. In Book I.V.5 he opposed the Aristotelians, probably Pomponazzi, who denied the soul's immortal nature. Calvin rejected that "frigid doctrine" of Aristotle that taught that the soul was united by the body "so as to be incapable of subsisting without it." Characterizing the view of men such as Pomponazzi, Calvin wrote: "For since the soul has organic faculties, they, by this pretext, bind the soul to the body so that it may not subsist without it, and by praising nature, they suppress God's name as far as they can." In Book I.15.6 Calvin repeated his attack against Aristotelians such as Pomponazzi who "so attach the soul's powers and faculties to the present life that they leave nothing to it outside the body."[50]

Calvin argued the opposite view. The powers of the soul, especially reason and the conscience, cannot be confined to the functions of the body and are proof of immortality. "Surely the conscience," he argued, "which, discerning between good and evil, responds to God's judgment, is an undoubted sign of the immortal spirit." So, too, the calculations of astronomy, the exercise of the memory, and the skill of invention all testify to the soul's immortality: "These are unfailing signs of divinity in man . . . What ought we to say here except that the signs of immortality which have been implanted cannot be effaced."[51] Calvin also marshalled scriptural proofs (Job 4:19, II Cor. 7:1, I Peter 1:9 and 2:25) to show that the soul has its own proper essence, separate from the body. And, finally, Calvin recalled Genesis 2:7; the *imago Dei* is "also a reliable proof of this matter," i.e., that the soul is immortal.[52] In his commentaries Calvin also argued that the levels of life evident in the creation of the human being illustrates the uniqueness of the human soul: "Three gradations indeed are to be noted in the creation of man; that his dead body was formed out of the dust of the earth; that it was endowed with a soul, whence it should receive vital motion; and that on this soul God engraved his image, to which immortality is added."[53] While the body is created though physical generation and birth, Calvin maintained that the soul is directly created by God. Arguing a creationist doctrine, Calvin wrote: "when God has created a human creature in the womb of the mother, it has as yet no soul; on the contrary we know that while the creature is shaped in the womb of the mother, God breathes into it a soul and certainly then there is a seed of life."[54]

In the *Institutes* Calvin opposed both this Aristotelian error and the implications of pantheism. He believed that the pantheistic error had resurfaced in the ravings of Osiander and Servetus, both of whom he accused of espousing the Manichaean belief that the soul emanates from God. He combated those aspects of their thought that implied any comingling of the divine essence and human nature. According to Calvin, because the Manichees misinterpreted Genesis 2:7 "they thought the soul to be a derivative of God's substance, as if some portion of immeasurable divinity had flowed into man."[55]

In Calvin's view this error had reemerged in the descriptions of regeneration found in Servetus and Osiander. Their talk of the indwelling Christ, the inner seed of God, and the essential righteousness of the saved, unnerved Calvin.[56] Any portrayal of the soul as a derivation of the divine essence or an inpouring of Christ's substance denied the truly *created* status of the soul: "to tear apart the essence of the Creator so that everyone may possess a part of it is utter folly. Therefore, we must take it to be a fact that souls, although the image of God be engraved upon them, are just as much created as are the angels." Calvin ended by reminding his readers that "creation is not inpouring, but the beginning of essence out of nothing."[57]

3. THE NATURE OF THE PREFALLEN SOUL

The struggle to define the soul as "created yet immortal" did not exhaust Calvin's analysis of its nature. Besides establishing its immortality, Calvin's main concern was to emphasize the radical difference between the human being's prefallen and fallen nature: "The knowledge of ourselves is twofold, namely, to know what we were like when we were first created and what our condition became after the fall of Adam."[58]

In order to explain this difference, Calvin postulated a basic understanding of the soul's faculties, which he then proceeded to evaluate according to their fallen and prefallen abilities. Although he left it to the philosophers "to discuss these faculties in their subtle way," Calvin did concede the following in a passage remniscent of classical and medieval psychology:

> Therefore I admit in the first place that there are five senses which Plato preferred to call organs, by which all objects are instilled into the common sense [*in sensum communem*] as a sort of receptacle. There follows fantasy [*phantasiam*], which distinguishes those things which have been apprehended by common sense; then reason, which is the power of universal judgment [*penes quam universale est iudicium*]; finally understanding [*mentem*] which in intent and quiet study contemplates that which reason ponders discursively. Likewise, to the understanding, reason, and fantasy (the three cognitive faculties of the soul), correspond three appetitive faculties: will [*voluntatem*], whose function consists of striving after what reason and understanding present, the capacity for anger [*vim irascendi*] which seizes what is offered it by reason and fantasy; the capacity to desire inordinately [*vim concupiscendi*], which apprehends what is set before it by fantasy and sense.[59]

Calvin refused to go beyond this description because he preferred a simpler definition "within the capacity for all," which divided the soul into only two faculties: the understanding and the will.[60] Having established these two faculties, he affirmed the primacy of the former: "Let the office of the understanding be to distinguish between objects as each seems worthy of approval or disapproval, while that of the will to choose and follow what the understanding pronounces good but to reject and flee what it disapproves."[61] The Reformer rejected the "minutiae of Aristotle" that the mind had no motion of itself but was moved by choice and insisted that the understanding is the "leader and governor of the soul and the will is always mindful of the bidding of the understanding and in its own desires awaits the judgment of the understanding."[62] Rather than pursuing a philosophical analysis, Calvin preferred to emphasize the ordered and harmonious nature of the prefallen soul:

> Accordingly the integrity with which Adam was endowed is expressed by this word [*imago*]. When he had full possession of right understanding, when he had his affections kept within the bounds of reason, all his senses tempered in right order, and he truly referred his exceptional gifts bestowed upon him by his Maker.

And although the primary seat of the divine image was in the mind and heart, or in the soul and its powers, yet there was no part of man, not even the body itself, in which some sparks did not glow. . . . From this we may gather that when his image is placed in man a tacit antithesis is introduced which raises man above all other creatures and, as it were, separates him from the common mass.[63]

In this context, the *imago Dei* is more than the soul's immortality. Calvin rejected the interpretations of Irenaeus, Chrysostom, and Augustine. Hebrew parallelism, he argued, does not allow for Irenaeus' distinction between image and likeness.[64] Augustine, he thought, had wandered into speculation with his idea that the image consisted in the psychological trinity of memory, understanding, and will, for, Calvin insisted, "in order that we may know of what parts this image consists, it is of no value to discuss the faculties of the soul."[65] He agreed with Chrysostom that dominion over nature was a part of the image but denied that it was the sole mark by which the human being resembled God.[66] Having rejected or corrected these interpretations, Calvin defined the image as the original order in the soul and the relationship whereby Adam "truly referred his excellence to the exceptional gifts bestowed on him by his Maker."[67] Because the soul was rightly ordered, the will was free to follow reason, the affections were kept within bounds, and the reason was capable of knowing and loving God. Human judgment, reason, and prudence sufficed, Calvin said, for the direction of earthly life and would have enabled the human being to rise up to God and eternal bliss.[68]

This "ascent" which was possible for the original image of God would have taken place through the contemplation of nature. In Calvin's view, the prefallen soul had been placed in a cosmos that was a "mirror," "theater," "open volume," or "book," displaying the glory of God.[69] Since, Calvin argued, the divine essence was unknowable, God manifested himself in the "visible language," "apparel," or "fabric" of the world "so that all people might know and praise him."[70] The order in nature would have led this prefallen, ordered soul to a knowledge of God and a life of obedience and praise. Therefore, the "skillful ordering of the universe," manifested in the regularities, continual order, and beauty of nature, was intended "as a sort of mirror in which we can contemplate God who is otherwise invisible."[71] Since the human body contained enough miracles to demonstrate God, one did not need to go beyond himself.[72] Consequently, the prefallen, immortal, and ordered soul was created for the purpose of knowing and praising God through a contemplation of nature.

4. THE NATURE OF THE FALLEN SOUL

Calvin's main purpose, of course, in describing the ordered nature of the prefallen soul was to contrast it with the deformity of the fallen soul. Adam did not "remain whole." Calvin's impatience with "the philosophers" went beyond their affection for subtleties; they failed, in his opinion, to recognize the radical difference between the fallen and prefallen soul. Consequently, Calvin attacked those who followed Plato and Aristotle and challenged their reliance on human reason and free will. He concluded by accusing the "philosophers" (including the Scholastics and the Renaissance humanists) of "seeking in a ruin for a building and in scattered fragments for a well-knit structure."[73]

In opposition to Plato, Calvin censured the reliance on human understanding. The knowledge of natural law, Calvin argued, disproved the Platonic theory that sin resulted from ignorance: "Natural law is that apprehension by the conscience which distinguishes sufficiently between just and unjust and deprives men of the excuse of ignorance while it proves them guilty by their own testimony."[74] Therefore, *coram Deo* the knowledge of natural law renders fallen men and women inexcusable: "The sinner tries to evade his own impression of the judgment between good and evil. Still he is continually drawn back to it and not even permitted to wink at it without being forced, whether he will or not, at times to open his eyes. It is falsely said, therefore, that man sins out of ignorance alone."[75]

Calvin also attacked the Scholastics for attributing to the human being any small ability to seek the good, which he said must be distinguished from our natural inclination toward well-being. In particular, Calvin censured the division between operating and cooperating grace, since it suggested a natural ability in human nature to seek the good. "The thing," Calvin explained, "that displeases me about this division is that, while he [Lombard] attributes the effective desire for good to the grace of God, yet he hints that man by his very own nature somehow seeks after the good, although ineffectively."[76] Calvin thought he spotted the same danger in Bernard: "Bernard declares the good will is God's work, yet concedes to man that of his own impulse he seeks this sort of good will."[77] For Calvin, any suggestion that human nature could seek the good mitigated the effect of the fall and blurred the radical disjunction between prefallen and fallen natures.

In the midst of these polemics, Calvin put forth his own view of fallen human nature, which was, of course, Augustinian in its emphasis on the bondage of the will. In order to understand Calvin's analysis of fallen human nature, two principles must be remembered: the distinction between the natural and the supernatural, and the inherently active character of human nature.

Despite his criticism of Peter Lombard, Calvin cited with approval Lombard's statement that in the fall supernatural gifts were effaced and natural gifts corrupted.[78] Faith, love of God, charity, and zeal for holiness were lost in Adam's defection. The human soul, which was disordered in the fall, is totally corrupt with respect to the spiritual realm. This loss of spiritual understanding is exemplified, in Calvin's view, by the inability of men and women to perceive God in the "book of nature." The fall, which was a "confusion" of the natural order, effected a corresponding confusion in the order of knowing.[79] Human beings no longer refer their excellence to God and consequently can no longer perceive God in nature. In short, the relational character of the *imago Dei* was destroyed.

The natural gifts remained; the human being did not become a brute animal in the fall. Nonetheless, the soundness of the mind and the uprightness of the heart were withdrawn:

> Since reason, therefore, by which man distinguishes between good and evil, and by which he understands and judges, is a natural gift, it could not be completely wiped out; but it was partly weakened and partly corrupted. . . . First, in man's perverted and degenerate nature, some sparks still gleam. These show him to be a rational being, differing from brute beasts because he is endowed with understanding. . . . Likewise the will, because it is inseparable from man's nature, did not perish but was so bound to wicked desires that it cannot strive after the right.[80]

For Calvin, the fact that human nature retains a will and a mind means both that a remnant of the divine image remains and that the human being is always active. This inherently active nature of the fallen soul is crucial for understanding Calvin's thought about the divine image, natural law, and the continuation of society, as well as his analysis of sin. According to Calvin, the active nature of sinful humanity is evident both in the mind and the will, as they direct themselves both to the supernatural and the natural realms.

Calvin believed that the activity of the fallen mind in the supernatural realm manifests itself most clearly in the sin of idolatry. The fallen mind, driven by the "sense of divinity," tries to find knowledge of its creator. But instead it becomes a "labyrinth" or a "perpetual workshop of idols" so that, incapable of finding God through nature, it conjures up a host of idols: "Just as waters boil up from a vast, full spring, so does an immense crowd of gods flow forth from the human mind. . . ."[81]

The fallen will is also, according to Calvin, inherently active. Adopting Augustine's formulation, Calvin stated that the original will, which could choose between good and evil, was weak and insecure. Nonetheless, Calvin insisted, "there was no necessity imposed on God of giving man other than a mediocre and transitory will, so that from man's fall, he might gather more occasion for his glory."[82]

In the fall, the will became so enslaved to sin that "it cannot move toward the good, much less apply itself thereto; for a movement of this sort is the beginning of the conversion to God, which in Scripture is ascribed entirely to God's grace."[83] Nevertheless, the will always sins willingly because it "remains with the most eager inclination, disposed and hastening to sin. For man, when he gave himself over to this necessity, was not deprived of will but the soundness of the will."[84] Calvin saw that because human nature remains inherently active, the continuing "movement" of the will must be distinguished from Adam's original freedom to choose between good and evil.

Calvin was not alone in making this distinction, as he well knew when he called upon the authority of St. Augustine. Augustine's earliest analysis of the nature of willing is found in *De libero arbitrio*, where he analyzed what it meant "to have something within one's power." He concluded that because the will was "present to" man, it was in his power and, therefore, free: "Wherefore nothing is so much within our power as the will itself. For it is present by absolutely no interval as soon as we will. . . . Because it is within our power, it is free."[85] The will, Augustine argued, is necessarily "within our power" because when we "will" [*volumus*], we do "effect" [*facimus*] the will. Therefore, Augustine explained, "compulsion" is a concept contradictory to the very nature of willing; since the will is always "present" [*praesto est*], human beings always exercise their wills both in sin and in grace.

By the time Augustine wrote to Simplician he had become increasingly aware of the insufficiency of knowledge, the power of habit, and the inability of the human being to create a delight in the good. Nevertheless, he remained convinced that sin did not eradicate the activity of the will. Commenting on Romans 7:7–19 ("To will is present with me, but to do that which is good I find not"), Augustine wrote:

> To those who do not rightly understand these words, he seems to take away free will. Yet how does he do that when he says, "to will is present with me"? If that is so, actual willing is certainly within our power; that it is not within our power to do that which is good is part of the desserts of original sin. . . . When he said, "to will is present with me," he was referring to its facility. There is nothing easier for man under the law than to will the good and yet to do evil; he has no difficulty in willing but it is not so easy to do what he wills.[86]

In *De spiritu et littera*, Augustine interpreted this verse as descriptive of the converted Christian life. The human being is born with a history, namely, original sin, which divides the will and disorders the loves of the soul. Because human beings cannot decide what will delight or motivate them, they are determined on the deepest level of their being and will only to sin. However, this "bondage" never destroys the fundamental activity of willing:

> Yet under examination it appears that even if you do something unwillingly [*invitus*], you do it by your will, if you do it at all. You are said to do it against your will, that is unwillingly, because you would prefer to act differently, but you are compelled to act [*facere compellitur*] because of some evil . . . and so you act under compulsion. . . . Therefore, if you act, though it may not be with a full or free will, it can never be without willing; since the will is carried into effect, we cannot say that the actor is powerless.[87]

In Augustine's thought the enslaved will is never merely passive; even when people can only will in the direction of evil, they always actively will. The active nature of the enslaved will caused Augustine to see that true freedom transcends the mere exercise of the will; freedom consists in the inability to sin and the gift of an immutable will. For Augustine, then, true freedom is an "inability," namely, the inability to will evil by a will rooted immutably in the good.[88]

Luther's use of this Augustinian analysis is most evident in his argument against Erasmus that the totally fallen will is never merely passive. Luther knew that the charge of passivity was one of Erasmus' strongest arguments and insisted that a will that sins necessarily still does so willingly. In Luther's view, both God and creatures are always active; God is in "movement" and employs instruments who are themselves inherently active:

> Now Satan and man, having fallen from God and having been deserted by God, cannot will the good . . . but instead are continually turned in the direction of their own desires, so that they are unable not to seek the things of the self. This will and nature of theirs, therefore, which is averse to God, is not something non-existent. Although their nature is corrupt and adverse to God, Satan and ungodly man are not nonexistent or possessed of no nature or will.[89]

Like Augustine, Luther recognized the distinction between freedom and activity; the necessitated will is always active. Evil men are "carried along" by their own evil nature "though without any violence being done to the will, since it is not unwillingly compelled [*quia non cogitur nolens*] but is carried along by the natural operation of God to will naturally in accord with its character (which, however, is evil)."[90]

Clearly, Calvin continued in this tradition with his insistence that the fallen, enslaved will sins actively. He relied not only on Augustine and Luther[91] but on St. Bernard's analysis of the will found in sermon 81 on the Song of Songs. In this sermon Bernard argued that the will is always "willing" and that in sin the will undergoes a "voluntary servitude." But, Bernard emphasized, this servitude does not hold the will against itself because the sinner always remains an actively willing being. Therefore, sinners are always inexcusable because they are subject to an internal necessity and not compelled or forced by another.[92]

Calvin cited Bernard approvingly and clarified the issue through his distinction between compulsion and necessity. According to Calvin, necessity is that inner state of the soul that determines the direction of the will; God necessarily wills the good, sinners necessarily will evil. Compulsion, he explained, is an external force, contrary to the nature of the will. Calvin concluded that people sin out of the inner necessity of their fallen wills, but never because of an external force or compulsion.[93]

> The chief point of this distinction, then, must be that man as he was corrupted by the Fall, sinned willingly, not unwillingly, or by compulsion [*non invitum nec coactum*] . . . but by the prompting of his own lust, not by compulsion from without. Yet he is so depraved in his nature that he can be moved or impelled only to evil. But if this is true, then it is clear that man is surely subject to the necessity of sinning.[94]

In summary, Calvin's analysis includes both the total corruption of human nature *coram Deo* as well as the continuing activity of the reason and will. In Calvin's view, the mind is trapped in error and produces only idols while the will moves only toward evil. Any suggestion that either of these faculties retain their original ordered integrity confuses the prefallen and fallen nature of the soul.

5. NATURAL MAN OUTSIDE OF REDEMPTION

Even in his early debate with Emil Brunner, Karl Barth agreed that "even as a sinner, man is a man and not a tortoise."[95] Calvin could not have said it better. The inherently active nature of the human being manifests itself not only in sin but in the activities, judgments, and contributions which men and women carry out in their natural, societal lives. The seemingly obvious fact that man did not become a tortoise played a rather large role in Calvin's thought about the natural order. It has also caused confusion regarding his use of the term *imago Dei*.

Calvin thought that if viewed from the perspective of the natural order, human beings remain the chief work of creation, "the most illustrious ornament and glory of the earth."[96] If the human race should vanish, there would be a scene of desolation and solitude, "no less hideous than if God should despoil the earth of all its riches."[97] The centrality of man in creation is also evident from the fact that nature still serves him: "For why do the stars shine in the heavens except to be of service to men? Why does rain fall from the heavens and why does the earth bring forth fruits, if it is not to provide man with food?"[98] In Calvin's view, sin perverted but did not destroy the fundamental order of creation; the cosmos still serves its head, namely, the human race.

The Reformer also emphasized the centrality of the human being in the universe by adopting the Renaissance commonplace that man is a microcosm. Containing a "little world" in himself, the human being is "a rare example of God's power, goodness, and wisdom and contains within himself enough miracles to occupy our minds . . ."[99] The human being possesses a body whose structure displays inconceivable skill. That such an intricate structure results from human procreation is itself, Calvin exclaimed, a source of admiration; from a mere seed comes the gradual, ordered formation of the flesh, skin, nerves, bones, and even human nails. Calvin's references to the body as a prison (as found in the *Psychopannychia*) find their balance in his comments on Psalm 139 and Job 10:7-15 where he praised its wonders.

The soul, of course, primarily gives the human race its central and preeminent position in creation. As Brunner pointed out, the Reformers adopted the notion of a "remnant" or "relic" to explain man's continued *humanum*.[100] Having rejected Irenaeus' distinction between image and likeness, Calvin, like Luther, agreed that sinners retain the human endowments of reason, will, and conscience which are remnants of the divine image and which raise fallen human beings above the brute creation. As Calvin well knew, enough of human reason remains "to distinguish us from brute beasts so that . . . in man's perverted and degenerate nature some sparks still shine."[101] Although, in Calvin's view, man is now much lower than the angels,[102] he remains human, distinct from the beasts; the head of creation. Calvin agreed with Melanchthon that John 1:9 ("the light that enlightens everyman") refers not to those born again by the Spirit, but to all people:

> But since the Evangelist mentions in general, "every man coming into the world," I prefer the other meaning: that rays from this light are shed upon the whole race of men, as I said. For we know that men have this unique quality above the animals, that they are endowed with reason and intelligence, and that they bear the distinction between right and wrong engraved in their conscience. Therefore, no man exists for whom some awareness of that eternal life does not shine. . . . Let us remember that this is only referring to the common light of nature, a far lowlier thing than faith.[103]

Calvin saw this common light manifest itself in the unredeemed mind in the universal drive to know, to create, and to develop laws and civilization. The inherently active nature of the fallen human being is clear from the formation of the arts, sciences, and laws of the state. Human reason and will did not shut down in the fall. For Calvin, to deny human perception and understanding would be to deny the empirical evidence that human beings everywhere seek out knowledge:

> Wretched people that we are, there are none of us who do not covet knowledge; it is a natural desire that burns in all men. And we see many who expend their wealth and who spare neither their bodies nor their lives. And to do what? In order to get knowledge. We see others running here and there. Why? To get knowledge. All men, then, have that desire, some more, some less, and there is not a person so as not to yearn for knowledge.[104]

In Calvin's view, to condemn human understanding so as to leave it no remnant of perception of any object whatsoever, not only goes against God's Word but also runs counter to the experience of common sense. Calvin believed that we see some sort of desire implanted in human nature for seeking out truth, to which man would not at all aspire if he had not already savored it. Therefore, human understanding possesses some perception, since it is naturally captivated by love of truth.[105]

But what is the function of this remnant or this "common light" which still drives the human being? Is it a "point of contact" between the human being and God? No. Does it render the human race only inexcusable before God? Certainly with respect to the spiritual realm, human reason, will, conscience, and judgment render human beings inexcusable. Are Calvin's statements about the accomplishments of this "common light" merely examples of his awakened "humanism"?[106] Certainly Calvin's "humanism" played an important role in his appreciation for the arts, sciences, and jurisprudence. But the remnant plays another essential function in Calvin's thought which goes beyond his appreciation for sixteenth-century humanism. As the various citations throughout this chapter have shown, Calvin continually stated that "man did not become a beast." In the following chapter we will see that the survival of reason, will, and conscience served to explain to the Reformer why human society did not dissolve into total confusion and chaos after the fall. In Calvin's writings, the fact that humanity did not become bestial was not merely a rhetorical phrase: it was the cause of wonder and gratitude.

6. CONCLUSIONS

Calvin's statements about human nature were often developed polemically and require attention to both this polemical context and to the perspective out of which he spoke. In these various contexts the notion of the *imago Dei* took on different, although not contradictory, meanings.

1. In his battles with Aristotelianism and psychopannychism, Calvin equated the *imago Dei* with immortality. The soul, he insisted, was not so attached to the body that it either died or "fell asleep" after the death of the body. The soul, he argued, is immortal and lives a conscious life independently of the "flesh" while awaiting the resurrection. If the image is equated with immortality then it cannot, by definition, be erased or lost.

2. Against the "philosophers" and the Scholastics, Calvin discussed human nature *coram Deo* and emphasized the disorder and depravity of the fallen soul. The image of God in the prefallen human being consisted of an ordered soul which referred its excellence to its maker. The ordered and relational character of the image has been defaced, with the result that the mind has fallen into idolatry, the will is enslaved to sin, and the supernatural gifts are destroyed.

3. Nonetheless, the human being remains active. With reference to the spiritual level, this activity of the soul is only sinful. On the natural level, however, human nature *qua* human still exists. Emphasizing the idea of the "remnant" or "relic," Calvin equated the image of God with the continued existence of such natural human endowments as reason and will. This "remnant" renders us inexcusable if we are referring to the knowledge of God, and as such it plays only a condemning role in the issue of "natural theology." But Calvin did not use the idea of a remnant only in the context of the knowledge of God. The dominance of this issue in modern Calvin scholarship threatens to overshadow the other, equally important, context in which Calvin employs the notion of the "remnant" or the natural endowments of human nature, namely, the continuation of human society. We will see that Calvin's fascination with this remnant stemmed not only from his humanism but from his awe before the continual survival of a human race that did not become bestial.

IV

THEIR CONSCIENCE ALSO BEARS WITNESS:
NATURAL LAW AND SOCIETAL LIFE

Having retained a remnant of the *imago Dei*, human beings remained human and continued to live in society. Calvin explored the nature of that society by means of natural law. Just as he inherited traditions concerning providence, angels, and the image of God, so too he received the legacy of natural law, derived from ancient and medieval theorists. This chapter will analyze the way in which Calvin used both this legacy and the belief in the remnant of the *imago Dei* to explain the continuation of societal life. We turn first to a brief history of the theory of natural law.

1. HISTORICAL BACKGROUND

Historians agree that the origin of natural law was not Roman. Natural law was borrowed from Greek philosophy, particularly Stoicism, and passed over into Roman thought and law.[1] In the following quotation from *De republica*, inspired by Stoicism and preserved by the Christian writer Lactantius, we find the famous Ciceronian definition of natural law.

> True law is right reason in agreement with nature; it is of universal application, unchanging and everlasting; it summons to duty by its commands, and averts from wrong-doing by its prohibitions. And it does not lay its commands or prohibitions upon good men in vain, though neither have any effect on the wicked. It is a sin to try to alter this law, nor is it allowable to attempt to repeal any part of it, and it is impossible to abolish it entirely. We cannot be freed from its obligations by senate or people, and we need not look outside of ourselves for an expounder or interpreter of it. And there will not be different laws at Rome and at Athens, or different laws now and in the future, but one eternal unchangeable law will be valid for all nations and for all times, and there will be one master and one ruler, that is God, over us all, for he is the author of this law, its promulgator, and its enforcing judge.[2]

Both Roman jurists and the Christian church took over the concept of natural law. The theory of natural law forms an important element of the *Corpus Iuris Civilis* (A.D. 534) which was compiled by Byzantine lawyers at the request of Emperor Justinian. However, the classifications of laws found in the Digest are not uniform; the differing opinions of Ulpian, Gaius, and Paulus are listed without any attempt at harmony. Gaius and Paulus presented a twofold definition of law. According to Gaius, law consists of the *ius civile* which is peculiar to each city or people and the *ius gentium* which is the law of nations, dictated by natural reason and commonly practiced by all nations.[3] Paulus, however, distinguished between natural law and civil law. The *ius civile* is that which "in each city is profitable to all or to many." The *ius naturale* is that which is always equitable and good.[4] Ulpian, however, defined the tripartite division of law, which in modified form was adopted by many theorists of the Middle Ages.[5] According to Ulpian, the *ius naturale* is that which nature teaches all animals (including humans) and includes the union of male and female, the procreation of the race, and the education of offspring. The *ius civile* is that which is proper to each people, namely, the law of the state. Finally, the *ius gentium* is that which is common to all peoples.

Isidore of Seville adopted Ulpian's threefold division but modified the definitions. For Isidore, the *ius civile* is that which is proper to each people. The *ius naturale*, however, is that which is common to all nations. And the *ius gentium* is that which is in usage among most people. Isidore defined the *ius naturale* as that which is characteristic of human beings and common to all peoples because he considered it as an inclination of nature, not a positive constitution of society. Consequently, Isidore's natural law encompasses "viri et feminiae coniunctio, liberorum susceptio et educatio, communis omnium possessio et omnium una libertas." Isidore further distinguished between divine and human laws. "All laws," he wrote, "are either divine or human. Divine laws are based on nature, human laws on custom." The reason why the latter sometimes varies, Isidore explained, is that "different nations adopt different laws."[6]

The *Decretum Gratiani* (c. 1140) became a principal source for the doctrine of natural law throughout the subsequent medieval period. Gratian reiterated Isidore's threefold division of *ius naturale, ius gentium*, and *ius civile*. For Gratian natural law pertained essentially to the human race. Gratian also emphasized that the moral law of the Scriptures was in accordance with natural law. "Mankind is ruled by two laws; Nature and Custom. Natural law is that which is contained in the Scripture and the Gospel." Identifying natural law with the "Golden Rule" of Matt. 7:12, Gratian added that natural law is that "by which everyone is commanded to do to others what he will to have done to himself, and forbids doing to others what he does not will to have done to himself." With the *Decretum Gratiani* we see the elevation of natural law. Natural law is binding and overrules all laws. It precedes them in time and remains unchangeable. If positive laws or customs contradict natural law, they must be considered as null and void.[7]

Thomas Aquinas, of course, formulated one of the fullest and most important explanations of natural law in the medieval period. In the *Summa Theologiae*, Thomas' teaching on natural law is a preliminary question for his discussion of the Old and New Laws which God made with his people. It is placed in the second part of the *Summa*, which begins with an analysis of how one obtains happiness. Thomas began his analysis in IaIIae 90 by explaining that law in general, as a principle of direction and measure, belongs to reason. In answer to the question whether natural law is a habit, Thomas answered that "since a habit is a quality whereby you act, it follows that a law cannot be a habit in the proper and essential sense of the term." However, Thomas added that "because the commandments of natural law sometimes are actually adverted to by reason and sometimes are just settled convictions, there, we may speak of natural law as a habit." He explained the role of the synderesis by stating that the "synderesis is called the law of our understanding inasmuch as it is the habit of keeping the precepts of natural law, which are the first principles of human activity."[8] And in S.T. IaIIae, qu. 91, art. 1–2 Thomas defined the position of natural law within the divine order. The whole universe, according to Thomas, is governed by providence or divine reason. The rational guidance of creation is God's eternal law. From this eternal law all creatures derive certain inclinations to those actions and ends which are proper to their nature. Rational creatures, above all others, participate in providence by providing for themselves and for others. In Thomas' view this participation of rational creatures in the eternal law is called natural law.[9]

According to Thomas, therefore, the objects to which human beings have a natural tendency are the concern of natural law. By its nature reason "apprehends the things towards which the human being has a natural tendency as good objectives." With this principle Thomas ranked the commands of natural law according to the natural tendencies of man. First, there is in human nature the desire for self-preservation, and natural law functions to maintain and defend the elementary requirements of human life. Secondly, following Ulpian, Thomas argued that the human being inclines toward that which he has in common with other animals. Hence, natural law teaches "the union of male and female, the bringing up of young, and so forth." Thirdly, human nature desires the good of its rational nature, i.e., to know truths about God and about living in society. Therefore, natural law dictates that one should shun ignorance, not offend those with whom he ought to live, and other such related requirements.[10] In answer to the question whether natural law is common to all, Thomas argued that "as for its first common principles, here natural law is the same for all in requiring a right attitude towards it as well as recognition. As for particular specific points, which are like conclusions drawn from common principles, here also natural law is the same for most people in their feeling for and knowledge of what is right." Nonetheless, Thomas added, the further one descends into detail, the more exceptions are admitted "so that you have to hedge it with cautions and qualifications."[11] And finally, Aquinas concluded by reaffirming Gratian's statement that natural right is that which is contained in the Old and New Laws: "By which everyone is commanded to do to others what he would have done to himself, and forbidden to do to others what he would not have done to himself."[12]

In his classifications of human laws, Thomas wanted to defend the sacred authority of Isidore. He argued that the *ius gentium* belongs only to human beings, in distinction from Ulpian's definition of natural law which extended to animals and humans. Thomas admitted that the *ius gentium* is natural to man "in the sense that he is reasonable and it is reasoned out like a conclusion from principles. . . ."[13] Throughout his definitions of the *ius naturale* and the *ius gentium*, however, are echoes of Roman law, namely, of Ulpian and Gaius.[14] As Lottin argued, in the midst of his defense of Isidore, Thomas was sympathetic to the formulations of Roman law.[15]

Late medieval theologians discussed whether the source of natural law was to be found in the divine will or divine reason. On this subject Otto von Gierke distinguished among several medieval views. The older view of the "Realists" depicted the law of nature as an intellectual act independent of the will. According to this view, Gierke argued, God was a teacher who worked by means of reason, "grounded in the Being of God but unalterable even by him." Nominalism, Gierke explained, saw the law of nature as a divine command rooted in the will of God. The commands of natural law were binding and right simply because God was their author. According to Gierke, Aquinas belonged to the "mediating opinion which regarded the substance of natural law as a judgment necessarily following from the Divine Being and unalterably determined by that Nature of Things which is comprised in God; howbeit, the binding force of this law but only its binding force, was traced to God's will."[16]

Reaffirming Gierke's general divisions, Francis Oakley contrasted Thomas with the "voluntarist" tradition of Occam and late medieval Nominalism.[17] Occam, d'Ailly, and Major, in their attempt to protect the biblical doctrine of God as free and sovereign against the philosophical determinism that resulted from the thirteenth-century reception of Aristotle, developed the implications of the "voluntarist ethics" of Duns Scotus. Fourteenth- and fifteenth-century thinkers emphasized God's freedom and omnipotence both in relation to his creation of the world and to his governance of the created realm. The voluntarist theory of natural law emphasized that the divine will, not reason, was the source of the law. Since God's will is the rule of justice, God is not under obligation to any law and may will anything that is not a logical contradiction. Oakley argued that when Occam spoke of an absolute and immutable law, he was thinking only within the framework of the ordained power of God.[18] *De potentia absoluta*, God could order the opposite of what has been forbidden.

Recent scholars, including Oakley, have demonstrated that this primacy of the divine will did not make God capricious or the created order, including the moral order, unreliable.[19] Occam and d'Ailly, for example, maintained the stability and the reliability of the moral order or natural morality through the distinction of God's absolute and ordained powers. God has condescended to work within the sphere of the moral law he ordained and to which right reason provides a guide, although by his absolute power God is not bound by that or any moral order.[20]

John McNeill has argued that the subject of natural law was not a source of controversy between the Scholastic tradition and the Reformers.[21] As did their predecessors, sixteenth-century Reformers assumed that Scripture, particularly Romans 2:15, affirmed the existence of natural law and that the Decalogue was the written and "clearer" form of that which was already true according to the law of nature.

In comparison with the medieval tradition, Calvin's discussions of natural law seem imprecise and unsystematic. He neither provided a systematic treatment of natural law nor did he analyze many of the issues commonly discussed by ancient and medieval thinkers. Nonetheless, he took over the traditional terminology and referred (sometimes interchangeably) to the "ius aequum," "lex naturae," "lex naturalis," and "ius gentium." The "ius gentium" referred to laws that govern the relations between the states, including the laws of marriage, security of ambassadors, theft, murder, and runaway slaves.[22] According to Bohatec, "die lex naturae ist vornehmlich der Inbegriff der praktischen, dem Menschengeist angeborenen rechtlichen und sittlichen Prinzipien (iustitiae ac rectitudinis conceptiones), die die Griechen als προλήψεις bezeichnet haben."[23] Often Calvin referred simply to "common sense," the "dictates of nature," or simply "nature." As we will see, throughout his writings Calvin emphasized the efficacy of such natural insight. Two of Calvin's most extensive statements regarding natural law are his comments on Romans 2:14–15 and the *Institutes* II.8.1:

> It is beyond all doubt that they have certain conceptions of justice and rectitude, which the Greeks refer to as προλήψεις and which are naturally inborn [*naturalites ingenitas*] in the minds of men. Therefore, they have a law without the Law; for although they do not have the written law of Moses they are not altogether lacking in knowledge of right and equity. Otherwise they could not discern between vice and virtue, the former of which they restrain by punishments, the latter they command, showing approval of it and honoring it with rewards. Paul opposes nature to the written law, meaning that the Gentiles had the natural right of justice which supplied the place of law by which the Jews are instructed so that they are a "law unto themselves."[24]

> Now that inward law [*lex illa interior*] which we have described is written, even engraved [*impressam*] upon the hearts of all, in a sense, asserts the very same things which are to be learned from the two tables. . . . Accordingly (because it is necessary both for our dullness and for our arrogance), the Lord has provided us with a written law to give us clearer witness of what was too obscure in the natural law, to shake off our listlessness and strike our mind and memory more vigorously.[25]

In these and similar passages Calvin relied on the traditional language of "natural law." Like his predecessors, he argued on the basis of Romans 2:14–15 that natural law was universally known but given in written form to Moses. Consequently in his exegesis of Exodus and Deuteronomy the commandments are seen as the divine formulation of natural law.[26] Calvin stressed, however, that the written Mosaic law was a necessity because of the effect of sin on natural perception. The Decalogue clarifies that which fallen reason can no longer understand or which it now perceives only dimly. This is particularly evident in the first table that requires a lawful worship of God. "Surely it [natural reason] does not at all comply with the principal points of the First table such as putting our faith in God, giving due praise for his excellence and righteousness, calling upon his name and truly keeping the sabbath. What soul, relying upon natural perception, ever had an inkling that the lawful worship of God consists in these and like matters."[27] In Calvin's view, even our knowledge of the second table of the Law is only partial and incomplete. In its demand that we obey unworthy rulers, the fifth commandment actually contradicts natural reason. Throughout its commandments the Decalogue, according to Calvin, demands not mere performance but the right motive, namely, the love of God and neighbor.[28]

Calvin also assumed other commonplaces of natural-law theory. He argued that "seeds" of law and conceptions of justice and equity have been implanted in all human minds so that we recognize the need for law and justice without a teacher or legislator.[29] For Calvin, as for Cicero, the principle that governs all laws is that of equity, and since equity is natural it is the same for all peoples.[30] Positive human laws, Calvin knew, are adapted to particular circumstances and may differ while equity remains the same. For Calvin, as for the previous Christian tradition, God, of course, was the author of this natural law and equity. When confronted by troublesome passages in which God appeared to command the opposite of natural and Mosaic law, Calvin insisted, in a way similar to late medieval Nominalism, that God's will is the rule of justice and that God is sovereign above all laws, including the law of nations and the law of nature. Eschewing all references to the nominalist terms "exlex" and "potentia absoluta," Calvin carefully maintained that in God's superiority to natural law his power is always conjoined with his justice.[31]

What importance do such statements possess in Calvin's thought? Are they, as Lang contends, superfluous and of no decisive significance?[32] Or were Bohatec, Doumergue, Beyerhaus, Brunner, Gloede, and McNeill correct in arguing that they play a central role in the Reformer's ethical, political, and social theory?

Calvin scholars have examined Calvin and natural law from various perspectives, including Calvin's relationship to classical and medieval sources, his similarity to his fellow Reformers, his belief in divine sovereignty, his position regarding natural theology, and his statements regarding the right of resistance. These important studies have discredited Lang's thesis and have clarified the multifaceted nature of Calvin's use of natural law. Bohatec has demonstrated that

Calvin repeatedly drew on the teachings of late antiquity. According to Bohatec, Calvin derived from Quintilian his division of laws into that which is given by nature to all peoples and that which is constituted by peoples and nations. From Cicero, Calvin learned the importance of equity as a fundamental component of all valid laws.[33] Beyerhaus and Bohatec have examined the role of Roman and natural law in Calvin's thought, often with differing results.[34] Bohatec and McNeill have documented the similarities and differences between Calvin and his fellow Reformers, especially in comparison to Melanchthon.[35] Both Brunner and Gloede have argued for the importance of natural law in Calvin's "natural theology" as a "concept of norm" in his statements about society, government, and the conscience.[36] And finally, both Bohatec and Beyerhaus have analyzed Calvin's rejection of any private right of resistance; only through legitimate or legally constituted means may a ruler be deposed.[37]

The focus of this chapter is somewhat different. We shall approach Calvin's statements about the "law" or "dictates" of nature as an extension of his doctrine of providence. In so doing we will see that his primary concern was not to formulate a theory of natural law but to use the idea of natural law as a way to explain the continuation of society after the devastating effects of the Fall. The recurrence of metaphors depicting the restraint of chaos and wickedness, so frequent in his discussions of providence, reveals that Calvin was keenly aware of the interconnection between the preservation of the cosmic and the societal realms. Like nature, the continuation of the civil realm was due to God's providence and the continual bridling of disorder. Calvin's statements about society reveal the same twofold attitude evident in his view of creation and history: fear of an ever-threatening chaos and awe before the continuation of stability and order.

2. NATURE AND SOCIETAL LIFE

Although God took less delight in creation after the vitiation wrought by sin, he continued to "take joy in his works."[38] As Calvin explained, "he did not cease to sustain by his power the world which he had made, nor to govern it by his wisdom, support it by his goodness, and regulate all things in heaven and in earth according to his good pleasure. . . ."[39] According to Calvin, sin could not alter the providential purposes of God; and, hence, Calvin repeatedly drew the reader's attention to the continuation of nature. The sun continues to shine and God's wisdom is still reflected in the order that prevails amidst the vast variety in nature. The seasons still change and appointed times remain for planting and for harvest. Animals are preserved with a hiddden instinct to search for food and no season is so barren that some food is not produced. Although vitiated by the Fall, the order of nature continues to be a mirror of God's glory and a testimony of his providence.[40] Calvin's presuppositions about secondary causality and the inherent fragility of nature meant that the mere continuation of creation is a sign to the believer that God still loves and preserves his creation.

Nature, however, was designed to serve its head, namely, the human being.[41] Unlike Augustine, Calvin lost no sleep over the fact that it took God "six days" to create the world. The order in the creation narratives teaches only that God did not create Adam until he had provided for his welfare. Like a diligent and caring father, God first disposed the movement of the sun and stars to human uses. God then filled the earth, waters, and air with living creatures. And finally, after providing fruits for food, God created Adam. The continuation of the order of nature after the Fall both reflected God's glory and provides for the human being who is the chief work of God's creation.[42]

In order to explain the preservation of the human race after the Fall, Calvin employed the concept of the *imago Dei*. God undertook to protect the life of men and women because they had been created in his image. Commenting on the divine punishment for murder, Calvin explained that God sought to preserve human life: "If anyone should object that this divine image has been obliterated, the solution is easy: first there yet exists some remnant of it; so that man is possessed of no small dignity. Secondly, the Celestial Creator himself, however corrupted man may be, still keeps in view the end of his original creation. . . ."[43] God could have created a world only of animals but, in order better to reflect his glory, chose to form some creatures after his own image.[44]

> God . . . willed to be magnified in heaven and earth, and in all his deeds, which we see, but much more so in man; and for this reason he imprinted his image in us more than in all the rest. For he did not say of the sun, stars, nor of some other creature as excellent as these, "I want to make here a chief work which is in my image and likeness."[45]

In Calvin's view, because God formed human beings in his image, God was affected by a fatherly love toward the human race; just as a worker loves his workmanship because he recognizes in it the fruit of his labor, so too God manifested his power and goodness in the formation of human beings and must embrace them with his love, "insofar as we are men . . . we are dear to God."[46] Here again Calvin argued from the nature of God. He repeatedly reminded his readers that the continued preservation of human beings was not due to their worthiness but to God's love for his own image and the fruit of his labor. Because people are created in the image of God, they remain, after the Fall, different from and superior to the animal creation.[47] God, Calvin repeated, did not allow either the cosmos to fall back into chaos or the human race to fall into bestial confusion. According to Calvin, God continues to support and preserve an ordered societal realm simply because he had once immutably decreed that "the earth shall be inhabited by man."

For how does it come about that God nourishes us and supplies us with everything that is necessary and even supports wicked men, except that he intended that his decree should stand by which he ordered the earth to be inhabited by men. For from any other point of view, it is strange that he bears with so many crimes and shameful things, and does not entirely destroy the human race in the universe; but he has regard to his own purpose and not to our dignity. Hence kingdoms and empires are sustained: these orders of society and forms of government are conserved even among barbarians and infidels. . . . Nevertheless, this disposition always holds in order that the earth may be inhabited because his decree is inviolable.[48]

Such statements have led scholars to formulate, on the basis of Calvin's thought, the doctrine of "common grace."[49] The assumptions governing such texts are threefold: God's love for his own image, his inherently providential nature, and his immutability regarding his purposes and decrees. Psalm 145:9 ("Jehovah is good to all") demonstrated to Calvin that human sin did not prevent God from displaying his merciful and fatherly nature or showering his goodness on both the good and the wicked.[50] Though the wicked have no regard for God's fatherly character, they are endowed with the knowledge that all good comes from him and that they too benefit from the order preserved in nature and society.[51] Unbelievers, Calvin explained, are nourished and clothed and profit from the light of the sun, the alternation of the seasons, and the fruitfulness of the earth.[52]

Nonetheless, in Calvin's view, the disorder ushered in by the Fall required that human society be more than simply sustained or preserved. The survival of the human race and its civilizations also required the restraining aspects of divine providence. We have seen above that for Calvin restraint was necessary from the beginning of creation to keep the stars and waters in their places. When Calvin discussed the survival of human society he stressed the divine restraint of the animals. When Adam rebelled against his creator, who was above him, so too the lower animals rose up against him.[53] The resulting savagery of the beasts was restrained by God's "secret bridle" so that their violence could not break forth and swallow up the human race. What, Calvin wondered, keeps the lions in their dens or the elephants content to feed on herbs in the mountains away from towns and people? "Whence comes this except that God has willed to subdue these beasts in order to give us a place to live here below? And, since when we are surrounded by all other types of savage beasts, would we be able to subsist one day in this world without being devoured except that God as a secret bridle [bride secrette] in order to restrain the fury of these savage beasts?"[54] Calvin characterized this "bridle" as a certain "fear and dread" divinely implanted or engraved in the animals after the Fall in order that they might continually fear the presence of people, thereby preserving a space in which human society might continue. The partial tameness of the animals and the fact that they could still be domesticated demonstrated to Calvin that although man's original dominion was lessened in the Fall, it was not entirely abolished, lest society perish instantly.[55]

To preserve order in human society, God placed the same mark of "fear and dread" in people so that they might obey the rulers and princes whom God has placed over them. Calvin carefully drew a comparison between the fear implanted in the beasts towards people and the fear implanted in people towards the civil authorities. In both cases Calvin saw God at work as he carved out and secured a place for society. In order that human society might survive, God granted humans dominion over beasts and over each other. Commenting on Genesis 9:2 ("And the fear of you will be upon all the beasts of the earth. . . .") Calvin explained the mark of fear and dread implanted by God. Note how easily he moves from the sphere of animals to that of rulers:

> This also has respect mainly to the restoration of the world, in order the sovereignty over the rest of the animals might remain with men. And although, after the fall of man, the beasts were imbued with new ferocity, yet some remains of that dominion which God conferred in the beginning were still left. . . . Indeed we see that wild beasts rush violently upon men . . . and if God did not wonderfully restrain their fierceness, the human race would be utterly destroyed. . . . Nevertheless, the bridle by which the Lord restrains the cruelty of wild beasts, to prevent them from falling upon men, is a certain fear and dread which God has implanted in them so that they might revere the presence of men. Daniel especially declares this reverence with respect to kings; namely, that they are possessed with dominion because the Lord has put the fear and dread of them in men and in beasts. But since the first use of fear is to defend the society of mankind, so to the extent that God has given a general authority over the beasts to men, there exists, in the greatest and least of men, I know not what hidden mark which does not allow the cruelty of wild beasts, by their violence to prevail.[56]

3. THE STATE AND THE ORDERED LIFE

In Calvin's view, all remaining traces of dominion testified to the divine preservation of human life. God ordained the restraint imposed by government because, if unbridled, the wickedness of men and women would destroy the human race. Repeatedly Calvin compared the wicked to the waters which, if unchecked, would "overflow" the land. Did the state, then, come into existence (in the Augustinian sense) with the Fall or, as Troeltsch and Dowey appear to suggest, was the state a part of creation and inherent in human society?[57] Scholars supporting this latter view rely on the following text:

> We should understand, furthermore, that the powers of the magistrate are from God, not as pestilence, famine, war, and other punishments for sin are said to be from him, but because he has appointed them for the just and lawful government of the world.[58]

Here Calvin confirmed the positive ordination of the state by God. So too he argued that "it has not come about by human perversity that the authority of all things on earth is in the hands of kings and other rulers but by divine providence and holy ordinance."[59] We should note, however, that both passages state only that God ordained the power of magistrates; Calvin did not unequivocally state that government was a prefallen institution. Clearly, for Calvin, the prefallen society would have been an ordered one, but to say that the state was necessary to human existence as such goes beyond the bounds of Calvin's texts. Bohatec correctly answered Troeltsch that sin was more than a secondary element in the role of the state; precisely in its function as a remedy or "bridle" for sin Calvin saw the state as a divinely willed order.[60] Calvin's functional view of the state as restraining disorder must be understood in its original sixteenth-century context. Calvin's primary concern was not to define the state as fallen or prefallen but to defend the authority of the magistracy against what he perceived to be the Anabaptist rejection of government.[61] He introduced his exegesis of Romans 13 by stating that "there are always some restless spirits who believe that the kingdom of Christ is properly exalted only when all earthly powers are abolished and that they can enjoy the liberty he has given them only if they shake off every yoke of human slavery."[62]

This charge, repeated in the first and subsequent editions of the *Institutes*, was aimed at the Anabaptists and, after February 1544, particularly against the Schleitheim Confession of 1527.[63] From those articles forbidding Christians to serve as magistrates, take part in warfare, or swear an oath, Calvin concluded that the Anabaptists were the "enemies of all order."

As Calvin himself occasionally admitted, the Anabaptists themselves did confess that government was necessary and ordained by God.[64] Neither Sattler nor his fellow Anabaptists concluded from their belief in pacifism or separation that the magistracy was to be abolished. They insisted only that the Christian baptismal community must be separated from the world; and, therefore, that the Christian could neither use the sword nor hold governmental office. Nevertheless, they affirmed that governing authorities were ordained to punish the wicked and protect the good. Hence they recognized that the state was necessary for the non-Christian world but dispensable for the Christian who was to be separated from this world.[65]

Fundamentally, Calvin and the Anabaptists differed in their views of creation, the role of the human being in society, and the sphere of God's redemptive purpose. These differences are seen most clearly in their respective ecclesiologies. According to the Anabaptists, the church was separated from the outside world of sin and darkness:

> We have been united concerning the separation that shall take place from the evil and the wickedness which the devil has planted in the world, simply is this; that we have no fellowship with them, and do not run with them in the confusion

of their abominations. So it is; since all who have not entered into the obedience of faith and have not united themselves with God so that they will to do his will, are a great abomination before God, therefore nothing else can or really will grow or spring forth from them than abominable things. Now there is nothing else in the world and all creation than good or evil, believing and unbelieving, darkness and light, the world and those who are [come] out of the world, God's temple and idols, Christ and Belial, and none will have part with the other.

To us, then, the commandment of the Lord is also obvious whereby he orders us to be and to become separated from the evil one, and thus he will be our God and we shall be his sons and daughters.

Further, he admonishes us therefore to go out from Babylon and from the earthly Egypt, that we may not be partakers in their torment and suffering, which the Lord will bring upon them.[66]

Despite his grim view of the disorder and wickedness in fallen human society, Calvin never advocated such separatism. He directed his polemic against what he perceived to be an otherworldly perfectionism inherent in Anabaptism. While Calvin recognized the need for discipline, his interest was in the purity of doctrine, not the purity of the church. His calls for meditation on the future life resulted not in a turning away from the world but advice on how to use the "present life and its helps."[67] These different attitudes toward "the world" grew out of two realizations: that Christians themselves remained imperfect and inextricably linked to the natural order and that creation itself was the object of God's preservation and redemption.

The awareness that the present life is always fraught with sin governed Calvin's thought; the believer always remains a sinner and the holiness of the church is incomplete.[68] Furthermore, Calvin saw that the believer coexists with the wicked in a natural order which has suffered the effects of the Fall:

Therefore, let us not deceive ourselves by imagining that a perfect church exists in the world, since our Lord Jesus Christ has declared that the kingdom will be like a field in which the good grain is so mixed with weeds that it is often not visible (Matt. 13:24). . . . For what is written about the Lord Jesus having shed his blood to cleanse the church in order that it might be free of spot and wrinkle (Eph. 5:26) does not mean that at present the church will be free from all stain. But rather she must grow and profit from day to day, moving toward this goal which she will never attain in this life.

Moreover, the church is tainted by vice in two ways. For not a member of the church is so pure or perfect as not to be surrounded by many imperfections. Thus all the faithful, as long as they live in this world, always carry about some impurities resident in their flesh. . . . The second way in which the church is soiled is that it always contains the good flock with evil hypocrites who infect the fellowship with their filthiness.[69]

This twofold imperfection necessitates, in Calvin's view, an unrelenting realism on the part of Christians; they must face the nature of the world and properly understand and take responsibility for that world. According to Calvin, this Christian realism required the believer to distinguish carefully between the spiritual and civil realms and to take seriously the fallen nature of the latter. In his discussions about the believer's role in the world Calvin expounded his theory of Christian freedom and the two governments. The "spiritual government" pertains to the life of the soul while the civil government is "political" and educates citizens for the duties of citizenship and humanity. The two governments are not antithetical but are never to be confused:

> Through this distinction it comes about that we are not to apply to the political order the gospel message about spiritual freedom, as if Christians were less subject regarding outward government to human laws because their consciences have been set free in God's sight; as if they were released from all bodily servitude because they are free according to the spirit.[70]

To Calvin's mind, Anabaptist perfectionism and separatism were dangerous to societal life. Calvin held this position from the time of his earliest writings, as the following citation from the 1536 *Institutes* makes clear:

> Certain men, when they hear that the Gospel promises a freedom . that acknowledges no king and no magistrate among men, but looks to Christ alone, think that they cannot benefit by their freedom so long as they see any power set over them. They therefore think that nothing will be safe unless the world is shaped to a new form where there are neither courts, nor laws, nor magistrates, nor anything which in their opinion restricts their freedom. But whoever knows how to distinguish between body and soul, between this present fleeting life and that future eternal kingdom, will without difficulty know that Christ's spiritual kingdom and the civil jurisdiction are things completely distinct.[71]

For Calvin the freedom of the conscience does not separate believers from coexistence with the wicked in the world. Only "certain beginnings" of the heavenly kingdom or the "spiritual government" have been initiated upon the earth.[72] Consequently, the natural realm continues to suffer the effects of disorder, for Christ's atonement restored neither the cosmos to its original order nor Christians to their original perfection. The believer, therefore, lives with his own lingering imperfection and within a society threatened by the forces of disorder.

However, in opposition to the Anabaptists, Calvin believed that imperfection and disorder rendered the created, civic order neither dispensable nor evil. The disorder of the world, including the presence of the wicked within the church, does not present a danger to God's redemptive purpose. The formation of the church is not a rejection of the past or of creation and, therefore, Christians are to live and participate in this earthly sphere. In short, Calvin believed that Christians must be willing to live in a world infected with disorder; they have to take sin seriously precisely because they cannot escape from it.

According to Calvin, one of the most serious effects of sin on society which believers must face is the presence of human rebellion. After the Fall, people turned against one another and lusted for dominion.[73] In Calvin's view, the fifth commandment taught that subjection was painful only to a depraved and sinful human nature; without sin, orderly submission would have been natural in society.[74] But now avarice and ambition continually threaten to destroy the ordered bonds of society; everyone now "wishes to go his own way" and to seek power and private profit.[75] People have separated themselves from one another and have overthrown the order originally instituted by God.[76] Calvin always feared anarchy and argued that unless the distinction of ranks within society are maintained, an anarchical confusion which will reduce human beings to beasts will result.[77] The fall of governments is a sign of divine wrath, for the human race cannot live in the ensuing disorder and confusion.

> It amounts to this, that the land of Edom shall resemble a mutilated body, and nothing can be seen in it but a dreadful confusion. This is the utmost curse of God, because if men have no political government, they will hardly differ at all from the beasts.[78]

We have seen above that Calvin believed God placed a mark of fear and dread in people so that they would obey their rulers. So, too, he thought the Lord preserved ranks and degrees in society in order that people might survive. In Calvin's view, the distinction of man in society must be maintained lest commerce and civil order be destroyed.[79] Although Calvin believed that individuals could change their vocations, he condemned all rash and restless moves that would destroy tranquility and order. He reminded his readers that Cicero himself taught that each one was to stay in his station and "not desert his sentry post" lest order and the ties of society be dissolved.[80] Calvin argued that without the distinction of ranks the life of men differs little from that of cattle and the beasts; or as Calvin said, we become "like cats and dogs."[81] Clearly, Calvin thought, God has not willed that "men should be jumbled together as would happen if there were no bridle [*bride*] but that some should rule and have authority to command others and that those who are subordinate obey them."[82]

Behind the "conservatism" exemplified in these social teachings lay Calvin's constant fear of anarchy and disorder, his conviction that in society "all change is to be feared," and that perversion of civil order is dangerous.[83] He insisted that people were to respect ranks and order because this principle preserved stability and kept at bay the disrupting forces of change and anarchy.

Calvin believed that a world characterized by the threats of disorder, greed, division, and tumult could not survive the abolition of government. In Calvin's view, such an idea (which the Anabaptists really did not propose) was dangerous and was based on a misunderstanding of the human situation in which Christians must participate. In a sense, Calvin shared the same dark view of society as that of his Anabaptist opponents: "For since the insolence of evil men is so great and their wickedness so stubborn that it can scarcely be restrained by extremely severe laws, what do we expect them to do if the wicked see that their depravity can go free, when no power can force them to cease from being evil."[84]

Perhaps Calvin was even more pessimistic since he believed that no one, not even the elect, possessed a perfection that made the state dispensable. According to Calvin, the Anabaptist vision was a dangerously optimistic one since it did not understand either the imperfection of society or that Christians too must live in this world threatened by the disorder of sin, "for nothing can be more cruel than man, if he be not held by some restraint."[85]

4. NATURAL LAW AND THE INSIGHT INTO ORDER

We have seen that Calvin explained the continuation of society after the Fall in terms of the restraint of God's providence effected both by his restraint of nature and the restraint imposed by the state. Continually Calvin depicted a world held in check by God. However, he believed that within this divinely preserved sphere men and women are able to conduct their temporal affairs without falling into a "bestial confusion." Calvin did not emphasize the external restraint of God only; he also assumed that the ordered civilized life in society flourished because of natural instincts, perceptions, dictates, and abilities still present within the fallen soul. The remaining ability of human beings to recognize the "dictates of nature" or the truths of natural law provided a means whereby they may participate in the formation of government and civic life.

According to Calvin, it is the human conscience that recognizes the need for order and the truths of natural law.[86] Repeatedly Calvin connected natural law to the "witness," "monitor," or "testimony" of the conscience. "The law of God," Calvin explained, "which we call the moral law is nothing else than that natural law and of that conscience which God has engraved upon the minds of men."[87] A remnant of the divine image, the human conscience serves not only to condemn the human being before the judgment of God but to conserve society by distinguishing good from evil, equity from injustice and order from disorder.[88] Calvin's statements about the natural discernment of the conscience form three general themes: the natural impulse for unity or the formation of society; the instinct for order within the family; and the necessity for an ordered civil government. Included in the latter are Calvin's comments about laws, property, and the wisdom of the pagans. Throughout these statements we will see that for Calvin, the human being's discernment of natural law functions as an internal bridle which fosters society.

In Calvin's view God created Eve in order that there might be "human beings on the earth who cultivate mutual society among themselves." Recorded in the book of Genesis, this beginning of human society exemplified a general principle, namely, that man was formed to be a social animal. This natural impulse toward the formation of society inclines people to care for the human race as a whole. Nature, Calvin argued, causes us to feel for one another since we are "inclined to mercy by some hidden impulse of nature." According to Calvin, murder is not only criminal but abhorrent to our natural instincts; since we are all made in the image of God, murder is contrary to the order of nature and to our "natural sentiment."[89]

Calvin also believed that the preservation of the human race is engraved in human nature and is a part of natural law. He interpreted Judah's instructions to Onan to go to his brother's wife as an "instinct of nature" whereby people are disposed naturally toward the preservation of the human race.[90] Even the pagans recognized the natural inclination for unity and preservation, since they knew that all people were born for the sake of one another.[91] He believed that the pagans also taught that the bonds of human society had to be maintained by mutual sharing. Throughout such discussions, Calvin relied on the integrity of human natural perceptions and instincts to account for the continued existence of society, for "since man is by nature a social animal, he tends through natural instinct to foster and preserve society. Consequently we observe that there exists in all men's minds universal impressions of a certain civic fair dealing and order."[92]

These "universal impressions" manifested themselves for Calvin in the bonds of marriage and family and in the submission to civil authorities and the rule of law. The original bonds of marriage and family ties are engraved in the eternal and inviolable laws of nature and, therefore, are understandable by all people without special divine revelation. In Calvin's view, the "order of nature" teaches that the woman should be the man's helper and willingly subservient to him.[93] Calvin also taught that adultery and promiscuity, which destroy the family, are not only violations of the morality commanded by Scripture but contrary to the "dictates of nature." "We gather, besides, from the words of Abimelech, that all nations have impressed on their minds the sentiment that the violation of holy wedlock is a crime worthy of divine vengeance and hence, they have a fear of the judgment of God."[94] According to Calvin, monogamy is inviolable and recognized by all societies. ". . . for the ignorant souls who had only natural understanding and behaved as their judgment [sens] directed them, have they not known that the wife was, as it were, a part of the husband and that there exists an inseparable bond between them so that they ought not to forsake each other unless they want to tear themselves to pieces?"[95]

Adultery, polygamy, and incest are immoral, "against nature," and contrary to the divinely established order. These unnatural acts also, Calvin argued, threaten to reduce people to the level of beasts. Polygamy is "disordered and confused," and adulterers are like neighing horses "for where such lasciviousness prevails, men degenerate into beasts."[96] For Calvin, the "pure sentiment of nature" condemns adultery which threatens the safety and stability of society.[97] And, by nature, "all men were instilled with a great horror of incest and natural reason judged it abhorrent for Judah to lie with Tamar."[98] Incestuous marriages, he stated, "trample upon all the laws of nature," and the horror of incest stems from the "natural feelings implanted in us by God." Even the "barbarism" of the East, Calvin insisted, cannot nullify the law against incest, for "what is natural cannot be abrogated by any consent and custom. In short, the prohibition of incest here set forth is by no means among those laws which are commonly abrogated according to the circumstances of time and place since it flows from the fountain of nature itself and is founded on the general principle of all laws, which is perpetual and inviolable."[99] A king, Calvin insisted, cannot command an incestuous marriage "for no legislator can effect that a thing which nature pronounces to be vicious should not be vicious; and if tyrannical arrogance dares to attempt it, the light of nature will presently shine forth and prevail . . . even among the heathen nations this law, as if engraved and implanted on the hearts of men, was accounted undissolvable."[100]

Consequently, for Calvin, familial ties among husband, wife, and children are grounded in the law of nature and recognized through natural reason.[101] These same appeals to "nature" recur in Calvin's arguments about civil government. Throughout his political discussions Calvin called on "nature," the "wisdom of the pagans," and the natural principles of justice and equity. According to Calvin, since the Spirit of God is the sole fountain of truth, the wisdom of the pagans should not be despised. "What then," he asked, "shall we deny that the truth shone upon the ancient jurists who established civic order and discipline with such great equity? . . . Those men whom Scripture calls 'natural men' were, indeed, sharp and penetrating in their investigation of things below. Let us, accordingly, learn by their example how many gifts the Lord left to human nature even after it was despoiled of its true good."[102]

Calvin often called on Plato, Seneca, and Cicero as authorities for his views of civic order and government; he did not present their theories in any coherent or systematic manner but drew on them at random to support his various arguments. To defend his view of a combined democracy and aristocracy he employed Plato's analysis of the types and dangers of different forms of governments.[103] He also cited Plato as teaching that no one was qualified to govern a commonwealth unless appointed by God.[104] According to Calvin, Seneca knew that the magistrate was the "father of his country" and must be obeyed.[105] Most importantly, however, Calvin thought that the pagans recognized the importance of laws. The art of government and the science of jurisprudence were handed down from the pagans, and Cicero taught that laws are the sinews of the state. Calvin prefaced his remarks about laws in the *Institutes* by saying: "Next to the magistracy in the civil state come the laws, stoutest sinews of the commonwealth, or as Cicero, after Plato, calls them, the souls without which the magistracy cannot stand, even as they themselves have no force apart from the magistracy. Accordingly, nothing truer could be said than that the law is a silent magistrate, the magistrate a living law."[106] Repeatedly, Calvin relied on the "wisdom of the ancients" to support the necessity of a strong and stable government, obedience to rulers, and the rule of law.

In Calvin's view, the rule of law or "order of justice" corresponds to the natural sense in the human being that recognizes the need for order. Nature itself teaches that human lives must be governed by law and ruled by the principles of equity and justice. "Equity, because it is natural, cannot but be the same for all; and, therefore, this same purpose ought to apply to all laws, whatever their object."[107] According to Calvin, the human conscience still retains insight into the natural principles of equity and justice and is thereby able to order society rightly.

In Calvin's discussions about the particular tasks or rules of government, arguments from natural equity were combined with arguments based on the threat of confusion. It was Calvin's belief that the rights of property and the necessity for boundaries are to be guarded carefully or else everything will dissolve into confusion. Against the communism held by some Anabaptists and Libertines, Calvin argued that God manifested his goodness in assigning territory to each nation and private property to each individual.[108] These "fanatics," Calvin insisted, who wanted to hold everything in common would overthrow the entire civil order and throw everything into confusion. In support of the right of private property, which was considered a "natural right," Calvin relied on Deuteronomy 19:14: "It is necessary that the landmarks be set up because the division of fields should remain untouched as if they were sacred." Calvin added that even the pagans knew that the right of property must be observed, for otherwise "there would be no equity among men and everything would be confused."[109]

> But insofar as we have seen this principle which nature always taught, namely, if boundaries were not held and observed, there would have been a horrible confusion among men and no laws would have been observed . . . for when someone wished to enlarge his own, it is as if he violated the order of nature. See, then, God who has distinguished peoples in order that all might live, communicating one with another in order that there may be no disordered confusion. See, therefore, how each person ought to be content with his limits.[110]

Such argumentation recurs frequently throughout Calvin's writings. If the order of nature is violated, society falls into confusion. The natural order and "sense of justice" teach that murder, false testimony, broken contracts, and dishonesty in business are against the order of nature and threaten, once again, to return the whole race "to the common confusion of all."[111] These passages demonstrate a reappearing set of assumptions and concerns in Calvin's mind: the natural mind's perception of the unchanging law of nature corresponded to the constant need for order and restraint so that society might continue after the Fall. Such insights keep the human race from falling to the level of beasts. Consequently, society is preserved not only by God's restraint of nature, wickedness, and rebellion, but also by human natural instincts which prevent the fall into anarchy.

5. THE ACTIVE LIFE

Calvin's various statements about societal life presupposed careful attention to perspective and to the difference between natural and supernatural gifts. Like Luther and Melanchthon, Calvin distinguished carefully between the issue of justification and the role of reason within the natural created order. Their belief in human depravity did not imply the annihilation or the uselessness of the natural. The Reformers were well aware that just as divine providence preserved the cosmos, so God left to the human being the ability to foster political and social life. Calvin carefully reminded his readers that the human intellect and will did not simply disappear in the Fall; they were condemned with reference only to justification and salvation but continued to function in the formation of civilized life. As Calvin never tired of saying, "we did not become beasts."

Luther's insistence on the proper distinction between the earthly and heavenly spheres was governed by his theological principle that the individual stood in two fundamental relationships: *coram Deo* and *coram hominibus*.[112] In Luther's view, retaining the proper perspective determined the proper understanding of justice, law, and reason.[113] Before God, the human being is always passive and receives an alien or imputed righteousness. Before the neighbor, however, the individual participates actively in political and social tasks. In his attacks on the doctrines of the medieval church, Luther argued that the devil and his cohorts, the "Sorbonnists," had caused the downfall of theology because they had confused these two fundamental relationships. Their failure to distinguish between the two realms of existence resulted, according to Luther, in a misunderstanding of the proper use of the Law and a belief in the merit of works.[114]

This fundamental distinction between the two spheres of existence also governed Luther's understanding of civil justice and the use of reason. *Coram Deo*, human nature is totally fallen; reason is unable to understand anything about God's free justification, and the will is incapable of making even one move toward salvation. The intrusion of reason into the spiritual realm results in a theology of glory and a misdirected trust in human works.[115] Since reason aligns itself with the Law, Luther argued that it must be broken down by the offense of the Gospel; before one can turn to the promise of salvation, he must be driven to despair.[116]

Nonetheless, Luther believed that within its own worldly realm reason functions legitimately and properly. On this point Luther and his fellow Reformers were not in controversy with the preceding Scholastic tradition. Just as they adopted the noncontroversial principle of natural law from the tradition, so too they assumed that the "natural light" left to the human mind functioned competently in its proper sphere. As Luther pointed out, we need not run to the Scriptures to learn how to build a house, make clothing, wage war, run the government, or navigate a ship.[117] In these "inferior things" the light of natural reason is sufficient. Luther was convinced that despite the radical effects of the

Fall, human reason is capable of fostering "civil justice" and "natural morality," which, although they can contribute nothing to justification, are necessary and proper on their own level.[118]

Melanchthon's important commentary on Colossians (1527) contains his clearest statements regarding the proper separation between the natural and spiritual realms. Melanchthon was eager to establish this separation in order to secure a place for the study of "natural philosophy." In Melanchthon's view, the use of human reason is legitimate and ordained by God as long as the limits of philosophy are recognized. But he agreed with Luther that if natural reason tries to enter a realm beyond its competence, a multiplication of errors results; human reason misunderstands God's governance in the world, the nature of justification, and the necessary help of the Spirit in combating sin.[119]

According to Melanchthon, the Gospel concerns the spiritual life, but philosophy pertains to the preservation of human society. When he turned his attention toward this lower sphere, Melanchthon was eager to prove that reason is capable of sure and certain knowledge.[120] In his view, the errors of the Epicureans, Stoics, and Aristotelians were not examples of philosophy at all because in these instances reason had strayed beyond its bounds and had fallen into that "deception" or uncertainty about which St. Paul warned. Still, Melanchthon argued, the natural mind can find certainty in the study of the arts, and can use these studies both in the discernment of certain aspects of natural revelation and in the preservation of the societal realm. Even after the Fall, Melanchthon insisted, the natural light of reason is suited for these studies and functions properly with reference to "natural things," such as numbers, measures, languages, medicine, building, navigation, agriculture, and government. Astronomy, medicine, arithmetic, eloquence, dialectic, rhetoric, ethics, and law are gifts of God in creation and gifts of divine providence for the preservation of society.[121]

Calvin also employed the distinction between the two realms of existence to discuss the role of reason in the temporal realm. In Calvin's view, our natural abilities and insights can contribute to the formation and preservation of an ordered life. As we have seen, divine restraint preserves a space for the human race amidst the threats of nature and of human wickedness. Furthermore, Calvin assumed that the natural instincts and perceptions of law help to preserve this society and to prevent the chaotic forces of human lust and greed from causing total confusion. When he reflected on the development of civilization within this societal realm, Calvin went beyond his references to natural law or the "dictates of nature" and recommended the use of natural reason in the arts and sciences.[122]

Many of Calvin's statements about the Christian's participation in the natural world were, once again, directed against the perfectionist and separatist arguments of the Anabaptists.[123] Against these "new Donatists" Calvin rejected any isolationism that condemned human participation in society. According to Calvin, the growth in holiness, necessary for Christians, does not remove them from the necessities and realities of life. Unlike the Anabaptists, for Calvin the realities of holiness and society are not antithetical. Condemning the Anabaptist withdrawal from the societal and political sphere, Calvin affirmed the institution of government and defined its tasks:

> Yet this distinction does not lead us to consider the whole nature of government a thing polluted, which has nothing to do with Christian men. That is what, indeed, certain fanatics who delight in unbridled license shout and boast: after we have died through Christ to the elements of this world (Col. 2:20), are transported to God's Kingdom, and sit among heavenly beings, it is a thing unworthy of us and set far beneath our excellence to be occupied with those vile and worldly cares which have to do with business foreign to a Christian man. To what purpose, they ask, are there laws without trials and tribunals? But what has a Christian to do with trials themselves. . . . But as we have just now pointed out that this kind of government is distinct from that spiritual and inward Kingdom of Christ, so we must know that they are not at variance. For spiritual government, indeed, is already initiating in us upon earth certain beginnings of the Heavenly Kingdom and in this mortal and fleeting life affords a certain foretaste of an immortal and incorruptible blessedness. Yet civil government has its appointed end so long as we live among men, to cherish and protect the outward worship of God, to defend sound doctrine of piety, and the position of the church, to adjust our life to the society of men, to form our social behavior to civil righteousness, to reconcile us with one another, and to promote general peace and tranquility. All of this I admit to be superfluous, if God's kingdom, such as it is now among us, wipes out the present life. But if it is God's will that we go as pilgrims upon the earth while we aspire to the true fatherland, and if the pilgrimage requires such helps, those who take these from man deprive him of his very humanity.[124]

In Calvin's view the kingdom of God does not "wipe out" the present life because the believer remains a part of the world. In his attack on the detachment of the Anabaptists, Calvin affirmed the goodness of societal life; like the spiritual government, it too is ordained by God. Not surprisingly, Calvin rejected the Anabaptist contention that a Christian cannot be a magistrate, and he approved of Christians participating in the ordered life of society. Believers, Calvin believed, are to engage in the economic and political life of society, to study the arts, to make use of the courts (but only with the motive of love), to use the oath, to bear arms, to become magistrates, and to protect the rights of their neighbors.[125] He even argued that the use of law and active participation in government are parts of the Christian duty of love since such activities protect order and the rights of one's neighbor.[126] In all of these exhortations to participate actively in society, Calvin presupposed that God never abandoned the created realm to the forces of darkness; just as God continued to love his image in the human being, so too he continued to provide for and to protect societal life. A well-ordered commonwealth, Calvin argued, is a singular gift of God. The divine presence is evident in that "order of justice" when judges,

senators, soldiers, captains, artificers, and teachers all aid one another and promote the general safety of all people.[127]

Consequently, Calvin believed that all the tools and gifts of this earthly life
were to be used. Believers are to despise no calling, including that of manual
labor. Calvin praised the mechanical arts, agriculture, architecture, and all
manual occupations because these pursuits promote the welfare and preservation
of human society. He also commended the arts, sciences, and wisdom of the
ancients.[128] Eloquence, for example, is necessary in public and private life to
demonstrate the truth of particular issues and principles.[129] According to
Calvin, Moses described all remaining blessings in this life as from God who
spread them throughout the whole human race. Hence, Calvin wrote, even the
sons of Cain, "though deprived of the spirit of regeneration, were still endowed
with gifts of no despicable kind, just as the experience of all ages teaches us
how widely the rays of divine light have shown on unbelieving nations, for the
benefit of the present life. . . ."[130] Calvin concluded that the liberal arts came
down to us from the heathen and we are "compelled to acknowledge that we have
received astronomy and other parts of philosophy, medicine, and orderly civil
government from them."[131] Calvin agreed with Melanchthon that St. Paul did
not condemn these arts in I Cor. 1:17; although useless for obtaining spiritual
wisdom, the arts are useful instruments for carrying out worthwhile activities
in the earthly realm.[132] After noting the use of Menander in I Cor. 15:33,
Calvin wrote that we are at liberty to borrow from every quarter because
everything comes from God: "He has put into the mouths of the wicked some
true and useful doctrine."[133] Therefore, far from condemning the natural realm,
natural wisdom, and natural insights into civic order, he affirmed the limited
integrity of the societal realm and encouraged human activity within it.

6. CONCLUSIONS

1. Throughout his writings Calvin adopted the common teachings about
natural law. He assumed the existence of the "lex naturae," whose author was
God. He believed that after the Fall God made this law clearer through the written form of the Decalogue. He argued that all peoples have certain conceptions
of justice and rectitude inborn in their minds. In particular, all human beings
recognize the need for equity, law, and order. Calvin was not interested in
natural law in and of itself. He did not develop a "theology of natural law" but,
rather, used the principle of natural law as an extension of his doctrine of providence to explain the survival of civilization. Therefore, his appeals to nature and
natural law were on the level of appropriation, not of doctrine. In his appropriation of these traditional ideas Calvin accounted for the survival of society by
means of two counterbalancing principles.

2. On the one hand, Calvin believed that the disorder caused by sin re-

quired God to restrain those natural and human forces which threaten to annihilate the human race. God exercises this restraint because he continues to love his own image in the human being and to take joy in his works. Remaining true to his own purposes in creation, God preserves the stability and order of the created realm. The restraint required for societal life is also exercised inwardly through the recognition by the conscience of natural law. According to Calvin, the "dictates" or insights of nature prevent men and women from falling into a bestial confusion. His frequent appeals to nature reveal a recurring form of argumentation: the natural mind still perceives the need for order and restraint. In Calvin's view, natural perception of natural law prevents people from killing one another, disobeying laws, committing adultery and incest, breaking contracts, stealing, lying under oath, rebelling against governmental and familial superiors, and abolishing private property. Such natural instincts serve as an internal bridle, so to speak, which keeps at bay those chaotic forces of lust and greed which lurk within human nature.

3. The survival of the *imago Dei* in the fallen soul helped Calvin account for the continuation of society in two ways. As noted above, Calvin believed that God preserves society because he continues to love his image in the human being. Also, however, the conscience and natural reason contribute to the order and stability of the civil realm. Not only do these remnants of the divine image act as a bridle but, occasionally, Calvin recognized a positive function in the instincts of nature which went beyond the idea of restraint. Nature, according to Calvin, causes us to propagate the race, raise our children, and even to recognize the image of God or a common human nature in our neighbor.[134] Calvin more frequently attributed a positive function to natural reason as it pursued the arts and sciences for the preservation and well-being of civilization. Like Melanchthon, he praised the knowledge and use of rhetoric, eloquence, medicine, law, and the sciences. Against the Anabaptists, Calvin insisted that the created world was not evil or alien to the believer. He stressed, therefore, not only the restraint of sin but also the remaining goodness and integrity of nature and society. Society was not, in Calvin's view, the realm of darkness but was that arena in which the Christian pursued holiness. Calvin's God did not reject his creation but continued to exercise providence over the "work of his hands" and to reveal his glory in this earthly "theater." In his polemics against the "fanatics," Calvin insisted on a Christian realism about societal life. This realism required both a respect for the threat of chaos and an appreciation for and activity within the world. The following chapter will show that the abilities and activities of human beings are, in Calvin's thought, the objects of redemption and the instruments for the renewal of creation.

V

CREATION SET FREE

Throughout his polemics against the Anabaptists, Calvin eschewed all views that would see the church as an oasis isolated from a lost creation or salvation as the rescuing of the elect from a demonic world. In this concluding chapter we will see that this rejection of the "new Donatism" also permeated Calvin's statements about the relationship between creation and redemption.

While Calvin's views of redemption and sanctification have been the object of intense study by Calvin scholars,[1] his ideas about the function of nature in God's salvific plan have received less attention. Several studies on this subject, however, are important. Quistorp has demonstrated Calvin's belief in the bodily resurrection and the restoration of the cosmos.[2] Milner, Richard, and Wallace have shown that "restoration of order" is a theme which governed Calvin's view of sanctification.[3] We will build on these studies in order to probe Calvin's view of the role of nature in redemption. Our task in this chapter is to draw together all of the elements of nature and the natural order which we have discussed thus far and to show that they reemerge and find their logical conclusion in Calvin's statements about the redemption of creation.

According to Calvin, God is reclaiming all of his creation: the cosmos, human nature, and history. This redemptive activity restores creation to its original purpose, namely, the praise and glory of God. In support of this view, Calvin argued that there is a fundamental, unbroken continuity of creation, a restoration of order in the world, and a reestablishment of the revelatory function of nature. We examine first the role of the cosmos in redemption and then turn to the activity of human nature in sanctification. Finally, we will analyze Calvin's understanding of the unity of history and the contributions human beings make to God's gradual restoration of order.

1. THE ROLE OF THE COSMOS IN REDEMPTION

In agreement with the traditional exegesis of Romans 8:20, Calvin argued that because of human sin, the cosmos was subjected to corruption and stood in need of renewal and renovation. All creatures, Calvin taught, tend by nature to their own preservation so that everything subject to decay "suffers violence against the purpose of nature and in opposition to it."[4] To demonstrate the all-pervasive effect of sin, he maintained that even the heavens are now "verging toward destruction" and awaiting their future renovation.[5] The Fall caused all of creation to stand in need of renovation "for the whole framework of the world is hastening to its end."[6]

Commenting on Romans 8:20, Calvin explained that this subjected creation now awaits the resurrection in hope: "No part of the universe is untouched by the longing with which everything in this world aspires to the hope of resurrection." In fact, the continued functioning of creation is itself due to hope:

> From hope comes the swiftness of the sun, the moon, and all the stars in their constant course, the continual obedience of the earth in producing its fruits, the unwearied motion of the air and the ready power of the water to flow. God has enjoined on each one its proper task and has not simply given a precise command to do his will, but at the same time has implanted inwardly the hope of renewal. In the sad dispersion which followed the Fall of Adam, the whole machinery of the world and all its parts would be dissolved at every moment were they not borne up from elsewhere by some hidden stability. . . . Therefore, however much created things incline naturally to some other course, since it has been God's pleasure to make them subject to vanity, yet they obey his command, and because he has given them hope of a better condition, they sustain themselves with this hope, postponing their longing until the incorruption which has been promised them is revealed.[7]

In Calvin's view, then, the cosmos is now verging toward destruction and waiting for future renewal and incorruption: "For to what purpose is that renovation promised, which even the heavens wait for with the strong desire like those in travail, except that they are now verging toward destruction?"[8] In opposition to the eschatological expectations and calculations of the Radical Reformers, Calvin refused to predict the day of the final judgment.[9] He also warned against speculation about the nature of this restored cosmos. It is neither useful nor "lawful," he said, "to inquire with great curiosity into the future perfection of the beasts, plants, and metals. If we give rein to these speculations, where will they finally lead us?" Calvin cautioned that readers were to be content with the doctrine that all creatures will be of such perfect constitution and order that "no appearance of deformity or impermanence will be seen."[10]

In the face of such a warning against further eschatological speculation it is important to note that Calvin did insist on one rather "speculative" point: the cosmos will be purified but not destroyed. His insistence appears to contradict passages such as II Peter 3:10–13 which states that the heavens will "pass away," that all things will be "dissolved," and that the elements will "melt with heat and the earth and all its works will be burnt up." But, probably in opposition to the speculation of Radical Reformers or the spiritualized eschatology of the Libertines, Calvin contended that God will not abandon creation; instead, God will renovate its original material. In Calvin's view, only the "corruptions" of the heaven and earth will be purified and melted by fire.[11] Interpreting I Corinthians 15:28, he rejected the view of those who imagine that "God will be all in all in this respect, namely, that all things will vanish and dissolve into nothing."[12] Paul's words, Calvin argued, mean only that all things will be brought back to God who is their beginning and end. In a rare comment about the future world, Calvin echoed Irenaeus' teaching and stated that: "I will say just one thing about the elements of the world, that they will be consumed in order to receive a new quality while their substance remains the same. . . ."[13] Therefore, in Calvin's view, the fires of judgment will not destroy creation but will purify its original and enduring substance. With this argument, Calvin portrayed God as faithful to his original creation. Just as God brought the cosmos into being, closely governs and restrains its natural forces, so too he will renew and transform its original substance.

2. THE REDEMPTION OF HUMAN NATURE

Calvin was, of course, primarily interested in the renewal or sanctification of the human being. In fact, he emphasized that renovation of the cosmos would follow the renewal of the elect. The oneness of humanity with creation is evident both in the Fall and in the restoration of creation; just as the cosmos became disordered in the Fall of Adam, so, too, it will be restored after the renewal of the human being: "Now subject to corruption, the creatures cannot be renewed until the sons of God are wholly restored; and while they seek for their renewal, they look for the manifestation of the heavenly kingdom."[14]

For Calvin, the renewal of the human being encompassed all of human nature: the body, mind, and will. In all of his discussions about this renewal the same principle emerges, as is evident in his view of the cosmos: the primary nature created by God remains, is reclaimed, purified, and transformed. In these passages, then, Calvin's concern with the endurance or continuity of nature resurfaces.

Calvin portrayed the redemption of the human body as parallel to the restoration of the cosmos. As Miles correctly argues, Calvin saw the body, by its subjection to corruption and death, as sharing the punishment of sin with the rest of creation.[15] According to Calvin the body is the victim of Adam's transgression and as such suffers disease, decay, and death, contrary to its original nature. But the body also shares with the cosmos the promise of that incorruption which follows the renewal of the soul. Unlike the soul, however, the body must first be subjected to physical death. Death is the separation of the soul from the body. But, Calvin explained, while the soul is "immortal" and consciously at peace, the body "sleeps" until the day of resurrection.[16]

Nonetheless, Calvin maintained that like the cosmos, the body does not suffer complete destruction. Interpreting I Corinthians 15:53 ("For this corruptible nature must put on incorruptibility and this mortal nature must put on immortality"), Calvin believed that we shall rise again in the "same flesh we now carry about with us."[17] Paul's argument, Calvin asserted, overthrows the errors of "those fanatics" who imagine that we will be given new bodies. Calvin was most likely referring to Laelius Socinus. In 1549, a few years after the publication of his commentary on I Corinthians, Calvin and Socinus exchanged letters on a number of issues, including the resurrection of the flesh. In a letter of July 26, 1549, Socinus asked Calvin whether the same body as we possess now would be restored in the resurrection. Socinus had argued that the scriptural promises of bodily resurrection intended "nothing more than, by the use of some physical terms, to make easily understandable to our senses, as it were, not only that ineffable blessedness but even our own selves, who would otherwise be invisible and incomprehensible to ourselves, until such a time as endowed with a more perfect light we may truly and not darkly behold God Himself in Christ as he is, bodily that is." Socinus then concluded the letter by asking Calvin to point out when the divine judgment and resurrection or transformation of the body would take place. "For," Socinus wrote, "unless I am mistaken, we should expect an alteration of the body, not its qualities, and a certain kind of passing of the soul, not a return to its old tabernacle."[18]

Calvin refused to be drawn into such forbidden speculation and referred Socinus to the discussion of resurrection found in his previous letter. Both in that letter and in the *Institutes* Calvin insisted that only the quality of bodies, but not their substance, will be transformed: the substance will remain but the quality will be changed.[19] Nonetheless, Calvin was clear that it was the originally created body that God will reclaim and renew. Arguing from Daniel 12:2 he answered Socinus that "God does not call forth new matter from the four elements to fashion men, but summons dead men from the grave."[20] He added that "if death, which takes its origin from the Fall of man is accidental, the restoration which Christ has brought belongs to the self-same body which began to be mortal."[21]

However, Calvin did not depict the body as being in a passive or waiting state, in contrast to his descriptions of the "groaning" creation. Although incorruptibility is not granted in this life, the body, along with the soul, must gradually be purified and dedicated to Christ. The human body, Calvin preached, must not be involved in drunkenness, fornication, or adultery because it too is destined to serve the glory of God. Christians "must not make themselves unclean again: having been washed, they must not sully themselves with fresh filth. Rather, they are to strive after purity, to continue in true holiness, and to detest the filthy things of their former life."[22] Calvin reminded his readers that Paul exhorted Christians to pursue holiness, a pursuit which includes the consecration of our bodies to a life of purity.

> Having shown that we are called to purity, he now adds that this purity should be evident in both body and soul. . . . He would have us pure from defilements, not only in our interior parts, which have God alone as our witness, but also in our external parts, which are subject to the senses of men. It is as if he said, "We should

not only have consciences which are pure in God's sight, but we should consecrate to him our whole body and all our members so that no impurities can be seen in any part of us."[23]

Since the primary seat of the divine image is in the soul, the mind and the will are the primary objects of sanctification. As Wallace and Richard have shown, Calvin defined sanctification as the gradual restoration of order in the soul.[24] This restoration is the renewal of the *imago Dei* described, according to Calvin, in Colossians 3:10. The soul, which became disordered in the Fall, is restored to order by the work of Christ, a restoration which reestablishes the soul's original rectitude and integrity. But sanctification is not only described by Calvin as a restoration to the original image with which Adam was created. As Richard Prins has shown, Calvin also talked about the transformation unto Christ which surpasses that of Adam.[25] In his exegesis of I Corinthians 15:44–50, Calvin made it clear that the life of sanctification "reforms" us not to Adam but to the superior image of Christ:

> In sum, Paul's meaning is, that the condition which we obtain through Christ is far superior to the lot of the first man because a living soul was conferred upon Adam in his own name and in that of his posterity, but Christ has procured for us the Spirit who is life. . . . All men were created in the first man, because whatever God decided to give to all, he conferred on that one man, so that the condition of mankind was settled in his person. He, by his fall, ruined himself and those that were his, because he drew them all, along with himself, into the same ruin. Christ came to restore our nature from ruin and to raise it up to a better condition.[26]

Describing the process of sanctification, Calvin had to interpret Paul's statements that Christians "put off the old man," "become new creatures," and "crucify" the "old man" with Christ. Calvin himself stated that in order to become the children of God, we must wipe out whatever we have from ourselves and that our common nature must die.[27] He interpreted such statements by means of II Corinthians 3:11, Ephesians 4:23, and Colossians 3:10, all of which describe the renewal of the human being. Calvin's understanding of sanctification is a continuation of his general view of redemption; namely, that nothing is lost. Consequently, he argued that the process of sanctification both retains and transforms human nature: the original natural faculties survive the Fall and function actively in the pursuit of holiness.

Calvin doggedly maintained that the will, which is inseparable from human nature, remains and plays an active part in the renewal of that nature. Just as the will is not annihilated by sin, so, too, it is not suspended by the action of the Spirit in the life of regeneration. This inherent activity of the will is evident in the struggle that characterizes the gradual transformation or progress in holiness.

While Calvin did not want to attribute any step toward justification to fallen human nature, he endeavored to protect the continued existence and functioning of the will. This wrestling on Calvin's part is clear in his polemics against the idea of "cooperative grace" in conversion or the life of grace. Calvin insisted that the Spirit must first activate the will to do good and that this grace is irresistible.

> Therefore we are robbing the Lord if we claim anything for ourselves either in will or in accomplishment. If God were to help our weak will, then something would be left to us. But when it is said that he makes the will, whatever of good is in it is now placed outside us. . . . It is the Lord's doing that the will conceives what is right, is jealously inclined toward it, is aroused and moved to pursue it. Then it is the Lord's doing that the choice, zeal, and effort do not falter but proceed even to fulfillment; lastly, that man goes forward in these things and perseveres to the very end.[28]

Such statements inevitably raise the suspicion of passivity. Has human nature been suspended by grace and the human will reduced to the level of a stone? While Calvin insisted that we did not become beasts, he seems to make us inanimate. Obviously, such implications were not lost on his opponents, since Calvin felt compelled to answer that he did not believe that grace eliminated the activity of the will:

> Now when they slander us that we make men like stones, when we teach that they have nothing good except from pure grace, they act shamefully. For we acknowledge that we have a will from nature; but as it is evil through the corruption of sin, it begins to be good only when it has been reformed by God. Nor do we say that man does anything good without willing it, but only when his inclination is ruled by the Spirit of God.[29]

Calvin was careful to maintain that the Spirit does not remove, cancel, or suspend the inherently active nature of the human will: "Man's action is not taken away by the movement of the Holy Spirit because the will, which is directed to aspire to the good, is of nature."[30] Claiming, as always, the authority of Augustine, Calvin argued that "grace does not destroy the will, but restores it."[31] The human being remains a willing being and is never compelled or borne along by an outside force. As Calvin insisted, "ours is the mind, ours the will, ours the striving which he directs toward the good."[32] Commenting on Ezekiel 36:26, he wrote:

> I say that the will is effaced; not insofar as it is will, for in man's conversion what belongs to his primal nature remains whole. I also say that it is created anew not meaning that the will now begins to exist, but that it is changed from an evil to a good will.[33]

In Calvin's view this godly will is called to purity and the pursuit of holiness so that it may attain to complete conformity with God's will. The knowledge of the Law of the divine will must penetrate the heart so that believers may pattern their lives after the imitation of Christ. The Law points out the goal towards which Christians are to strive throughout their lives so that "this whole life is a race."[34]

But this purity of life is attained only gradually; holiness is actively and daily pursued by the continual striving of the redirected human will. Calvin reminded his readers that they were far removed from perfection and must "steadily move forward and, though entangled by vices, daily fight against them." The ideas of "growth," "struggle," "combat," and "striving" governed Calvin's view of the spiritual life.[35] Believers are to "strive manfully" to keep pure until the day of the Lord.[36] Perfection is the goal toward which Christians must "strive and struggle" throughout life.[37] He exhorted his readers to "aspire" to their goal by "continuous effort."[38] Each person was to proceed "according to the measure of his puny capacity and set out in the journey we have begun."[39] We are, Calvin said, to make "unceasing progress in the way of the Lord."[40] Such descriptions of the sanctified life demonstrate that Calvin assumed the activity of the natural but redirected will in the life of regeneration.

The mind too must be renewed. This renewal was, according to Calvin, accomplished through faith. His understanding of faith makes clear the continuity and activity of the natural mind in redemption: "So then, in various respects, faith is a part of our regeneration, and an entrance into the kingdom of God, that he may reckon us among his children. The illumination of our minds by the Holy Spirit belongs to our renewal. . . ."[41] Calvin's exhortations to purity and holiness do not refer only to the decisions of the will or the passions of the lower appetites but to the mind as well. All aspects of Calvin's doctrine of sanctification show that "reason," "knowledge," and "discernment" are elements in the renewed life of faith. The mind, he said, "must be healed and put on a new nature."[42] As Calvin stated, we must be "totally renewed, beginning with the mind, which appears to be most noble and excellent."[43]

This renewal of the mind begins with submission to Christ which renders the mind teachable [docilitas]. The natural fallen mind, which Calvin likened to a labyrinth, a workshop of idols, and a runaway horse, is hemmed in by the "bridle" of the Law.[44] This submission and restraint empties Christians of their own wisdom, counsels, and desires so that they may be guided by the Spirit:

> "A fool in this world," is someone who renounces his own understanding, and as if with closed eyes he allowed himself to be guided by the Lord; who, lacking confidence in himself, leans entirely on the Lord; who bases all his wisdom on him; who yields himself obedient and docile to God. Our wisdom must vanish in this way, so that God's will may reign over us and we must be emptied of our own understanding, so that we may be filled with the wisdom of God.[45]

Once again such statements appear to render human nature useless or inactive. But Calvin's teachings about self-denial do not render the mind of the believer inactive because the restoration of God's image consists in a renewed mind and an increased knowledge of God. Calvin's concern for the progress of the mind is clear in his attacks on the "weak" or "ineffective" faith of the Scholastics. These attacks aimed at the idea of passivity and the submission of the mind which Calvin associated with the Scholastic notion of "implicit faith."[46] "Is this what believing means," Calvin asked, "to understand nothing provided only that you submit your feeling obediently to the church?"[47] He repeatedly rejected such passivity; if faith consists merely of some general assent to the truths of Scripture, the mind does not really know anything or strive after greater understanding. Consequently, Calvin argued that "faith rests not on ignorance but on knowledge."[48]

Calvin also knew that faith is always surrounded by error and unbelief but insisted that "the height of wisdom" was "to go forward quietly and humbly, to strive still further."[49] The submission of the mind is only the beginning of a gradual progress of knowledge. The continual renewal and advance of the mind, he thought, brings us closer to God, "so we see that the mind, illumined by the knowledge of God, is first wrapped up in much ignorance which is gradually dispelled."[50] This gradual, progressive increase in the knowledge of God is, according to Calvin, threefold: (1) increased knowledge regarding God's will for human life, (2) increased certainty of salvation, (3) restored ability to see God in nature.

For Calvin, the "teachable mind" is gradually redirected toward a deeper and deeper knowledge of God's will. The illumination of the Spirit and the "third use of the Law" lie at the center of Calvin's portrayal of the mind's renewal. The Spirit is an "inner teacher" who illumines the mind so that one may be certain of the authority and the meaning of Scripture.[51] The Law, in particular, grants a more and more penetrating knowledge of God's will for the sanctified life.[52] The Law, Calvin taught, is the best instrument for Christians "to learn more thoroughly each day the nature of the Lord's will to which they aspire and to confirm them in an understanding of it."[53] Because the mind is not yet fully renewed and is still liable to fall into wild speculations, forging new and "unlawful" means of worship, the believer must be careful and not "wander outside God's law."[54]

Calvin frequently extolled this "growth," "advance," or "progress" in the knowledge of divine Law. The continued imperfection of the mind required daily learning "for no man has heretofore attained to such wisdom as to be unable to make fresh progress toward a purer knowledge of God from daily instruction in the Law."[55] Believers, Calvin argued, are enlightened with the "spirit of discernment" which enables the mind to judge what should be done or avoided.[56] In these discussions, Calvin saw Christians as moving beyond the mere restraint caused by the knowledge and shame imposed by natural law or the dictates of nature. In the life of regeneration, Calvin portrayed Christians as actively learning, discerning, and pursuing the good.

The Reformer especially associated the renewal of the human mind with the certainty of salvation. The knowledge of God's benevolence is a faith that is never merely cognitive but rather penetrates to the heart and renders the believer confident and assured. As Calvin stated in his famous description of faith: "for as faith is not content with a doubtful and changeable opinion, so it is not content with an obscure and confused conception; but requires a full and fixed certainty such as men are wont to have from things experienced and proved."[57] According to Calvin, the renewed mind can perceive more and more clearly that God is a "propitious Father" whose benevolence and goodness is "beyond doubt." Since they know themselves "to be God's children," believers are no longer uncertain about God's love or will towards them, nor even of their own perseverance.[58] Such certainty, available to the purified perception of the mind, allows believers to cry, "Abba Father!"

The reality of growth resurfaces in Calvin's recognition that the certainty of faith remains incomplete and under attack in the present life. Consequently, Calvin explained, the mind is always involved in a constant struggle against doubt about salvation.[59] Not surprisingly, Calvin equated temptation with doubt about God's benevolence and will to save. Satan, he thought, suggests to us that we are not saved or that God is not merciful: "Surely, while we teach that faith ought to be certain and assured, we cannot imagine any certainty that is not assailed by some anxiety. On the other hand, we say that believers are in perpetual conflict with their own unbelief."[60] The believer must "struggle with his own weakness," or "press on toward faith," and "rise up" from his own doubt and uncertainty.[61] Calvin knew, then, that believers experience a mental or spiritual conflict between fear and faith. For Calvin this conflict is exemplified in the question "can fear and faith dwell in the same mind?"[62] Calvin's idea of spiritual warfare included not only the angelic defense of the church against demons but also the inner conflict of the gradually illumined and renewed mind. He perceived this struggle between faith and doubt as a part of that Christian warfare which characterizes the present life. The renewed mind is engaged in a *battle* against the doubt instigated by Satan. Again Calvin drew on military imagery to describe the daily fight against doubt or unbelief, a fight which gradually drives this satanic fear from the mind.

> To bear these attacks, faith arms and fortifies itself with the Word of the Lord. And wherever temptation of any kind assails us, suggesting that God is our enemy because he is unfavorable toward us, faith, on the other hand, replies that while he afflicts us, he is also merciful because his punishment arises out of love rather than wrath. . . . Unbelief does not hold sway within the hearts of believers but assails them from without. . . . Faith, then, as Paul teaches, serves as our shield. . . . When, therefore, faith is shaken, it is like a strong soldier forced by the violent blow of a spear to move his foot and to yield a little. When faith itself is wounded, it is as if the soldier's shield were broken at some point from the thrust of the spear, but not in such a way as to be pierced.[63]

Finally, Calvin also included the contemplation of nature in the renewal of the mind. In Calvin's theology, the restoration of the *imago Dei* allows nature to regain its revelatory function. In fact, the ability to study nature profitably (without falling into idolatry) is a part of this restored image. As Dowey and Brunner have argued, the mind which is bridled by Scripture is enabled once again to read the "book of nature."[64] Earlier we saw that the natural, fallen mind, directed only by the light of nature, was quite competent in the "investigation of lower things" such as astronomy and the other sciences. Scripture, then, does not function to make nature more knowable in a scientific way. Scripture only allows the contemplation of nature to become again a legitimate religious activity. The "original order of knowing" is not thereby restored, since Scripture must continually function as "spectacles" which correct the noetic failure caused by sin.[65] But as order in the soul is gradually restored, the mind is once again able to perceive the order and beauty still present in nature and, once again, to refer this "theater" back to God.

The reader can see Calvin applying the spectacles of Scripture throughout his writings, especially in the sermons on Job and the commentary on the Psalms. Despite his insistence about man's inexcusability before nature, Calvin felt perfectly free to call upon the wonders of nature to describe the majesty, glory, wisdom, and power of God. The universe struck him as a constant source of revelation:

> The little birds singing are singing of God; the beasts cry unto him; the elements are in awe of him; the mountains echo his name; the waves and fountains cast their glances at him; the herbs and flowers praise him. Nor do we need to labor or seek him far off, since each of us finds [God] within himself, inasmuch as we are all upheld and preserved by his power dwelling in us.[66]

Illustrations and arguments from nature fill Calvin's writings: human generation and motherhood are examples of God's wise providence; the variety found throughout the cosmos in the different species of animals or changes in the weather are signs and images which reveal that God is the Creator, Governor, and Preserver of the universe.[67] The whirlwind speech in the book of Job (from which these illustrations are drawn) is for Calvin a vast theology of nature. Calvin believed that in this speech God showed Job his majestic nature through the wonders of the visible creation. As we saw in the first chapter of this book, the geocentric world view also served Calvin well in his descriptions of God's providence and power; the fact that God upholds the stable, heavy mass of the earth, guides the revolutions of the stars around the earth, and restrains the waters all demonstrate his constant presence, wisdom, power, and care for the human race.[68] Not only did Calvin himself draw on the order of nature but he expressly exhorted his congregation and readers to do the same:

> While it is true that God declares himself to us by his Word, nevertheless we are inexcusable when we have not at all considered him in his works. He does not at

all leave himself without witness here, as St. Paul says in the 14th chapter of Acts concerning the order of nature which is like a mirror in which we are able to contemplate that which is of God. Let us note then that St. Paul says (Acts 14:17) that when God causes the sun to shine, sends the diverse seasons, fructifies the earth, that he does not at all leave himself without good testimony. . . . It is not at all necessary that they allege ignorance for in the order of nature they have been able to perceive a little that there is a Creator who disposes everything. Let us then only open our eyes and we will have enough arguments for the grandeur of God, so that we may learn to honor him as he deserves.[69]

God's nature, of course, transcends human reason and comprehension. But this must not turn us away from finding God since he has "accommodated himself" to us in the natural order. In Calvin's interpretation, Psalm 104 teaches that we need not "pierce the clouds" in order to find God since he "meets us in the fabric of the world and is everywhere exhibiting to our view, scenes of the most vivid description."[70] Calvin's view of Scripture parallels, therefore, his understanding of God in Scripture: just as God "lisps" to us in Scripture, so too he clothes himself in the fabric of the world or the robe of nature for our sake. Both language and the cosmos are means by which God covers his majesty so as not to blind his creatures. The antispeculative thrust of Calvin's thought, therefore, did not function to prohibit the contemplation of nature. The noetic effect of sin is gradually corrected when the soul is reordered so that once again the cosmos can serve as a "stage," "theater," or "book" from which believers are encouraged to learn about their Creator.

3. THE REDEMPTION OF HISTORY AND SOCIETY

Calvin believed God was reclaiming not only the cosmos and human nature but history as well. The renewal or "reconstitution" of which he spoke included the renovation of society and the historical order. This all-encompassing scope of God's redemption is clear in Calvin's statements about the unity of the Testaments, the gradual restoration of the world to order, and the contribution of believers to the restoration of society.

In teaching about the relationship between the Old and New Testaments, Calvin reacted against the general tendency of the Anabaptists to give the Old Testament a lower position than the New Testament.[71] According to the Anabaptists, the period of the Old Testament was radically different from the Christian or New Testament era. Consequently, Anabaptist theology stressed the discontinuity between the Jewish religion with its rite of circumcision and the Christian church which practiced baptism and a strict church discipline. Against this view of discontinuity, Calvin emphasized the unity and similarity of the two covenants: "The covenant made with all the patriarchs was so much like ours in substance and reality that the two are actually one and the same. Yet they differ in the mode of dispensation."[72]

For our purposes, the importance of Calvin's argument lies in the implied view of history. Calvin's opposition to the Anabaptist separation from the outside world is also reflected in his opposition to their rejection of the past. Such a rejection constituted, in Calvin's eyes, a rejection of creation. In contrast, Calvin argued for the continuity of God's historical plan. The two Testaments are to be differentiated by their chronological position in God's plan of salvation. The Old Testament was a "witness" or "promise" of that which was fulfilled in the New Testament.[73] Those under the Law were not confined to earthly life or pleasures but shared in the same promises of eternal life as do Christians: "Adam, Abel, Noah, Abraham, and the other patriarchs cleaved to God by such illumination of the Word. Therefore, I say, that without any doubt, they entered into God's immortal kingdom. For theirs was a real participation in God which cannot be without the blessing of eternal life."[74] His interpretation of Ezekiel 16:61 argues that Christ only renewed and restored the same covenant he had formerly made with Israel. In the following passage Calvin roots the promise of Ezekiel 16 and the New Covenant of Jeremiah 31:31–33 in the one imperishable covenant of God. This passage demonstrates Calvin's determination to preserve the unchangeable historical unity of God's all-encompassing plan of salvation throughout history.

> And when [God] says, "I will establish a covenant," we may explain it as though he said "I will set it up again, or restore it to its former condition [*in integrum*]." For we said that the New Testament was so distinguished from the Old that it was founded upon it. . . . Since, therefore, Abraham is at this time the father of all the faithful, it follows that our safety is not to be sought elsewhere than in that Covenant which God established with Abraham. But afterwards the same covenant was ratified by the hand of Moses. A difference must now be briefly noted from Jeremiah [31:32], namely, because the ancient covenant was abolished through the fault of man, there was need of a better remedy, which is shown to be twofold, namely, that God would bury men's sins and inscribe his Law on their hearts. That was also done in Abraham's time. Abraham believed in God; faith was always the gift of the Holy Spirit and, therefore, God inscribed his covenant in Abraham's heart. . . . We see then that the difference which Jeremiah points out was really true and yet the new covenant so flowed from the old that it was the same in substance, while distinguished in form.[75]

Calvin's arguments for the fundamental unity of the Old and New Testaments are inseparable from his view of providence and redemption. In Calvin's view, God's redemptive purpose encompasses creation to the second coming. As the realm of God's creation and action, all of history unfolds under the divine plan of salvation. There is an "Irenaean" sense of history in Calvin's thought: God is reclaiming, renewing, or "recapitulating" the whole of creation and history.

Not surprisingly, Calvin saw this reconstitution or "renovation of the world" (Acts 3:21) as a restoration to order.[76] Simultaneously with the restoration of the image of God, God is restoring history or "the affairs of men" to order. Since all things were "perverted" and "confused" in the Fall, the work of redemption brings the world back to its original order. In Calvin's theology, the reestablishment of this order is now being accomplished gradually through the work of Christ. Repeatedly he depicted Christ as the one who has come to restore all things to order. Commenting on Isaiah 65:25 Calvin wrote:

> But since it is the office of Christ to bring everything back to its state and order, that is the reason why he [the prophet] declares that the confusion or ruin that now exists in human affairs shall be removed by the coming of Christ; because at that time, corruptions having been taken away, the world shall return to its first origin [*primam originem*].[77]

This restoration of order is not, of course, complete, but only gradually accomplished. Occasionally, biblical passages led Calvin to describe the restoration of the world in the past tense. Explaining Ephesians 1:10 Calvin said that "all was restored" or "brought back to a fixed order again at the coming of Christ."[78] Through the atonement, Calvin believed, God "has gathered together all things that had been scattered before and then the world was, in a manner, changed."[79] Nonetheless, Calvin was clear that although Christ initiated the restoration to order, the renewal of the world still awaits completion:

> Christ, by his death, has already restored all things as far as the power to achieve this and the cause of it are concerned; but the effect of it is still not fully visible because that restoration is still in the process of completion and so, too, our redemption, insofar as we still groan under the burden of servitude. For just as the kingdom of Christ has only begun and the perfection of it is still deferred until the last day, so too, the benefits that are joined to it are now seen only in part. Therefore, if, at the present time, we see much confusion in the world, let that faith encourage us and revive us, the faith that Christ shall one day come and restore all things to their former condition [*in integrum*].[80]

In the same way, Calvin described the final judgment as the final restoration of order to the world. Declining to interpret the term "judgment" as "condemnation," he preferred to think of the last judgment as a final restoration of the order initiated by Christ:

> The word "judgment" is interpreted by some as "reformation" and by others as "condemnation." I agree with the former interpreters who explain it such that the world must be restored to legitimate order [*legitimum ordinem*]. The Hebrew word "mishpat" which is translated as "judgment" means a rightly ordered constitution. Now we know that outside of Christ there is nothing but confusion in the world; and although Christ has already begun to set up the kingdom of God, his death was the true beginning of a properly ordered state [*status rite compositi*] and the complete restoration of the world.[81]

Moreover, in Calvin's thought, the restoration of history and the societal order is, like that of the cosmos, inseparably linked to the renewal of the elect.

However, unlike the renovation of the cosmos, the efforts and activity of the elect directly contribute to the restoration of the world's order. Calvin believed that Christians are called to a well-ordered life in the world, not only to guarantee the survival of society but for the glory of God and the upbuilding of the church. As Richard has argued, Calvin portrayed the pious Christian as one who, taking his place within God's order, lives a life of order.[82]

This ordered life contributes to the gradual restoration of an ordered world. Christians again live according to natural law in the fullest sense of the term. In Calvin's view, believers obey the law of nature or the "ordre de nature" not because of the restraint and shame it imposes nor because of the mere necessity for survival which it guarantees. The elect obey the divine and natural law out of love, because such a life promotes the will and glory of God. The elect understand the coherence among the order of nature, the revealed law of God, and the example manifested in the life of Christ.[83] They live "according to nature" precisely because they are being returned to the nature intended for them by their Creator. This original nature demands that all intellectual and social activities of the Christian are redirected to their proper goal, namely, the praise of God. Calvin believed that human knowledge can be recognized as a good when it is "subordinated to Christ" and becomes futile and idolatrous only when Christ ceases to be its foundation.[84] According to Calvin, Paul was not condemning knowledge nor "telling us to be skeptics, always uncertain and doubt-ridden. Nor does he approve a false, counterfeit modesty when we pretend that we are doing a fine thing in adopting the attitude of not understanding the things that we do know."[85] Paul's teaching referred to the original "relation" between God and his creation, a relation of dependence and gratitude. According to Calvin, Paul was instructing Christians to refer the source of all knowledge to the Creator who is its source.

Not only is human knowledge "reordered," according to Calvin, but the activities of Christians are also reclaimed by God. In Calvin's thought, the ordered life of the church bears a social and ecclesiastical dimension which includes, but also goes beyond, the restraint of evil imposed by natural law. The life of charity and justice helps to restore society to order and to the praise of God. The "meditation on the future life" requires a self-renunciation which results not in withdrawal but in helpfulness toward the neighbor. The imitation of Christ is not an individualistic, isolating pursuit but a social ordering of the world, a life of service and love of the neighbor, a reestablishing of justice, and a relieving of poverty.[86] The sermonic exhortations to charity and justice, the exposition of the Sermon on the Mount, and the provisions of the *Draft Ecclesiastical Ordinances* are only several signs of Calvin's concern with the social dimension of the sanctified life that contributes to the restoration of society.

Ultimately the institutions in society that secure and advance order in the world will be abolished. Calvin envisioned a future life of uncoerced, spontaneous harmony in which God will rule *directly* instead of through Christ, the angels, or the institutions of society.[87] In the end, secondary means are unnecessary because then we will see God "face to face." Commenting on I Corinthians 15:24, Calvin wrote:

> Hence as the world will have an end, so will all governments, and magistracy, and laws, and distinction of orders, and different degrees of rank, and everything of that order. There will be no more distinction between servant and master, between king and peasant, between magistrate and private citizen. Indeed, there will be then an end put to all angelic principalities in heaven and to ministries and superiorities in the church, in order that God may exercise his power and sovereignty by himself alone, and not by the hands of men or angels.[88]

The means of order and restraint present in the world are divinely ordained but aimed at their own dissolution. Even the role of angels will end. As the angels, bishops, teachers, and prophets resign their office and cease to rule, "all things will be brought back to God alone as their beginning and their end."[89] But Calvin knew that this was an eschatological goal. Until the time of God's direct rule, Christians are called to service in the world. In the Reformer's thought there is a release of energy. Calvin's doctrines of predestination, the certainty of salvation, spiritual combat, and sanctification directed Christians outward toward the world. The elect are turned toward creation for the good of the neighbor, the upbuilding of the church, and the restoration of society. Concepts of order, stewardship, service, charity, equity, and justice governed Calvin's ethic and demonstrate the high evaluation he placed on the active, ordered, and sanctified activity of Christian life.

4. CONCLUSIONS

1. Calvin's belief in God's faithfulness to his original purpose in creation governed his understanding of the role of creation in redemption. In Calvin's theology, God is reclaiming all of his creation: the cosmos, human nature, and society. In his discussions about this redemptive activity, we can see that Calvin's attacks on the "Manichees" and the "Donatists" were real: he rejected any notion that creation was evil, the cause of sin, or to be repudiated. He most often saw the recurrence of Manichaeism and Donatism in the Anabaptist movement. His attacks on the Anabaptists involved not only their views of baptism and ecclesiology; underlying his polemic was the conviction that they fundamentally misunderstood God's relationship to the created order. In an attempt to rectify this misunderstanding, Calvin continually argued that as the object of God's love and redemption, the created order was not to be shunned.

This polemical and theological context helps to explain that tension which Quistorp perceived in Calvin's theology. According to Quistorp, there is a tension between Calvin's loyalty to the biblical message of the return of Christ and the kingdom of God as a visible, all-encompassing reality, and his tendency to spiritualize and individualize the hope of salvation. Quistorp points out that Calvin viewed heavenly life as beginning with death and the liberation of the immortal soul. As a result, Quistorp argues, Calvin referred "only occasionally" to the new creation.[90]

This tension may well be present in Calvin's thought; it is somewhat difficult at times to see why the resurrection of the body and the renewal of creation are necessary if the immortal soul already enjoys, to a large measure, the joy of God's presence. (However, this criticism can also be directed to any part of the Christian tradition that accepts the natural immortality of the soul.) Nevertheless, it is important to recall that the Reformer's insistence on the renovation of the cosmos and of the body was a polemical point fundamental to his view of creation. When Calvin defended the renewal of the material creation, his concern was not primarily with debates about the immortality of the soul. He was, rather, defending the goodness of God's original creation. He also recognized that the salvation of the individual was not the ultimate goal. All of creation (including the soul) existed not for its own redemption but in order to reflect the glory of God. Consequently, in his renovation of the world Calvin's God preserved the original matter both of the cosmos and of human nature – not to do so would be a failure of God's purpose in creation. Basing his comments on Romans 8:20, Calvin repeatedly argued that creation subjected now to disorder would not be abandoned but, rather, that its original substance would be restored to order.

2. Also on the basis of Romans 8:20, Calvin maintained that the renovation of nature would follow that of the head of creation, namely, the human being. The life of sanctification, which renews human nature, is a restoration of the image of God in the soul. According to Calvin, the original mind and will are retained and actively participate in their own transformation. The will is brought back into conformity with God's Law and the mind is renewed as it increases in the knowledge of God, certainty of salvation, and the restored contemplation of nature. In this restored condition, the mind gains mastery over the self, is granted the "life-giving Spirit," and refers its gifts back to God. The relational character of the *imago Dei* is thereby reestablished. Although he attacked the philosophers for not recognizing the effects of sin, Calvin adopted their view as the *goal* of sanctification:

> For how is the whole man entire, except when his thoughts are pure and holy, his affections all honorable and well-ordered, and when his body also devotes its energies and services to good works alone? The philosophers hold that the faculty of understanding is like a mistress, while the affections are means of exercising command and the body renders ready obedience. We see now how well all things fit together. For man is pure and whole if he thinks nothing with the mind, desires nothing with the heart, nor does anything with the body except that which is approved by God.[91]

3. This gradual internal restoration of the soul enables the believer to find again a richer knowledge of God from the contemplation of nature. This Christian theology of nature cannot be separated from Calvin's understanding of a sanctified, restored order within the soul. The renewed ability to perceive God in nature is dependent on this restored internal order. The "redeemed" eye or the reordered soul alone is able to refer the order in the cosmos back to its Creator. With the soul's restoration, nature once again serves God's original purpose: to manifest the divine majesty to the human creation in praise of their common Creator.

4. The contemplation of the historical order, however, is not so simple. Here the reader of Calvin must be careful. For Calvin, the disorder in history obstructed the view of providence more than did the disorder in nature. Because the restoration of order in the historical realm was only begun by Christ, Calvin warned that providence in historical affairs was not an empirical doctrine. In the *Institutes* Calvin admitted that the events of the world appear to our mind as fortuitous since the "order, reason, and necessity" of things lie hidden in God's plan and are "not apprehended by human opinion."[92] Throughout the sermons on Job, he distinguished between nature and history; nature manifests the power of God but providence in human affairs (particularly Job's life) often remains hidden behind the confusion and tumults of earthly historical life.[93] Calvin, therefore, was ambiguous about the contemplation of *history*. On the one hand, he was reserved and warned Christians not to depend on empirical evidence for their trust in providence. After all, the wicked often prosper while the just (Job) suffer. However, he could at times encourage the contemplation of "God's works" in history. In such cases he was anxious to insist that although these *opera Dei* often transcend our ability to understand, nonetheless believers are to seek God in the "theater" of God's historical providence. Often such exhortations referred not to the "revolutions" and changes of the everyday world but to the "mystery" of God's salvific plan, as in the following sermon on Ephesians 3:9–12:

> For it is said that it is the wisdom of men to search out God's works, and to set their minds wholly upon them. And God has also ordained the world to be like a theater upon which to behold his goodness, righteousness, power, and wisdom. Therefore, there seems to be some contradiction between these two things: that we should be diligent and attentive in considering God's works and yet that our minds are overcome when we think about them. To answer this is very easy. If we desire to know soberly only the things which God wills to reveal to us, and which are useful to us, we shall have sufficient understanding and we shall rightly perceive that he means to teach us by his works to come to him and to put our whole trust in him, to know how to call upon him, to discern between good and evil, and to walk according to his will. . . . And that is the reason why it is said in the Book of Job chapter 26, that we shall have done very much if we can perceive "parts of God's ways." We may taste then of God's wisdom, righteousness, power and

goodness by considering simply in outline the works of God. But if we must get down to plumbing their depths, we shall find there the mystery already mentioned, which is able to engulf our understanding.[94]

Calvin's emphasis, however, remained on the inscrutability of providence which functions as a "veil" that clouds or obscures our view of God's providence.[95] Providence, for Calvin, is most clearly "seen" only from the "watchtower" of faith.

5. The gradual restoration of the historical order will be complete only in the afterlife when "God will be all in all." Meanwhile the restoration of internal order in the soul has an effect on the surrounding world. In his reclaiming of creation, Calvin's God makes use of the societal and ecclesiastical activities of Christians. While Calvin charged the Anabaptists with Donatism, his own ecclesiology and spirituality was the reverse of isolationism. The church was not a pure body in the midst of a dark and dangerous creation. Schulze's contention that Calvin's pessimistic, negative, and ascetic attitude devalued earthly existence has been disproven by scholars such as Doumergue, Wallace, and Richard, all of whom point to Calvin's concern with and appreciation for the present life.[96] The Reformer's "activist" piety must be seen in terms of his theology of creation as a whole. The renovation of creation renews all of life. Therefore, after submitting their knowledge and will to Christ, the elect are encouraged to turn outward for the common upbuilding of the church and the good of their neighbors. Such ordered outward activity, Calvin assumed, contributes to the sanctifying or reordering of the world. Instead of positing a church that stood in isolation from a threatening world, Calvin saw the church as the organ that led the renewal of both the cosmos and society.

VI

CONCLUSION

The preceding chapters have shown that although Calvin rejected certain "speculative" questions about creation, he stood in a line of continuity with the tradition and defended the orthodox teaching on creation against sixteenth-century challenges. While he criticized the Augustinian exegesis of Genesis 1:1 and Eccl. 18:1, Calvin taught the doctrine of *creatio ex nihilo*. Against the influence of Aristotelianism, Averroism, Epicureanism, and Stoicism, he insisted on a doctrine of providence that both protected divine sovereignty and involved God directly in the sublunar realm of nature and history. In opposition to what he considered the dangers of pantheism, Calvin opposed the Libertines and defended the reality of angels and demons. Amidst sixteenth-century speculation about the state of the soul after death, Calvin reaffirmed the doctrine of immortality. And, finally, he opposed what he viewed as the Donatist tendency of the Anabaptists and upheld the continuity of God's providence in history, the participation of believers in government, and the activity of the church in the world. In the course of these discussions Calvin formulated an essentially Irenaean vision of creation and redemption. In Calvin's theology, God is the Lord of nature and of history and is reclaiming his creation so that nothing of its original substance will be lost or destroyed.

Calvin shared his interest in creation with his fellow Reformers. One should not conclude a work such as the present one without taking note of the fact that concern with the created order is a prominent feature in all Reformation theologies. The God of the Reformers is one who is guiding history, is true to the "work of his hands," and faithful to his purposes in creation. A brief survey of the general features of the creation theologies of Luther, Zwingli, and Melanchthon will demonstrate this common concern and serve as a comparison to those traits emphasized by Calvin.

Like Calvin and the preceding tradition, Luther argued that the Fall was decisive for understanding the created order. Luther described the relation between humanity and creation by stressing the impact of sin on the cosmos. According to Luther, the prefallen world was characterized by perfection and harmony. The original creation differed from that which we see today: the air was purer, the light of the sun was brighter, and all the plants were fruitful. No harmful vermin or savage beasts existed and Adam and Eve lived in perfect harmony with nature.[1] Luther defined their perfection in terms of a perfect knowledge of God, society, and nature. Adam, Luther explained, was a perfect philosopher, jurist, and "medicus." Just as he knew God, so too he possessed a complete and instantaneous knowledge of the nature over which he was to exercise dominion. He also possessed a perfect knowledge of how to organize society and govern human relationships.[2]

According to Luther, the image of God, in which Adam and Eve were created, enabled them both to understand creation and to know God through his revelation in nature. Luther argued that God had revealed himself through the Word (the Law given in Genesis 2:16) and the works of nature. The knowledge of God and that of nature were inseparable: "The knowledge of all other creatures necessarily followed this knowledge [of God]; for where the knowledge of God is perfect, there also the knowledge of the other things that are under God is also necessarily perfect."[3]

Luther also argued that this harmonious and joyful state was altered dramatically by the Fall. Not only did human beings lose the original image of God but they lost the knowledge of creation. Now only a trace remains of their original dominion over nature. According to Luther, the human being now transfers his allegiance from God to creation. Fallen men and women, he argued, trust in themselves and created things rather than in God alone. Humanity can no longer find a knowledge of God through creation, but instead worships and relies on creation itself.[4]

In a manner consistent with the traditional exegesis of Romans and Genesis, Luther explained that Adam's sin brought about the progressive decay of nature. After the entrance of sin into the world, the earth was cursed and plants became unfruitful; thorns, thistles, and vermin appeared and the animals became savage. "Even the sun and moon appear as though they put on sackcloth."[5] As sins increased, nature continued to deteriorate in a long and steady decline, as God's continual punishment was added to the original curse of the earth. Luther believed that mountains came into being after the flood and were, therefore, a sign of God's later punishment for sin.[6] According to Luther, creatures have now become the "sermons" or preachers of divine wrath. Because of the noetic or perceptual effects of sin, however, we are unable to understand these sermons of wrath.[7]

Marjorie Nicolson and George Williams have analyzed Luther's statements about the curse on creation and the continual decay of nature.[8] This aspect of Luther's thought, however, must not overshadow his belief that the goodness, love, and power of God still shine forth in creation. Heinrich Bornkamm and Werner Elert have studied Luther's many references to the great and wonderful works of God in nature and his extensive use of nature imagery.[9] Luther too believed that God brought all of creation into being through the Word and that God now continually sustains, preserves, governs, and works through every creature. More so than Calvin, Luther dramatically emphasized God's presence in every leaf, rock, tree, animal, cloud, and section of creation to such an extent that he sometimes sounds pantheistic. According to Luther, all creatures are the masks [*larvae*] of God under which God both hides himself and works in creation. Human beings cannot know the naked God [*Deus nudus*]. They can only find God in his works and his words.[10]

Both Luther and Calvin, however, argued that one must stand in the right relationship to God in order to understand creation. After the Fall, humanity cannot understand either the mercy nor the anger of God through the contemplation of nature. For the unredeemed mind, the search for God in nature results only in idolatry. Therefore, Luther explained, only the upright are capable of studying, meditating, and searching out the works of God in creation. This search, moreover, requires the Word of God which now must explain God's works. Although fallen humans retain a conscience, a knowledge of natural law, and the ability to regulate society, they have lost that perfect, instantaneous knowledge of God, nature, and society characteristic of the prefallen world. Humanity now responds to God's words and works in faith.[11]

Zwingli's discussions of nature are somewhat less extensive than those of Luther and Calvin. Nonetheless, he demonstrated a lively interest in the doctrine of providence, the realm of the cosmos, and the function of natural reason and pagan wisdom. Because of the limitations of space, I restrict myself to his statements about providence and secondary causality found in his sermon *De providentia*.

Throughout his treatment of providence, Zwingli described a God who is an immediate presence to the world, upholding and sustaining it in being, and immediately governing all creatures. He insisted that God's power never withdrew, rested, or wavered but continued to move and direct all creatures. Moreover, Zwingli's universe needed such a God. Calvin's portrayal of a fragile cosmos threatened by chaos was anticipated by Zwingli. However, Zwingli was more sympathetic to the ancient identification of nature with God. Defending Pliny's statement that the power of nature is properly called God, Zwingli argued:

> For what he [Pliny] called nature, we call Deity. For what is that nature whose power he proclaims as so vast? Are we to suppose that, according to the habit of atheistic philosophers, he was speaking of that nature which belongs to each individually? Who, then, could establish peace and harmony in the vast discord of things? Who will prevent a chaotic confusion of things? Especially when we see that not only men but the elements are so mutually antagonistic to each other that, unless you harmonize them by means of some neutral mediator, you will never succeed in making fire and water, for example, work together. If, then, anyone believes that Pliny means by nature the natural characteristic of individual things, we shall find everything in chaos. For everything is so antagonistic to its opposite that without some outside force nothing can exist. . . . Even the original elements, therefore, are by their nature ἀσπ'ο δια, that is, incapable of leaguing and uniting themselves together. . . . For thus no two things could unite together so that a third would result from their union, since the natures of things are so antagonistic that no one will receive a second unto it, unless compelled by some stronger outside

force. He seems to understand by nature that power which moves and unites or separates all things. And what is that but God?[12]

Zwingli stressed the immediacy of God to creation to such an extent that secondary causes lost their reality or function: "Secondary causes are not properly called causes."[13] There is, according to Zwingli, only one true cause of all things so that all other means and instruments are so called only by metonymy. Other things are not truly causes any more than the representative of a potentate could truly be a potentate or the hammer the artificer. God, then, is the only effective force in nature, ". . . we assign to the sun and the stars things that belong to God alone. For he is in the stars themselves, nay, the stars being of him and in him, do not have their own essence, power, activity, but God's."[14] Zwingli admitted that God uses creatures, including the angels, as "instruments" but true causality, he insisted, belongs only to God.[15] Repeatedly Zwingli described a cosmos in need of a God who directly governs and sustains it. Just as God created the world, so too the world remains "in him and from him." For, Zwingli argued, if God ceased to exist "all substances, all bodies, stars, earth, and seas, in short, the whole structure of the universe would collapse in an instant and be reduced to nothing."[16]

In Zwingli's view, nothing in the universe escapes or evades this divine providence. The divine attributes guarantee, so to speak, the all-encompassing power of providence. If one argued that something escaped God's knowledge or power, then God would be lacking in omniscience and omnipotence.[17] Poverty, illness, childlessness, and all events must be attributed to God's providence. According to Zwingli, this proper recognition of providence as the cause of all events brings comfort in the midst of misfortune.[18] Knowing that all events come from providence allows one to rise above the events of the world. "For when we see these things we are in the habit of calling them goods of fortune, so variable and uncertain that they cannot remain in any fixed place, we shall, unless unbalanced in mind, bind all of our efforts to standing firm ourselves and not tossing about with them. . . . Hence what can strengthen us against the buffetings of these misfortunes but the contemplation of Providence? It suggests to the stoutest heart the thought 'Believe not that these things happen by accident. They are done at my command. They had to be. They could not be otherwise.' "[19] Despite their many differences, therefore, Zwingli and Calvin shared similar views of the cosmos, a belief in the necessity for a strong doctrine of providence, and the conviction that by attributing every event to God the believer would find comfort.

A third reformer whose writings demonstrate a lively and consistent interest in providence and the natural order is Philip Melanchthon. Like Calvin, Melanchthon defended his understanding of God's relation to creation against the resurgence of Epicurean and Stoic philosophies. In these polemics he appealed to the ordered regularity of nature against Epicurean notions of chance and fortune. God, he argued, is an orderly being who created and sustains order both in the cosmos and in society.[20] Melanchthon maintained that it is "impossible that there be perpetual order in nature, having arisen from matter. The principal parts of nature are ordered and remain in perpetual order. . . . Therefore nature does not exist by chance but has arisen from some mind which understands order."[21] Against the Stoics, he argued that God is the most free of all beings and independent of the realm of secondary causality so that order is preserved in the world by a providential but transcendent Deity.[22]

Melanchthon was also intensely interested in the continual functioning and limited integrity of human nature after the Fall. Sensitive to the criticism that the Protestant emphasis on the depravity of sinful nature rendered humanity inactive, Melanchthon argued that the human being still retained a will and natural reason or that "natural light" which, though weakened in the Fall, still functioned admirably in the earthly realm.[23] According to Melanchthon, this natural light and the "notitiae" in the mind are the basis for certitude in the sciences and are evident in man's inborn knowledge of natural law, morality, measure, order, and number. The "lex naturae" is part of the order of creation, and natural reason is quite capable of perceiving its contents and ordering human relationships in accordance with its teachings.[24]

In Melanchthon's view, the natural light was created by God in order that man might discern the divine nature in creation. He believed that the world was "growing old," but this encroaching senility did not hinder creation from being a testimony of God.[25] God impressed traces of his nature in creation; these *vestigia Dei* consisted of the order in nature and even functioned as proof of God's existence. The days, seasons, years, stars, and even procreation and government are all signs of God's orderly nature and are meant to be objects of study and contemplation.[26] Natural reason is suited to the study of "physics" or natural philosophy, which investigated this order embedded in nature. Astronomy, medicine, arithmetic, and geometry are all gifts of God designed for the contemplation of God's wisdom in creation.

Even this brief survey shows that in many points Calvin's fellow reformers shared his view of creation. The drastic effect of sin on the cosmos, the fragility of the universe, the need for a correct doctrine of providence, the remaining integrity of creation and human reason, and the revelation of God in the order and beauty of nature were themes expressed throughout the Reformation theology of the sixteenth century.

This study has attempted to show what concerns governed Calvin's understanding of creation and how the created order functioned theologically in his thought. Students of Calvin's theology must never lose sight of that argument against Sadoleto that the primary concern of the Christian is not the salvation of his individual soul but the glory of God.[27] Without minimizing the importance of sin, justification by faith, or the certainty of salvation in Calvin's thought, we must remember that he knew the glory of God extended beyond the individual and encompassed all aspects of creation. God created the world as a theater of his glory, and although the human being stands at the head of that creation, he is never the whole of creation itself. From the orderly course of the stars to the limited stability of governments, God's nature and glory are displayed in every part of creation. The suggestion that "the world" has become a sphere of darkness alien to the church implied, for Calvin, that God's purpose for his creation as a mirror or theater has been overturned. To refuse participation in this earthly realm or to neglect to contemplate nature is a failure to understand God's commitment, purpose, and governance of his created order. And, finally, to limit Calvin's vision to the total depravity of human nature, justification by faith, and the condemning function of nature is to impose on him a mentality that he resisted throughout his writings. In Calvin's view, the human race belongs to the order of creation which reveals or reflects the power, wisdom, and glory of God; and not surprisingly, the entire creation plays an important role in his understanding of God's nature and purposes.

As we have seen, this all-encompassing vision of creation found expression in the recurrence of several themes throughout Calvin's statements about the natural realm. Central to all his discussions is the wonder that order continues in the creation. Sin has not annihilated what was a beautiful but fragile creation. The sun and stars still revolve around the earth, the waters (usually) remain within their bounds, and the earth hangs suspended in its place. Cities and governments continue to exist and to retain the order and justice necessary for the survival of the human race. Since, in Calvin's view, order, stability, and the continuation of nature are not self-sufficient, these realities demonstrate the power, immutability, faithfulness, and reliability of God. Without the restraining bridle of God's power the devil and his legions would overwhelm society just as the raging waters would rush forth from their shores. Consequently, the very survival and continuation of nature are a revelation of God's nature and commitment to creation.

Calvin was equally conscious of the continuation of human nature. People remained human and in possession of a will and reason which distinguished them from beasts. After the Fall this reason and will remained active in sin, grace, and the preservation of society. Calvin's uncompromising insistence that "before God" human nature is totally depraved and a willing source of evil never blinded him to the natural gifts left to the fallen soul. Insight into order, natural law, the dictates of nature, the arts and sciences, and the preservation of civil life are indisputable evidence that human nature continues to function competently in this earthly sphere. Calvin also believed that since God is the source of all knowledge, pagan wisdom can be legitimately appropriated as an aid in investigations of nature and for governing society.

Calvin recognized not only that the remaining natural gifts of man function quite well within the earthly realm but argued also that this lower sphere is the proper realm of activity for the believer. Christians are not to crucify all natural knowledge but are to submit their minds to Christ, after which they are to use their knowledge within the world. Neither the meditation on the future life nor the "spiritualizing tendency" in Calvin's thought led him into isolationism from the natural order. Believers, he insisted, are to be active in whatever calling they find themselves. Creation, moreover, is to be used not only out of necessity but "for delight and enjoyment."

> In grasses, trees, and fruits, apart from their various uses, there is the beauty of appearance and pleasantness of odor. For if this were not true, the prophet would not have reckoned them among the benefits of God, "that wine gladdens the heart of man and oil makes his face to shine. . . ." Has the Lord clothed the flowers with the great beauty that greets our eyes, the sweetness of smell that is wafted upon our nostrils, and yet will it be unlawful for our eyes to be affected by that beauty or our sense of smell by the sweetness of that odor? What? Did he not so distinguish the colors as to make some more lovely than others? What? Did he not endow gold and silver, ivory and marble, with a loveliness that renders them more precious than other metals or stones? Did he not, in short, render many things attractive to us apart from their necessary use?[28]

Calvin believed that this created realm can be enjoyed properly and is the legitimate sphere in which Christians are to act, study, and exercise their considerable talents and abilities; the church does not call the Christian away from the world created by God.

All of these teachings are founded on the conviction that God is still true to his creation and continues to take joy in the works of his hands. Calvin's is a salvation-history theology. Christianity begins with creation and is the story of God's covenant with Israel, a covenant that is renewed in Christ and encompasses all peoples. Throughout this history, God governs his creation both in the cosmos and in human history. So, too, Calvin's God not only secures the salvation of the elect but reclaims all aspects of his creation. Although Calvin did not like to speculate about the end of time, he was careful to insist that the fires of judgment will "purify" the universe but not destroy it. As a result, Calvin maintained that "the same substance" of both our bodies and material creation will remain and be restored. He expressed the same concern in his belief that everything primal to human nature will remain throughout the process of sanctification. To deny the continuation of nature was, in Calvin's view, to be a Manichaean.

Finally, the gradual restoration of human nature is presupposed in Calvin's various statements about "natural theology." As the human soul is gradually restored to (and even surpasses) the original order characteristic of the image of God, so too the believer returns to that originally intended activity: namely, the contemplating of God's revelation written in the book of nature and revealed in the visible splendor of the world. As the perceptual breakdown caused by sin is healed through the Spirit and Scriptures, nature regains its revelatory function as a mirror, a painting, and a theater of the divine glory.

Nonetheless, the remaining sinfulness of the believer and the imperfection of the world still limit the completeness of this final restoration; the bridle of Scripture must still hem in the mind, and nature still suffers the disorder caused by sin. The main problem for a "Christian natural theology" is not the disputed "point of contact" debated by Barth and Brunner. Calvin clearly stated that the work of the Spirit and of Scripture corrects the noetic effect of sin insofar as one remains within the bounds of Scripture. Most Calvin scholars now agree with Brunner, Torrance, Gloede, Dowey, and Parker that Calvin allowed for the pious contemplation of nature.[29] The problem lies in Calvin's statements that the atonement has not yet restored order to nature and to history. This means that the believer contemplates a nature that suffers confusion and corruption caused by human sin. In the sermons on Job, Calvin explained that the remaining disorders in the historical sphere act as a "cloud" which prevents providence from being an empirical reality always discernible in the present time. Nonetheless, Calvin believed that providence preserved nature as a presently empirical revelation of God's glory, power, wisdom, and goodness. God remained faithful to his creation such that it continued to reflect his nature despite the intrusion of disorder after the Fall. Hence, Calvin can argue that "moreover, although the blessing of God is never seen as purely and clearly as it appeared to man in his innocence, yet if what remains behind be considered in itself, David truly and properly exclaims 'The earth is full of the mercy of God.' "[30]

As we have seen, Calvin believed that this creation is to function as the arena of Christian activity and contemplation. For Calvin, the need for salvation does not leave believers analyzing their own condition; justification by faith and predestination release their energies and direct them outward to the world. The certitude of salvation experienced through union with Christ allows Christians to combat the devil as well as to look at the book of nature surrounding them in creation. Christians are to be active in the ordering of society, the upbuilding of the church, the combating of demons, and the study of nature, not because this world can offer salvation or fulfillment but because these activities express the glory of God within his created order.

NOTES

INTRODUCTION

1. David C. Steinmetz analyzes the influence of Luther's view of Christ's presence in the world after the ascension, expressed in his doctrine of the Eucharist, in *Luther in Context* (Bloomington: Indiana U. Press, 1986), pp. 81–83.

2. Richard Stauffer, *Dieu, la création et la Providence dans la prédication de Calvin* (Berne: Peter Lang, 1978).

3. Josef Bohatec, *Calvin und das Recht* (Feudingen: Buchdruck und Verlags-Anstalt, 1934); idem, *Budé und Calvin: Studien zur Gedankenwelt des französischen Frühhumanismus* (Graz: Böhlau, 1950); idem, *Calvins Lehre von Staat und Kirche* (Breslau: Marcus, 1937).

4. Ronald S. Wallace, *Calvin's Doctrine of the Christian Life* (Edinburgh & London: Oliver and Boyd, 1959); Lucien Joseph Richard, *The Spirituality of John Calvin* (Atlanta: John Knox, 1974). See also: T. F. Torrance, *Calvin's Doctrine of Man* (London: Lutterworth, 1949).

5. Benjamin Charles Milner, Jr., *Calvin's Doctrine of the Church* (Leiden: E.J. Brill, 1970), p. 190.

6. *Praefationes bibliis gallicis Petri Roberti Olivetani*, CO 9:793–795.

7. *Inst.* (1539) I.11–18, CO 1:286–291.

8. *Inst.* (1559) I.17.1–2. The 1559 edition of the *Institutes* will be cited throughout this book unless otherwise indicated.

9. *Calvin's Commentary on Seneca's "De clementia"*, Introduction, translation, and notes by F.L. Battles and A.M. Hugo (Leiden: E.J. Brill, 1969), 19.2, 41ff., 50ff., 87.10ff., 112.6ff.

10. *Inst.* (1536), OS I.39–40.

11. *Inst.* (1536), OS I.39; *Inst.* (1539) III.2, CO 1:371–2.

12. Comm. on Rom. 2:14; T.H.L. Parker, *Iohannis Calvini Commentarius in Epistolam Pauli ad Romanos*, Vol. 22 of *Studies in the History of Christian Thought* (Leiden: E.J. Brill, 1981), p. 45. CO 49:37–38; sermon on Deut. 19:14–15, CO 27:568; sermon on Job 28:1–9, CO 34:503; Harmony on the Five Books of Moses, CO 24:209–260; *Inst.* II.8.1–2; IV.20.16.

13. *Calvin's Commentary on Seneca's "De clementia"*, 6.9ff.

14. *Inst.* (1536), OS I.756.

15. *Inst.* (1539) XIV.38–41, CO 1:889–891.

16. *Inst.* I.16–18.

17. Throughout this book I will use the term "rationalist" to refer to the thinkers such as Dolet and Rabelais studied by Bohatec (*Budé und Calvin*) and Henri Busson, *Le rationalisme dans la littérature Française de la Renaissance 1533–1601* (Paris: J. Vrin, 1957).

18. *Consensus Genevensis* CO 8:294. See also *Inst.* I.5.1–2, 8.10; I.6.2–4; I.14.20.

I. PROVIDENCE: THE PROSCENIUM ARCH

1. Alexander Schweizer, *Die Glaubenslehre der evangelisch-reformierten Kirche*, 2 vols. (Zurich: Orell, Fussli, 1844–47); M. Scheibe, *Calvins Prädestinationslehre*, (Halle: Max Niemeyer, 1897); Albrecht Ritschl, "Geschichtliche Studien zur christlichen Lehre von Gott," *Jahrbücher für deutsche Theologie* (1868):67–133; Reinhold Seeberg, *Lehrbuch der Dogmengeschichte*, 5th ed., 4 vols. (Basel: B. Schwabe, 1954), IV.2.

2. Josef Bohatec, "Calvins Vorsehungslehre," in *Calvinstudien. Festschrift zum 400. Geburtstage Johann Calvins* (Leipzig: Rudolf Haupt, 1909), p. 414. Bohatec here agrees with Albrecht Ritschl, "Geschichtliche Studien zur christlichen Lehre von Gott," p. 108, who also saw Calvin's foundational doctrine as providence. Cf. Paul Jacobs, *Prädestination und Verantwortlichkeit bei Calvin* (Neukirchen, Kreis Moers: Buchhandlung des Erziehungsvereins, 1937), p. 69; Emile Doumergue, *Jean Calvin—Les hommes et les choses de son temps*, 7 vols. (Lausanne: G. Bridel et Cie, 1897–1927), IV:111–118, 351–416.

3. Theopholus of Antioch, *Autol.*, II.2, cited by Jaroslav Pelikan, "Creation and Causality in the History of Christian Thought," *Journal of Religion* 40 (Oct. 1960):246–255. See also Glenn F. Chesnut, *The First Christian Histories: Eusebius, Socrates, Sozomen, Theodoret, and Evagrius* (Macon: Mercer, 1986). On the history of doctrines of creation and providence see: Lloyd G. Patterson, *God and History in Early Christian Thought* (New York: Seabury, 1967) and Leo Scheffczyk, *Creation and Providence*, tr. Richard Strachan (New York: Herder and Herder, 1970).

4. Henry Austryn Wolfson, "Patristic Arguments Against the Eternity of the World," *Harvard Theological Review* 59 (1966):351–367, reprinted in *Studies in the History of Philosophy and Religion*, ed. Isidore Twersky and George H. Williams, 2 vols. (Cambridge, MA: Harvard U. Press, 1973), I:182–198.

5. Irenaeus, *Adv. haer.* II.9.1; III.11.1; V.1.1.

6. Ibid., III.11.1.

7. Ibid., V.2.

8. Ibid., IV.32.2.

9. Ibid., V.19.1.

10. Ibid., V.36.1.

11. Chrysostom, *Ad eos qui scandalizati sunt*, can be found in PG 52:479–528 and *Sources chrétiennes*, intr. and tr. Anne-Marie Malingrey (Paris: Les editions du Cerf, 1961), vol. 79. The text was first edited separately in 1658. *Ad Stagirium a daemone vexatum* PG 47:429ff.

12. Ibid., VII.3–6.

13. Ibid., VII.26. Cf. Seneca, *De providentia* I.2–5. On the use of creation as a proof of providence in Stoic arguments see M. Spanneut, *Le Stoïcisme des Pères de l'Église* (Paris, 1957).

14. Chrysostom, *Ad pop. Antioch* IX.4.

15. Chrysostom, *Ad eos qui scandalizati sunt* IXff.

16. Chrysostom, *Ad Stagirium* I.3; I.4; I.10.

17. Chrysostom, *Ad eos qui scandalizati sunt* X–XIII.

18. Ibid., XXIII–XXIV.

19. Ibid., IX.7.

20. Ibid., X.7.

21. Ibid., II.1.

22. Ibid., II.14.

23. Ibid., I.4–6.

24. Ibid., II.4; *Ad Stagirium* I.5.

25. The following section is taken from my essay "Eve as Mother: Reaching for the Reality of History in Augustine's Later Exegesis of Genesis," in *Genesis 1–3 in the History of Exegesis* (Lewiston, NY: Edwin Mellen, 1988), pp. 135–186.

26. Augustine, *De Genesi ad litteram libri duodecim* (*The Literal Meaning of Genesis: Commentary in Twelve Books*) [hereafter *De Genesi ad litteram*]. V.11.27–XII.12.28; Bibliotheque augustinienne, Latin text with French translation and notes by P. Agaesse and A. Solignac (Paris: Études augustiniennes, 1949–), vol. 48–49 [hereafter B.A.], pp. 680–682; Jean Guitton, *Le temps et l'éternité chez Plotin et saint Augustin*, 3rd ed. (Paris: J. Vrin, 1959), 146ff.

27. Augustine, *De Genesi ad litteram* IV.23.51–24.56; VI.3.4.

28. Ibid., V.3.1–6.

29. Ibid., V.5.12.

30. Augustine, *De civ. Dei* XII.13.17, 20; R.W. Dyson, "St. Augustine's Remarks on Time," *The Downside Review* 100 (1982):221–230.

31. Augustine, *De Genesi ad litteram* V.5.12.

32. Ibid., IV.22.39; VI.32.50. See also: G. Pelland, *Cinq études d'Augustin sur le début de la Genèse* (Tournai: Desclée, 1972), 189ff.; Solignac, "Exégèse et Métaphysique Genèse 1:1-3 chez saint Augustin," *In Principio*, Centre d'études des religions du livre (Paris: Études augustiniennes, 1973), pp. 164–171; Jacques de Blic, "Le processus de la création d'après saint Augustin," *Mélanges offerts au R.P. Ferdinand Cavallera* (Toulouse, 1948), pp. 179–189.

33. Augustine, *De Genesi ad litteram* V.23.44–46.

34. Ibid., IV.33.51–52; V.23.44–45.

35. Ibid., V.4.11; VI.6.19–VII.20; V.11.27; V.20.40.

36. Guitton, *Le temps et l'éternité chez Plotin et saint Augustin*, pp. 187–188; B.A. 48, pp. 678–680.

37. On the theory of the causal reasons, see B.A. 48, pp. 653–668; Michael McKeough, "The Meaning of the Rationes Seminales in St. Augustine," Ph.D. dissertation, Dept. of Phil., Catholic U. of America, 1956; Jules Brady, "St. Augustine's Theory of Seminal Reasons," *The New Scholasticism* 38 (1964):141–158; Christopher J. O'Toole, "The Philosophy of Creation in the Writings of St. Augustine," Ph.D dissertation, Dept. of Phil., Catholic U. of America, 1944, 70ff. Scholars have debated whether causal reasons are passive or active principles and whether Augustine's philosophy supports a static or evolutionary view of nature. For a defense of the active role of causal reasons see Brady and McKeough. Gilson, and later O'Toole, minimized (although they do not appear to deny completely) the role of causal reasons as efficient causes. They effectively argue, however, that Augustine's theory cannot be viewed as evolutionary because the reasons cannot bring new *forms* into being; all future effects of the *rationes* are fixed in form at the moment of their creation. Gilson, however, grants that the *rationes* possess a principle of activity and development; no creature possesses *creative* efficacy. See: E. Gilson, *Introduction à l'étude de saint Augustin* (Paris: J. Vrin, 1929), pp. 270–271.

38. Augustine, *De Genesi ad litteram* IV.12.32.

39. Ibid., V.20.41; VIII.24.45; IX.14.25–XV.28; XII.36.69.

40. See also: William Christian, "Augustine on the Creation of the World," *Harvard Theological Review* 47 (1953):1–25; Alois Wachtel, *Beiträge zur Geschichtstheologie des Aurelius Augustinus* (Bonn:Ludwig Röhrscheid, 1960), pp. 27–100.

41. John F. Wippel, "The Condemnations of 1270 and 1277 at Paris," *Journal of Medieval and Renaissance Studies* (1972):169–201. Wippel identifies three philosophical movements, each of which developed between 1250 and 1270. I limit myself to the second of these groups, which is sometimes known as "Latin Averroism," "Heterodox Aristotelianism," or as Wippel identifies it, "Radical Aristotelianism." See also, F. Van Steenberghen, *La Philosophie au XIIIᵉ siècle* (Louvain, 1966), 356ff.

42. Bonaventure, *Collationes de decem praeceptis* (Quaracchi, 1882-1902), V.514; idem, *Collationes de septem donis Spiritus sancti*, V.497, 43; ibid., cited by Wippel, "The Condemnations," p. 180.

43. Wippel, "The Condemnations," 180ff.

44. Bonaventure, *Collationes in Hexaemeron* VI.2–5.

45. Aquinas, S.T. Ia.45.1., SCG II.16.1ff.

46. Ibid., Ia.46.2, SCG III.65.8.

47. Ibid., S.T. Ia.104.1. Thomas is citing Gregory's *Moralia* XVI.

48. Aquinas, *Quaestiones disputatae de potentia Dei* III.5; Cf. SCG I.22.9, II.15.5, III.65.7, III.66.7.

49. Aquinas, *De substantiis separatis*, C.15.

50. John O. Riedl, "The Nature of Angels," in *Essays in Thomism*, ed. Robert E. Brennan (New York: Sheed & Ward, 1942), p. 139.

51. Aquinas, S.T. Ia.104.1.

52. Ibid., Ia.22.2. Aquinas explained that Maimonides exempted humans from the group of corruptibles because of the excellence of their intellect. Thomas' reference is to *Dux neutrorum* III.18 (Paris, 1520).

53. Aquinas, S.T. Ia.22.2.

54. Ibid., Ia.22.3.

55. Ibid.

56. Wippel, "The Condemnations," 179ff.

57. For a history of scholarship on Nominalism see William J. Courtenay, "Nominalism and Late Medieval Religion," in *The Pursuit of Holiness in Late Medieval and Renaissance Religion*, ed. C. Trinkaus with H.A. Oberman (Leiden: E.J. Brill, 1974), pp. 26–59. On the dialectic of the two powers in God, see H.A. Oberman, "Some Notes on the Theology of Nominalism with Attention to its Relation to the Renaissance," *Harvard Theological Review* 53 (1960):46–76. Francis Oakley, *Omnipotence, Covenant, and Order* (Ithaca: Cornell U. Press, 1984), 48ff.

58. Francis Oakley, "Pierre d'Ailly and the Absolute Power of God," *Harvard Theological Review* 56 (1963):59–73. See also William J. Courtenay, "Covenant and Causality in Pierre d'Ailly," *Speculum* 46 (1971):94–119. Courtenay points out that d'Ailly was not willing to draw the radical conclusions about causality suggested by Autrecourt. According to Courtenay, d'Ailly argued that in natural causation the effect resulted from a power in the cause as well as from the will of God.

59. Courtenay, "Covenant and Causality in Pierre d'Ailly"; Oakley, "Pierre d'Ailly and the Absolute Power of God"; David C. Steinmetz, "Scholasticism and Radical Reform: Nominalist Motifs in the Theology of Balthasar Hubmaier," *The Mennonite Quarterly Review* 45 (1971):123–143.

60. H.A. Oberman, *Harvest of Medieval Theology* (Cambridge, MA: Harvard U. Press, 1963); Paul Vignaux, *Justification et prédestination au XIVᵉ siècle. Duns Scot, Pierre d'Auriole, Guillaume d'Occam, Grégoire de Rimini* (Paris: Leroux, 1934).

61. *Inst.* I.14.20. See also Richard Stauffer, *Dieu, la création et la Providence dans la prédication de Calvin*, p. 181.

62. Comm. on Gen. 1:2, CO 23:15–16.

63. Argument to Genesis, CO 23:10.

64. Comm. on Gen. 1:5, CO 23:17. See also Stauffer, *Dieu, la création et la Providence dans la prédication de Calvin*, p. 179.

65. Ibid.

66. Comm. on Gen. 1:26, CO 23:25–26.

67. *Inst.* I.14.22.

68. Leontine Zanta, *La Renaissance du Stoïcisme au seizième siècle* (Paris: Edouard Champion, 1914). See also Quirinus Breen, *John Calvin: A Study in French Humanism* (Grand Rapids: Eerdmans, 1931); William J. Bouwsma, "The Two Faces of Humanism: Stoicism and Augustinianism in Renaissance Thought," *Itinerarium Italicum*, ed. H.A. Oberman (Leiden: E.J. Brill, 1975), pp. 3–60; Henri Busson, *Le rationalisme dans la littérature Française de la Renaissance 1533–1601*.

69. Breen, *John Calvin: A Study in French Humanism*, 67ff.; Zanta, *La Renaissance du Stoïcisme*, 47ff.

70. Charles Partee, "The Revitalization of the Concept of 'Christian Philosophy' in Renaissance Humanism," *Christian Scholar's Review* 3/4 (1974):360ff.

71. Zanta, *La Renaissance du Stoïcisme*, pp. 47–73; Victor L. Nuovo, "Calvin's Theology: A Study of Its Sources in Classical Antiquity," Ph.D dissertation, Columbia University, 1964, pp. 136–161; Charles Partee, *Calvin and Classical Philosophy* (Leiden: E.J. Brill, 1977), pp. 104–125; Alexandre Ganoczy and Stefan Scheld, *Herrschaft, Tugend-Vorsehung* (Wiesbaden: Franz Steiner, 1982), pp. 46–53. For a detailed discussion of the meaning, appeal, and deficiencies of Stoicism in sixteenth-century humanism, see: William J. Bowsma, *Itinerarium Italicum: The Profile of the Italian Renaissance in the Mirror of Its European Transformation*, ed. by

Heiko A. Oberman and Thomas A. Brady, Jr., *Studies in Medieval and Renaissance Thought* 14 (Leiden: E. J. Brill, 1985), pp. 3–60.

72. Ibid. Calvin rejected the Stoic teaching on the passions as early as his *Commentary on Seneca's "De clementia"* II.151–154. On Calvin's relationship to the Stoics see Charles Partee, *Calvin and Classical Philosophy*, pp. 105–125. On Calvin's use of Cicero see also: Egil Grislis, "Calvin's Use of Cicero in the *Institutes* I:1–5 – A Case Study in Theological Method," *Archiv für Reformationsgeschichte* 62 (1971):1–36.

73. Comm. on Dan. 2:21, CO 40:576. Cf. *Inst.* I.5.5.

74. On the deification or elevation of nature by Dolet and Rabelais, see Josef Bohatec, *Budé und Calvin*, 174ff., 225ff.

75. *Inst.* I.16.8.

76. *Inst.* I.5.4–6, I.16.3, I.16.8; Comm. on Acts 17:28, CO 48:405.

77. *Inst.* I.16.8.

78. *Contre la secte phantastique et furieuse des Libertins qui se nomment spirituelz*, CO 7:149–248.

79. George H. Williams, *The Radical Reformation* (Philadelphia: Westminster, 1962), 351ff. Williams characterizes the Netherlandish Spiritualizers (including the Loists, Libertines, Familists, Spirituals, and Sacramentists) as "a loosely interrelated antinomian movement of the sixteenth century, compounding variously the self-deification of Rhenish mysticism, the libertarianism of the medieval Brethren of the Free Spirit and other groups, the ecclesiastical indifferentism of Erasmus and the Christian antinomianism of Luther, and in some places, at least, the Averroism of Padua. They were alike in attaching little or no importance to external sacraments," p. 351. Busson argues that the Libertines were the descendents of thirteenth-century German mysticism, *Le rationalisme*, 297ff.

80. *Contre la secte phantastique et furieuse des Libertins*, CO 7:183–198. See also Allen Verhey and Robert G. Wilkie, "Calvin's Treatise 'Against the Libertines,'" *Calvin Theological Journal* 15 (1980):190–219. For an analysis of the alleged "pantheism" of the Libertines see Busson, *Le rationalisme*, 305ff.

81. *Contre la secte phantastique et furieuse des Libertins*, CO 7:178ff.

82. Ibid., 178–183ff.

83. Ibid., p. 186.

84. Ibid.

85. Ibid., p. 187.

86. Ibid., p. 188.

87. *Inst.* I.17.4.

88. Ibid., I.16.2–3.

89. Bohatec, "Calvins Vorsehungslehre," 360ff. Bohatec argues that Calvin assumes the psychological freedom of the will. See also Doumergue, *Jean Calvin – Les hommes et les choses de son temps*, IV:111ff.; Henri Strohl, "La pensée de Calvin sur la providence divine au temps où il était réfugié à Strasbourg," *Revue d'histoire et de philosophie religieuses* 22 (1942):154–169. For a discussion of determinism in Calvin's thought compared to late medieval thinkers, see Karl Reuter, *Das Grundverständnis der Theologie Calvins* (Neukirchen: Verlag des Erziehungsvereins, 1963), 157ff. The question of Calvin's determinism was raised by Max Scheibe, who argued that Calvin's "fatalism" was influenced by Stoic determinism, *Calvins Prädestinationslehre*.

90. *Inst.* I.16.3.

91. *Inst.* I.16.4.

92. Ibid.

93. OS III.193. Barth and Niesel propose Pomponazzi's *De fato, libero arbitrio et de praedestinatione* (1520) II.1.5 as *one* of Calvin's possible sources. On this work see Busson, *La rationalisme*, pp. 52–64.

94. Partee, *Calvin and Classical Philosophy*, p. 99.

95. Bohatec, "Calvins Vorsehungslehre," 344ff.

96. Busson, *Le rationalisme*; Bohatec, *Budé und Calvin*, 149ff.

97. Busson, *Le rationalisme*, 123ff. The philosophical identification of God and providence with "movement" can be discerned in the writings of Zwingli. In his sermon, *De providentia*, Zwingli described God as the mover and author of all things in a manner reminiscent of the Aristotelianism of the late Middle Ages: "If we listen to the philosophers discussing about their heavens, about spheres and circles and their powers, yet finally we must come to only one sole and first κινγτῆ, that is mover. This is the Deity" (*De providentia* CR 93:91 [*Huldreich Zwinglis sämtliche Werke* VI]). Nonetheless, Zwingli also combated the view that would merely identify God with life and motion of all things "in such a way that he himself blindly puts breath or motion into things or they who breathe or move ask blindly of him, motion or life." See *De vera et false religione*, CR 90 (*Huldreich Zwinglis sämtliche Werke*, III), p. 647. Transl. found in Zwingli, *Commentary on True and False Religion*, ed. Samuel Macauley Jackson and Clarence Nevin Heller (Durham, NC: Labyrinth, 1981).

98. Wippel, "The Condemnations," 179ff.

99. *Inst*. I.16.3.

100. Busson, *Le rationalisme*; Bohatec, *Budé und Calvin*; Marc Lienhard ed., "Les Épicuriens à Strasbourg entre 1530 et 1550 et le problème de l'épicurisme au XVIe siècle," in *Croyants et sceptiques au XVIe siècle* (Strasbourg: Librairie Istra, 1981), pp. 17–56; Jean Wirth, "Libertins et Épicuriens: Aspects de l'irréligion au XVIe siècle," *Bibliothèque d'Humanisme et Renaissance* 39 (1977):601–627.

101. Lucien Febvre, *Le problème de l'incroyance au XVIe siècle* (Paris, 1947).

102. *De scandalis* CO 8:43ff. Critical edition found in Jean Calvin, *Des scandales*, ed. Olivier Fatio with C. Rapin (Geneva: Librairie Droz, 1984), p. 138. For a discussion of Rabelais' humanistic religion see the comments on pages 138 to 139. Calvin's earliest attack on the Epicureans can be found in his *Commentary on Seneca's "De clementia"* 1.6.10 (p. 31): "The Epicureans, although they do not deny the existence of the gods, do the closest thing to it; they imagine the gods to be pleasure-loving, idle, not caring for morals, lest anything detract from their pleasures; they deride Stoic providence as a prophesying old woman. They think that everything happens by mere chance." Cf. Comm. on Dan. 2:21, CO 40:576ff. See also Bohatec, *Budé und Calvin*, 165ff.; Busson, *Le rationalisme*, 106ff. and 233ff.

103. *De scandalis* CO 8:43ff. See also Fatio's comments in *Des scandales*, pp. 137–138.

104. Marc Lienhard, "Les Épicuriens à Strasbourg," pp. 17–56.

105. Ibid. See also Partee, *Calvin and Classical Philosophy*, pp. 97–104.

106. Ibid., p. 38. Cf. Melanchthon, *Philosophiae moralis epitome* CR 16:32; Fritz Büsser, "Zwingli und Laktanz," *Zwingliana* XXII (1971):375–399.

107. Cicero, *De natura deorum* I.52.

108. Comm. on Gen. 1:2, CO 23:16. See also Comm. on Nahum 1:5, CO 21:42–43; sermon on Deut. 5:9–14, CO 38:376; Werner Krusche, *Das Wirken des Heiligen Geistes nach Calvin* (Göttingen: Vandenhoek & Ruprecht, 1957), 15ff.

109. See also Günter Gloede, *Theologia naturalis bei Calvin* (Stuttgart: Kohlhammer, 1935), pp. 332–334; Benjamin Charles Milner, *Calvin's Doctrine of the Church*, pp. 1–25; Melanchthon, *Initia doctrinae physicae*, CR 13:200; *Loci praecipui theologici 1559*, MW II/1:220–221.

110. Calvin may reflect the decline in hierarchical thinking characteristic of the late Middle Ages. On this decline see Edward P. Mahoney, "Metaphysical Foundations of the Hierarchy of Being According to Some Late Medieval and Renaissance Philosophers," in *Philosophies of Existence, Ancient and Medieval*, ed. Parvis Morewedge (New York: Fordham, 1982), pp. 179–186, 204–206; C.A. Patrides, "Renaissance Thought on the Celestial Hierarchy: The Decline of a Tradition," *Journal of the History of Ideas* 20 (1959):155–156. It may be noted that Calvin did not adopt Augustine's rather "fluid" hierarchical schemes in his understanding of the order of nature. Augustine, for example, equated God's immutability with supreme existence above the realm of time

and change. Calvin, on the other hand, interpreted divine immutability in terms of reliability in nature and salvation. See Augustine: *De Genesi ad litteram* VIII.29-30; *De civ. Dei* XII.2.4-5; *Conf.* XI.12, XII.7.28. On Calvin see: *Inst.* I.14.1, I.14.7-8, 10-14. This lack of influence on Calvin by Augustine is another example of the way in which Augustine influenced Calvin on some dogmatic questions but less so on philosophical issues and exegetical method. For a general discussion of the varying degrees of Augustine's influence on Calvin, see Lucien Smits, *Saint Augustin dans l'oeuvre de Jean Calvin*, 2 vols. (Assen: van Gorcum, 1957-58), I:254-269.

111. *Inst.* I.5.2, I.14.21. Cf. Cicero, *De natura deorum*, II.15-17; Seneca, *De providentia*, I.2-5; Chrysostom, *Ad eos qui scandalizati sunt*, VII.1ff.

112. For the debate about Calvin's knowledge of or attitude toward Copernicus see the following (listed chronologically): Edward Rosen, "Calvin's Attitude toward Copernicus," *Journal of the History of Ideas* 21 (1960):431-441; Joseph Ratner, "Some Comments on Rosen's 'Calvin's Attitude toward Copernicus,' " *Journal of the History of Ideas* 22 (1961):382-385; E. Rosen, "A Reply to Dr. Ratner," *Journal of the History of Ideas* 22 (1961):386-388; Rosen, "Calvin n'a pas lu Copernic," *Revue de l'histoire des religions* 31 (1972):183-185; Pierre Marcel, "Calvin and Copernicus: The Problem Reconsidered," *Calvin Theological Journal* 15 (1980):233-243; Stauffer, *Dieu, la création et la Providence dans la prédication de Calvin*, p. 188. Rosen argues that since Calvin had never heard of Copernicus, he had no attitude about him. While we cannot conclude that he had never heard of Copernicus (Ratner and Stauffer), it is clear that we possess no evidence to prove that he had read—or rejected—his writings.

On the reception of Copernicus in the Reformation see Heinrich Bornkamm, "Kopernikus im Urteil der Reformatoren," *Archiv für Reformationsgeschichte* 40 (1943):171-183; Robert S. Westman, "The Wittenburg Interpretation of the Copernican Theory," in *The Nature of Scientific Discovery: A Symposium Commemorating the 500th Anniversary of the Birth of Nicholaus Copernicus*, ed. Owen Gingerich (Washington, DC: Smithsonian, 1975), pp. 393-429; J.R. Christianson, "Copernicus and the Lutherans," *Sixteenth Century Journal* 4/2 (1973):1-10; John Dillenberger, *Protestant Thought and Natural Science* (Garden City: Doubleday, 1960), 39ff.; Brian A. Gerrish, *The Old Protestantism and the New* (Chicago: U. of Chicago Press, 1982), pp. 163-178. On the downfall of the Aristotelian and Ptolemaic world views and the emergence of Copernicus see Edward A. Burtt, *Metaphysical Foundations of Modern Physical Science* (London: Routledge & Kegan, 1950); H. Butterfield, *The Origins of Modern Science, 1300-1800* (London: G. Bell & Sons, 1975); William Cecil Dampier, *A History of Science* (Cambridge: Cambridge U. Press, 1961).

113. *Inst.* I.14.21.

114. Comm. on Is. 48:13, CO 37:180.

115. Pierre Duhem, *Le système du monde. Histoire des doctrines cosmologiques de Platon a Copernic* (Paris: Hermann, 1958), IX:88.

116. Ibid., 109ff.

117. Aquinas, *Expositio super Iob ad litteram*, In *Opera omnia iussu impensaque Leonis XIII.P.M. edita* (Rome, 1965). IV:5.10.207, 7.10.137-139, 38.8.176-183. For Thomas' analysis of the effect of the moon on the waters see Duhem, *Le système du monde*, IX.20ff. Duhem studied Thomas' treatise *De occultis operationibus naturae, ad quendam militem ultramontanum*. In this letter Aquinas explained that the activities of natural bodies are natural either because of some inherent or intrinsic principle or by powers instilled by the heavenly bodies. The movement of the waves, then, is due not to the element of water per se but the influence of the moon.

118. Duhem, *Le système du monde*, IX:148-150.

119. Comm. on Jer. 5:22, CO 37:631-632. In this passage Calvin refers to God's "perpetual ordinance" whereby he commands the sea, once and for all, to remain within its limits. Elsewhere, however, Calvin made it clear that the waters stay within their bounds only insofar as God continues to will them to do so: "He [the Psalmist] celebrates a signal and remarkable miracle which we see in looking on the surface of the earth; namely, that God gathers together the element of water, fluid and unstable as it is, into a solid heap and holds it so at his pleasure. . . . In this we certainly

perceive that God, who is ever attentive to the welfare of the human race, has enclosed the waters within certain invisible barriers and keeps them shut up to this day; the prophet elegantly declares that they stand still at God's commandment as if they were a heap of firm and solid matter." Going on to describe the subterreanean waters, Calvin concluded "the fact that so many hollows and channels and gulfs, accordingly should not swallow up the earth every moment, affords another magnificent display of divine power; for although some cities and fields are not engulfed, yet the body of the earth is preserved in its place," Comm. on Ps. 33:7, CO 31:328. Calvin usually combined the idea of God's perpetual decree or ordinance with the necessity for the continual restraint of the waters; he was aware, after all, of the obvious fact that in floods God "releases" or "lets loose" this original command. These passages show again that Calvin took traditional cosmological explanations but heightened the precariousness of creation and its absolute dependence on God. For a discussion of the waters in Calvin's sermons see also Stauffer, *Dieu, la création et la Providence dans la prédication de Calvin*, pp. 186–187.

120. Duhem, *Le système du monde* II.487ff.

121. Basil, *Hexaemeron* III.4.

122. Ibid.; cf. Ambrose, *Hexaemeron* II.3.9–11.

123. Chrysostom, *Hom. in Gen.* IV, cited by Duhem, *Le système du monde* II:490.

124. Augustine, *De Genesi ad litteram* II.4.8. See also Duhem, *Le système du monde*, II:491–494.

125. Comm. on Gen. 7:11, CO 23:131–132.

126. Comm. on Gen. 1:9, CO 23:19.

127. Comm. on Gen. 1:8–9, 7:11, CO 23:18–19, 131.

128. Aristotle, *De caelo*, II.13, 294a–295b and II.14ff. See also: Leo Elders, *Aristotle's Cosmology* (Assen: Van Gorcum, 1966).

129. Ibid., II.13.296a.

130. Basil, *Hexaemeron* I.9. (Fathers of the Church, Vol. 46). Calvin recommended both Basil and Ambrose on the exegesis of the creation account: *Inst.* I.XIV.20.

131. Comm. on Ps. 104.5, CO 32:86–87.

132. Sermon on Job 38:4–10, CO 35:366–367.

133. Sermon on Ps. 119, CO 32:620.

134. Comm. on Ps. 104:32, CO 32:97.

135. Comm. on Gen. 3:1, CO 23:55.

136. Comm. on Gen. 2:20, 3:17–18, 8:22, CO 23:48, 72–73, 141. See also Milner, *Calvin's Doctrine of the Church*, pp. 37–43; Arnold Williams, *The Common Expositor: An Account of the Commentaries on Genesis, 1527–1663* (Chapel Hill: U. of North Carolina Press, 1948), pp. 112–138.

137. Comm. on Is. 24:5–6, CO 36:402; Comm. on Ps. 8:7, CO 31:94; Comm. on Genesis 2:10, CO 23:40.

138. Comm. on Jer. 5:25, CO 37:635.

139. Comm. on Rom. 8:20, *Commentarius*, p. 174.

140. Sermons on Job 1:6–8, 21:7–12, 24:21–26, CO 33:57, CO 34:220, CO 35:171; sermon on Eph. 3:7–9, CO 51:457; Comm. on Ps. 36:6, CO 31:361–362.

141. Comm. on Ps. 17:15, CO 31:167. Comm. on Is. 34:4, CO 36:581, 585–586; sermon on Job 9:23–28, CO 33:450–451.

142. On Calvin's view of history see: Heinrich Berger, *Calvins Geschichtsauffassung* (Zurich: Zwingli-Verlag, 1955); Bohatec, *Budé und Calvin*, pp. 280–300; idem, "Gott und die Geschichte nach Calvin," *Philosophia Reformata* (1936):129–161; Charles Trinkaus, "Renaissance Problems in Calvin's Theology," *Studies in the Renaissance*, ed. W. Peery (Austin: U. of Texas Press, 1954) I:59–80. Trinkaus stresses Calvin's emphasis on the perceptual problems of viewing providence in history.

143. Sermon on Job 24:19–25, CO 34:397–398.

144. Sermon on Job 5:3–7, 9:23–28, CO 33:221, 450; sermon on Job 17:6–16, 21:7–12, 21:16–21, 25:1–6, 29:1–7, CO 34:58ff., 219–221, 247, 252, 405–406, 533–535; sermon on Job 36:1–7,

CO 35:263. See also: *Inst.* I.16.9; Comm. on Ps. 73:1, 16, CO 31:674–675, 682; sermon on Eph. 1:7–10, CO 51:283ff.

145. Sermon on Job 8:13–32, CO 33:403; Comm. on Gen. 9:2, CO 23:143–144; sermon on Job 5:19–27, CO 33:275–276; sermon on Job 21:16–21, CO 34:243; sermon on Job 40:7–19, CO 35:462; sermon on Job 37:7–13, CO 35:145.

146. *Inst.* I.14.17; I.17.11; sermon on Job 1:6–8, CO 33:57–69.

147. *Inst.* I.18.1–2. Lombard formulated the distinction between the operative and permissive will of God in *Libri quattuor Sententiarum* I.45–46. He drew on Augustine's statement in the Enchiridion 24.95 that "nothing, therefore, happens unless the Omnipotent wills it to happen. He either allows it to happen, or he actually causes it to happen." This distinction was employed by Thomas Aquinas to explain that the reprobate are condemned justly because God allowed them to fall into sin, S.T. I.23.4.ad2 and S.T. I.19.6ad1. Calvin specifically attacked the notion of "foreknowledge" and "permission" as ways of accounting for the fall into sin in *Inst.* II.4.3 and III.23.8, where he insisted that Adam's fall and the rejection of the reprobate are due to God's will and not merely to his permission.

148. *Inst.* I.16.4.

149. *Inst.* I.17.9; *Contre la secte phantastique et furieuse des Libertins*, CO 7:186ff.

150. *Inst.* I.17.1.

151. *Advertissement contre l'Astrologie qu'on appelle iudiciaire*, CO 7:518. Cf. pp. 516–517, 524.

152. Bohatec, *Budé und Calvin*, pp. 270–280.

153. *Advertissement contre l'Astrologie*, 527ff.

154. Ibid., 523ff.; Bohatec, *Budé und Calvin*, p. 273.

155. Bohatec demonstrates, however, that Melanchthon distinguished among types of providence. Like Calvin, Melanchthon condemned Stoic fate but permitted the stars to influence certain qualities of living creatures. Unlike Calvin, however, Melanchthon believed the stars exercise power according to a person's birth. With this knowledge of the stars, Melanchthon believed that a person can avoid illness and exercise foresight in economic and political affairs: *Initia doctrinae physicae*, CR 13:329ff.; Bohatec, *Budé und Calvin*, pp. 276–279. Melanchthon did argue, however, that God stood as First Cause above the stars, CR 13:325. Like Calvin, Melanchthon also depicted God as caring, watching, guarding, and actively guiding the human order; see, Manfred Büttner, *Regiert Gott die Welt?*, pp. 49–50.

156. *Inst.* I.16.2–4; Comm. on Ps. 135:7, CO 32:360: ". . . quoties pluit, non id fieri caeco naturae instinctu: sed quia Deus ita decrevit, cuius est pro suo arbitrio coelum ex sereno reddere obnubilum, et caligine discussa puram lucem reddere."

157. *Inst.* I.16.2.

158. Ibid. *Consensus Genevensis*, CO 8:348. Cf. Comm. on Ps. 18:3, 147:15, CO 31:177, CO 32:430–431; Comm. on Dan. 1:14–15, CO 40:550–552; sermon on Job 37:14–24, CO 35:341–342; sermon on Deut. 28:9–14, CO 38:371ff.

159. *Consensus Genevensis*, CO 8:348–349.

160. It should be noted that Calvin does not equate universal or general providence simply with a general divine "concursus." In the *Consensus Genevensis*, for example, Calvin distinguished several degrees of providence; namely, God's care of nature, the human race, and the church. However, even in his care of nature, Calvin's God directly cares for, sustains, governs, and gives power to each individual creature. In fact, Calvin can use the term "special providence" to refer to Matt. 10:29 and God's care of the natural order: *Consensus Genevensis* CO 8:348ff. "General providence," then, referred to God's particular and immediate governance of the natural order; cf. Comm. on Ps. 135:6, CO 32:359; Comm. on John 1:4, CO 47:5. To relegate "special providence" to God's saving grace is confused and overlooks the issue with which Calvin struggled in his polemics against such groups as the "Epicureans." See: Partee, *Calvin and Classical Philosophy*, pp. 126–145. Cf. Etienne de Peyer, "Calvin's Doctrine of Providence," *Evangelical Quarterly* 10 (1938):30–44; François Wendel, *Calvin, The Origins and Development of His Religious Thought*,

tr. Philip Mairet (New York: Harper & Row, 1963), pp. 179–180.

161. *Inst*. I.16.8.

162. *Inst*. I.16.9.

163. Bohatec, *Budé und Calvin*, pp. 283–285; Trinkaus, "Renaissance Problems in Calvin's Theology."

164. Comm. on Ps. 73:1, 94:15, 116:11, CO 31:673, CO 32:26, 196; sermon on Job 12:14–16, CO 33:585–586; sermon on Job 21:22–34, CO 34:255–256; sermon on Job 34:26–29, CO 35:192, passim. See also: Stauffer, *Dieu, la création et la Providence dans la prédication de Calvin*, pp. 118–119.

165. *Inst*. I.16.2.

166. *Inst*. I.17.10.

167. Melanchthon also identified providence in history as a belief known only to faith. Like Calvin, however, he distinguished between the providence revealed in nature and the providence perceptible in history. *Scholia in Epistulam Pauli ad Colossenses*, MW IV:230–242; *Initia doctrinae physicae*, CR 13:191, 204. In the 1559 *Loci* he explained that because the events in life do not always reflect clearly God's providential care, Scripture is necessary to strengthen faith in providence: "Mens humana convincitur demonstrationibus, ut fateatur hunc mundum a Deo conditum esse. Sed Deum adesse moderatorem, etsi huius sententiae etiam quaedam habet argumenta ut poenas atrocium scelerum, tamen hoc obscurius est. Quia igitur difficilior est assensio, divinis testimoniis fides in animis excitanda et confirmanda est. . . ." MWII/1:219.

168. Comm. on Ps. 73:20, CO 31:684. Sermon on Job 38:6–8, CO 35:493–494. Cf. Comm. on Ps. 73:20, CO 31:684. On the hiddenness of God in history see also Berger, *Calvins Geschichtsauffassung*, pp. 51–55, 237ff.; Bohatec, *Budé und Calvin*, 292ff.

169. Sermon on Job 22:18–22.

170. Comm. on Ps. 25:6, CO 31:253. Cf. Comm. on Ps. 102:14, 119:126; CO 32:67, 270–271.

171. Comm. on Ps. 7:9, CO 31:83. For a discussion of the attributes of God in Calvin's sermons see Stauffer, *Dieu, la création et la Providence dans la prédication de Calvin*, 105ff. Stauffer points out that Calvin stressed the power of God throughout his sermons, pp. 112–116. Cf. Comm. on Ps. 9:10, 25:5, CO 31:100, 252; Comm. on Rom. 3:6, *Commentarius*, pp. 60–61. Comm. on Dan. 9:9, CO 41:11–12.

172. *Inst*. II.8.16.

173. Comm. on Is. 40:12, 45:7, 61:11, CO 37:15–16, 25–26, 133–134, 380; Comm. on Ps. 33:6–7, 75:3, 104:5ff., CO 31:327, 701, 32:86ff.; *Inst*. I.16.1.

174. *Inst*. I.16.8, I.18.1–2.

175. *Inst*. I.17.2. See also H.A. Oberman, "Some Notes on the Theology of Nominalism."

176. Sermon on Job 7:15–21, 9:16–21, 11:7–12, CO 33:438–440, 539; sermon on Job 20:16–20, 23:8–12, 24:1–9, 27:1–4, CO 34:174, 342, 345, 382, 446; sermon on Job 34:21–26, CO 35:167ff.; *Inst*. I.17.2.

177. Sermon on Job 9:7–15, CO 33:428: ". . . non point une puissance tyrannique, comme ils l'ont imaginé: mais une puissance infinie, laquelle ne se monstre point à nostre sens pour dire, Dieu est-il iuste ou non selon que nous le comprenons tel?" See also: sermon on Job 9:7–15, sermon on Job 11:7–12, sermon on Job 12:14–16, CO 33:428, 539, 584; sermon on Job 21:16–21, CO 34:246.

178. *Inst*. I.17.2. This is a major theme in the Job sermons: Sermon on Job 9:16–22, 12:17–26, sermons on Job 14:1–4, CO 33:539, 602, 687; 20:16–20, 23:13–17, CO 34:175, 357ff.; 24:10–15, 37:1–6, 38:4–11, CO 35:143ff., 315, 369. For a discussion of the alleged influence of Scotus on Calvin, see Doumergue, *Jean Calvin—Les hommes et les choses de son temps* IV:119–125; A. Lecerf, *Études Calvinistes* (Neuchâtel: Delachaux et Niestlé, 1949), pp. 11–28; R. Seeberg, *Lehrbuch der Dogmengeschichte* II:151; Stauffer, *Dieu, la création et la Providence dans la prédication de Calvin*, pp. 114–116; Wendel, *Calvin, The Origins and Development of His Religious Thought*, pp. 127–129. Doumergue and Lecerf denied all Scotist dependence. Wendel has shown that both Scotus and Calvin held that God was bound to his previous decrees but not subject to any external

restraint or causality. For Scotus' view of God and divine power see P. Minges, *Der Gottesbegriff des Duns Scotus auf seinen angeblich exzessiven Indeterminismus* (Vienna: Von Mayer, 1907).

179. *Inst.* I.17.12.

180. *Inst.* I.16.3.

181. *Inst.* I.16.7-9; I.17.11.

182. *Inst.* I.17.11.

183. This is particularly clear if one compares Calvin's descriptions of nature with those by Seneca or Cicero. Cicero, for example, portrayed a much more benevolent view of nature than did Calvin. To Cicero the sea was not a source of potential chaos but one more example of beauty found in the universe. The regular revolutions of the stars demonstrated no potential for disorder but only the evidence of design. He explained the position of the earth by its natural gravitation toward the center with no appeal to a divine power that would prevent its collapse into disorder. Although Calvin obviously adopted many descriptions of nature from Cicero, his view of the cosmos was fundamentally different. Cf. Cicero, *De natura deorum*, I.21.87, I.26.100, II.5.15, II.16.43, II.38.39, II.45-46, 115-119.

II. THE ANGELS WHO DO HIS BIDDING

1. *Inst.* I.14.3.

2. Benjamin Warfield, *Calvin and Calvinism* (London: Oxford, 1931), p. 309.

3. Wilhelm Niesel, *The Theology of John Calvin*, tr. Harold Knight (Philadelphia: Westminster, 1956), p. 63; Doumergue, *Jean Calvin—Les hommes et les choses de son temps*, IV:106; Wendel, *Calvin, The Origins and Development of His Religious Thought*, p. 172.

4. Karlfried Fröhlich, *Gottesreich, Welt und Kirche bei Calvin* (Munich: Reinhardt, 1930), p. 27; Wilhelm Kolfhaus, *Vom christlichen Leben nach Johannes Calvin* (Neukirchen, Kreis Moers: Buchhandlung des Erziehungsvereins, 1949), pp. 434-481; Charles Hall, *With the Spirit's Sword* (Richmond: John Knox, 1968), p. 162.

5. Warfield, *Calvin and Calvinism*, 307ff.

6. Stauffer, *Dieu, la création et la Providence dans la prédication de Calvin*, pp. 190-195.

7. On the development of angelology in the Patristic and Scholastic authors see: *Dictionnaire de théologie catholique* (Paris, 1909-1950), s.v. "Angé. D'après les Pères" by G. Bareille and "Angé. D'après les scolastiques" by A. Vacant, Vol. I, cols. 1195-1248 [hereafter DTC]; Jean Daniélou, *The Angels and Their Mission*, tr. David Heimann (Baltimore: Newmann, 1957); and *Dictionnaire de spiritualité, ascétique et mystique doctrine et histoire* (Paris, 1932-), s.v. "Anges" by Joseph Duhr, Vol. I, cols. 581-625 [hereafter DS]; Lothar Heiser, *Die Engel im Glauben der Orthodoxie* (Trier, 1976).

8. D. Petau ("De angelis," in *Opus de Theologicis Dogmatibus*, ed. J.-B. Thomas [Bar-le-Duc, 1868], Vol. I, 5-20) names Justin, Clement, Origen, Hilary, Ambrose, and Augustine as those who believed that angels possess some type of body. Petau cites Gregory of Nyssa, Eusebius, Epiphanius, Theodoret, and Chrysostom as among those who denied that angels possess bodies. Gregory wrote ". . . ipsi illorum spiritus comparatione quidem nostrorum corporum, spiritus sunt sed comparatione summi et incircumscripti spiritus, corpus," *Moralia* II.3.3. Compare, however, *Moralia* II.7.8 where he denies any composition in angels. *Corpus Christianorum* CXLIII (Turnhout, 1979), pp. 61, 64.

9. Peter Lombard, *Sent.* II dist. VIII. Although he was ambivalent on this issue, Bernard seemed to prefer the theory that angels have ethereal bodies. Bernard of Clairvaux, *De considera- tione* V.iv.7; idem, *On the Song of Songs* V.2-4, 7, tr. Kilian Walsh (Shannon, Ireland: Irish U. Press, 1971), pp. 26-30.

10. Ps.-Dionysius, *De coelesti hierarchia* XV. See also René Roques, *L'univers dionysien, structure hiérarchique du monde selon le Pseudo-Denys* (Aubier: Éditions Montaigne, 1954), pp. 154–158. Against the Albigensians and the Cathars, the Fourth Lateran Council reaffirmed that God created all things "visible and invisible, spiritual and corporeal . . . formed out of nothing the spiritual creature and the corporeal creature, that is the angelic and terrestrial and then the human creature, composed of both spirit and body." The Council also stated that God created Satan and the devils, all of whom were originally created good but of themselves became evil.

11. S.T. Ia.50.2. See also James D. Collins, *The Thomistic Philosophy of the Angels* (Washington, DC: Catholic U. of America Press, 1947), 13ff. Thomas does, however, repeat the Gregorian statement ". . . et hac ratione dicitur quod angeli Deo comparati sunt materiales et corporei, non quod in eis sit aliquid de natura corporea," S.T. Ia.50.1. obj.1. He uses this commonplace to locate the incorporeal substances midway between God and corporeal things.

12. Augustine, *De Genesi ad litteram* I.3.7, I.9.15–17, II.8.16. See also A.H. Armstrong, "Spiritual or Intelligible Matter in Plotinus and St. Augustine," *Augustinus Magister* I (1954):277–283; R. Connelly, "Light in the Reality of St. Augustine," *The Modern Schoolman* 51 (1979):237–251.

13. S.T. Ia.61.3.

14. Daniélou, *The Angels and Their Mission*, pp. 45–48; Cf. Tertullian, *De patientia* V.5–6.

15. *De Genesi ad litteram* XI.23.30, Cf. XI.15–16. Augustine rejected the specific theory that the devil's first sin was envy by arguing that pride always precedes envy: XI.14. "Therefore, it was because of his pride that the devil envied man," *De Genesi ad litteram* XI.16. On the devil's fall see also *De civ. Dei* XI.13.

16. *De Genesi ad litteram* XI.26.33.

17. S.T. Ia.63.3. See also S.T. Ia.63.2. Here Thomas, like Augustine, states that the first sin was pride which then gave rise to envy. "Therefore after the sin of pride he fell also into the evil of envy, detesting the well-being of mankind; and detesting too the majesty of God inasmuch as God makes use of man to further his own glory, against the devil's will."

18. *Strom.* VII.7; DTC, col. 1203.

19. *De virg. vel.* 7; DTC, col. 1203.

20. *De Spir. sancto* XIX.49; DTC, col. 1204.

21. *In Psal.* CXVIII; DTC, col. 1204.

22. *De Genesi ad litteram* XI.17; *De civ. Dei* XI.13.

23. S.T. Ia.62.8.

24. *Adv. Marcion* V.15; *Collationes* VIII.13; DTC, col. 1201.

25. *In Eph. hom.* VII.1. See also Ambrose, *De mysteriis* VII.36.

26. *Hom. in Ascen.* 4. See also Daniélou, *The Angels and Their Mission*, pp. 34–43; Heiser, *Die Engel im Glauben der Orthodoxie*, pp. 128–135.

27. Sermon CCXLIII; DTC, col. 1202.

28. *De Genesi ad litteram* XII.22.48.

29. *De civ. Dei* IX.22; DTC, col. 1202.

30. *De Genesi ad litteram* IV.22.39–24.41; *De civ. Dei* XI.29.

31. D.N. VII, XI; Roques, *L'univers dionysien*, pp. 158–167.

32. C.H. III.1; E.H. I.2; Roques, *L'univers dionysien*, p. 165. Roques explains that because of his concept of the "aeon," Dionysius could speak of the increase or progress of angelic knowledge without inserting time into the celestial world.

33. S.T. Ia.50.1 and S.T. Ia.51.2.

34. S.T. Ia.54.4.

35. Ibid.

36. S.T. Ia.55.2.

37. Ibid.

38. S.T. Ia.57.2: "If they had not knowledge of individual things they could exercise no providential government over events in this world, since these always imply individuals at work; and this

would contradict what we read in Ecclesiastes, 'Say not before the angels: there is no providence.' "
Thomas is here disputing an opinion that Albert the Great attributed to Maimonides. On
Maimonides' conception of providence see A.J. Reines, "Maimonides' Concepts of Providence and
Theodicy," *Hebrew Union College Annual* 43 (1972):169–206.

39. On medieval hierarchical thought see Arthur Lovejoy, *The Great Chain of Being: A Study
in the History of an Idea* (Cambridge, MA: Harvard U. Press, 1936); Edward P. Mahoney,
"Metaphysical Foundations of the Hierarchy of Being According to Some Late-Medieval and
Renaissance Philosophers," in *Philosophies of Existence, Ancient and Medieval*, ed. Parvis
Morewedge (New York: Fordham, 1982), pp. 165–257.

40. C.H. VI–IX; Roques, *L'univers dionysien*, pp. 92–115, 135–146. Roques points out that
"Mais, avec les hiérarchies angéliques, pourtant constituées d'ordres supérieurs, moyens et
inférieurs, il apparaît que les trois fonctions de perfection, d'illumination et de purification se
retrouvent en chacun d'eux, bien qu'à des degrés différents," p. 98.

41. C.H. IX.2.

42. Chrysostom, *Hom. in Gen.* IV.5; Clement of Alexandria, *Strom.* VII.2. Like Clement,
Jerome (Comm. on Eph. 1:21) believed this was a hierarchy of function, not of nature. Origen
believed in a hierarchy based on the inequality of merits, *De princ.* I.8.4. G. Bareille points to the
hesitation among early fathers to specify the nature and number of angelic orders: DTC, col. 1206.

43. Daniélou, *The Angels and Their Mission*, pp. 24–43.

44. Tertullian, *De bapt.* 6; Chrysostom, *De sacr.*, VI.4; *Hom. in Eph.* I.3. See also Daniélou,
The Angels and Their Mission, pp. 55–67; Heiser, *Die Engel im Glauben der Orthodoxie*,
pp. 147–156. Daniélou points out that Thomas later argued that angels cannot be ministers of the
sacraments in the proper sense of the word, S.T. IIIae.64.7.

45. For a history of the idea of guardian angels see DS, cols. 586–598; Daniélou, *The Angels
and Their Mission*, pp. 68–82.

46. C.H. IX.2.

47. S.T. Ia.106.4. For Thomas' description of the angelic hierarchy see S.T. Ia.108.1–6. On
Thomas' relationship to Dionysius see J. Durantel, *Saint Thomas et le Pseudo-Denys* (Paris, 1919).

48. S.T. Ia.112.2.

49. S.T. Ia.113.3; Cf. S.T. Ia.113.1–113.8.

50. On the angelic cult, see DTC, cols 1219–1222; DS, cols. 598–619; Heiser, *Die Engel im
Glauben der Orthodoxie*, pp. 192–198.

51. *De vera relig.* 55.

52. *Regula* VII.

53. *On the Song of Songs IV*, tr. Irene Edmonds (Kalamazoo: Cistercian, 1970), 78.1.1, p. 130.

54. DS, cols. 602–603; Heiser, *Die Engel im Glauben der Orthodoxie*, pp. 166–169.

55. DS, cols. 603–604.

56. DS, col. 617.

57. Comm. on Gen. 1:5, 2:1, CO 23:18, 31–32.

58. *Inst.* I.14.4.

59. C.A. Patrides, "Renaissance Thought on the Celestial Hierarchy: The Decline of a Tradition." Idem, "Renaissance Views on Unconfused Orders Angellick," *Journal of the History of Ideas*
23 (April 1962):265–266.

60. *Inst.* I.14.8; Comm. on Col. 1:17, CO 51:86.

61. Comm. on Eph. 1:21, CO 51:158. Cf. Comm. on Dan. 12:5–7, CO 41:295–298: "The
philosophy of Dionysius ought not to be admitted here, who speculates too cunningly, or rather too
profanely, when treating of angels. But I only state the existence of some difference, because God
assigns various duties to certain angels, and he dispenses to each a certain measure of grace and
revelation according to his pleasure," CO 41:296.

62. Comm. on Eph. 1:21, CO 51:158.

63. *Inst.* I.14.6–7.

64. Comm. on Matt. 18:10, CO 45:504.

65. Comm. on Dan. 3:28, CO 40:643.

66. *Contre le secte phantastique et furieuse des Libertins*, CO 7:179-186.

67. *Inst*. I.14.3.

68. *Inst*. I.14.9, 16. See also Stauffer, *Dieu, la création et la Providence dans la prédication de Calvin*, pp. 190-191.

69. *Inst*. I.14.16.

70. Comm. on Col. 1:20, CO 52:88-89; sermon on Eph. 1:7-10, CO 51:283-4; sermon on Job 1:6-8, CO 33:57ff.; sermon on Job 21:22-34, CO 34:257; sermon on Job 23:1-7, CO 34:337.

71. Sermon on Job 1:6-8, CO 33:58.

72. *Inst*. I.14.5, 11-15.

73. Comm. on Ez. 1:21, CO 40:48.

74. Comm. on Ez. 1:24, CO 40:50.

75. Comm. on Ez. 1:21, CO 40:48.

76. Heinrich Berger, *Calvins Geschichtsauffassung*, pp. 135-167; Fröhlich, *Gottesreich, Welt und Kirche bei Calvin*, pp. 19-27; Charles Hall, *With the Spirit's Sword*, 77ff.; Kolfhaus, *Vom christlichen Leben nach Johannes Calvin*, pp. 451-453.

77. Comm. on Luke 10:18, CO 45:315; Comm. on I Peter 5:8, CO 55:289.

78. *Inst*. I.14.13.

79. *Inst*. I.14.15.

80. Comm. on Daniel 10:13, CO 41:206.

81. Comm. on Zech. 2:3, CO 44:154; See also Comm. on Ps. 68:18, CO 31:626; Comm. on Acts 5:19, CO 48:106.

82. Comm. on Is. 37:36, CO 36:641-642.

83. Comm. on Ps. 34:8, CO 31:339. See also Comm. on Ps. 55:19, CO 31:542; *Inst*. I.14.11.

84. Hall, *With the Spirit's Sword*, pp. 194-197.

85. Sermon on Job 1:6-8, CO 33:60. "Satan est d'autre costé adversaire, car combien qu'il comparoisse devant Dieu, et qu'il faille qu'il rende conte, neantmoins ce n'est pas qu'il plie de son bon gré, ce n'est pas qu'il demande d'estré, subiet à Dieu: ains il s'esleve à l'encontre, il est enflammé d'une rage si enorme qu'il voudroit avoir ruiné la puissance de Dieu, s'il luy estoit possible. Ainsi donc il retient son naturel corrompu, c'est d'estre tousiours ennemi: mais si est-il forcé par contrainte de venir faire hommage à celuy qui a tout empire souverain sur ses creatures. Or Satan est aussi subiet à Dieu, d'autant qu'il ne faut point imaginer que Satan ait aucune principauté que celle qui luy est donnee de Dieu."

86. Sermon on Job 1:6-8, CO 33:61.

87. *Inst*. I.14.17.

88. Ibid., I.14.18.

89. Ibid. Comm. on Gen. 3:15, CO 23:70.

90. Ibid., I.17.11. Cf. I.14.17-18.

91. Ibid., I.14.3, 10-12.

92. Compare Calvin's attack on angelic devotion with his attack on the cult of saints: *Inst*. I.12.1-2, I.14.10-12, III.20.21-23; Comm. on Ps. 50:15, CO 31:503; sermon on Eph. 1:19-23, CO 51:335-336. In both cases Calvin attacks the notion of intercessors.

93. *Inst*. I.12.1, I.14.3.

94. Sermon on Eph. 4:7-10, CO 51:548; sermon on Job 7:7-15, CO 33:348; sermon on Job 15:11-16, CO 33:725-726.

95. Sermon on Job 4:12-19, CO 33:205-206; sermon on Eph. 3:9-12, CO 51:470; Comm. on Dan. 8:13-14, CO 41:104-109; Comm. on Col. 1:17, CO 52:86.

96. *Inst*. I.14.4.

97. Comm. on Heb. 1:14, CO 55:20; see also Comm. on Dan. 7-10, CO 41:56.

98. Comm. on Ez. 1:22, CO 40:49.

99. Comm. on Ez. 10:1, CO 40:207.

100. Comm. on Ez. 10:8, CO 40:213: "Alae enim haud dubie in angelis directionem repraesentant, qua Deus testatur angelos non habere proprium vel intrinsecum aliquem motum, sed gubernari arcano suo instinctu."

101. Comm. on Is. 63:9, CO 37:398–399.

102. *Inst*. I.14.11.

103. Comm. on Heb. 1:13–14, CO 55:19–20.

104. Comm. on Eph. 1:10, CO 51:151.

105. Comm. on Col. 1:20, CO 52:89. See also Stauffer, *Dieu, la création et la Providence dans la prédiction de Calvin*, pp. 191–192.

106. Cf. Gregory the Great, *Moralia in Iob* V.38.68, *Corpus Christianorum* Series Latina CXLIII (Turnhout, 1979), pp. 267–268; Thomas Aquinas, *Expositio super Iob ad litteram* IV.18.410–420.

107. Sermon on Job 4:18, CO 33:206–207; sermon on Job 13:16–22, CO 33:630–633; sermon on Job 15:11–16, CO 33:725–726.

108. Cf. Chrysostom, *Hom. in Col.* III; Thomas Aquinas, *In epistolam ad Ephesios* Lectio III, *Opera omnia* XIII (Parma, 1852), p. 449.

109. Stauffer points out that on this point Calvin is in agreement with Ignatius of Antioch (Stauffer, *Dieu, la création et la Providence dans la prédication de Calvin*, p. 230, note 115). See also DTC, col. 1203.

110. Comm. on Daniel 8:13–14, 12:5–7, CO 41:104–109, 295–298; sermon on Eph. 3:9–12, CO 51:468; sermon on Job 10:1–6, CO 33:467–468; Comm. on I Timothy 3:16, CO 52:290–291.

111. Comm. on I Timothy 3:16, CO 52:290–291.

112. Comm. on Col. 2:18, CO 52:111–112; *Inst*. I.14.2.

113. Comm. on Zechariah 1:12, CO 43:140–143.

114. Comm. on Heb. 8:4, CO 55:98; Comm. on Gen. 24:49, CO 23:338; Comm. on Ps. 89:8, CO 31:814.

115. Comm. on Gen. 28:12, CO 23:391; *Inst*. I.14.12. This identification of the ladder as Christ does not originate with Calvin but is found in medieval exegesis. On Genesis 28:12 in the history of interpretation see David C. Steinmetz, "Luther and the Ascent of Jacob's Ladder," *Church History* 55 (June 1986):179–192. Here again Calvin applied a traditional exegetical argument in a polemical manner against the adoration of angels.

III. IMAGO DEI: THOU HAS MADE HIM
A LITTLE LOWER THAN THE ANGELS

1. Karl Barth, "No! Answer to Emil Brunner," in *Natural Theology*, 80ff.; Niesel, *The Theology of John Calvin*, pp. 67–68; Torrance, *Calvin's Doctrine of Man* (London: Lutterworth, 1949), pp. 23–81, 106–115. Brunner argues that in Barth's later works the differences between them lessened: Brunner, "The New Barth: Observations on Karl Barth's *Doctrine of Man*," *Scottish Journal of Theology* 4 (1951):123–135.

2. Torrance, *Calvin's Doctrine of Man*, p. 36. Torrance emphasizes that Calvin saw the divine image in terms of a mirror that reflects its object, namely, God. On the relational character of the divine image see also Brian A. Gerrish, *The Old Protestantism and the New*, pp. 150–159.

3. Brunner, "Nature and Grace," in *Natural Theology*, 20ff.; Gloede, *Theologia naturalis bei Calvin*, pp. 72–146; Stauffer, *Dieu, la création et la Providence dans la prédiction de Calvin*, pp. 201–205.

4. On the history of the concept of the divine image (from an Evangelical perspective) see David Cairns, *The Image of God in Man* (London: S.C.M. Press, 1953, repr. Fontana Library, 1973),

and Brunner, *Man in Revolt: A Christian Anthropology*, tr. Olive Wyon (London: Lutterworth, 1939), pp. 499–515.

5. *Adv. haer.* IV.4.3, V.6.1, V.16.1.

6. Brunner, *Man in Revolt*, p. 93.

7. *De trinitate* XIV.4.

8. Ibid. XIV.8.

9. Ibid.

10. Ibid. XIV.12.

11. Cairns, *The Image of God in Man*, pp. 102–103.

12. S.T. Ia.93.2, 93.6.

13. S.T. Ia.93.8.

14. S.T. Ia.93.4.

15. S.T. Ia.93.8.

16. S.T. Ia.12.1.

17. S.T. IaIIae.85.1, 87, 109.7.

18. For a summary of the Averroistic movement (Radical Aristotelianism) in the West, see F. van Steenberghen, *La philosophie au XIIIe siècle* (Louvain, 1966); James A. Weisheipl, *Friar Thomas d'Aquino, His Life, Thought, and Works* (Washington, DC: Catholic U. of America Press, 1983), pp. 272–285. I have used the phrase "Radical Aristotelianism" to refer to men such as Siger because, as F. van Steenberghen has argued, the Aristotelianism condemned in 1270 and 1277 was less directly Averroistic than purely Aristotle. The main source for Siger and Boethius was Aristotle, not Averroistic commentaries, *Aristotle in the West*, tr. L. Johnston (Louvain: E. Nauwelaerts, 1955), 219ff.

19. Thomas challenged Siger on the basis that Siger's interpretation was not the proper understanding or exegesis of Aristotle. Moreover, according to Thomas, Siger's position on the unicity of the intellect was not philosophically defensible. Thomas believed that the immortality of the soul could be demonstrated from its functions in life. Through a knowledge of psychology, i.e., human knowledge and will, the natural philosopher could know the fact of immortality. For a review of the controversy between Thomas and Siger see E.P. Mahoney, "Saint Thomas and Siger of Brabant Revisited," *Review of Metaphysics* 27 (1974):531–553. See also: Weisheipl, *Friar Thomas d'Aquino*, 233ff.

20. *De unitate intellectus contra Averroistas* (Paris, 1270) is found in the Parma edition, vol. 16, pp. 208–224. English translation can be found in Thomas Aquinas, *On the Unity of the Intellect against the Averroists*, tr. Beatrice H. Zedler (Milwaukee: Marquette U. Press, 1968). On Thomas' Parisian periods see James A. Weisheipl, *Friar Thomas d' Aquino*, pp. 53–140, 241–292. On March 18, 1277, the University of Oxford became involved in controversy. Archbishop Robert Kilwardy of Canterbury condemned 13 propositions, a number of which touched on the unicity of the substantial form in man. Scholars debate how many of the Oxford condemnations were directed at Thomas. See D. Callus, *The Condemnations of St. Thomas at Oxford* (Oxford, 1946); Wippel, "The Condemnations of 1270 and 1277," pp. 169–170, particularly note 3. On references to Bonaventure see St. Bonaventure, *Collationes in Hexaemeron*, Opera Omnia, Quaracchi V, pp. 327–454. See also *Collationes de decem praeceptis* (1267) and *Collationes de septem donis Spiritus sancti* (1268), Opera Omnia, Quaracchi V, 497ff.; Wippel, "The Condemnations of 1270 and 1277," p. 180; P. Robert, "Saint Bonaventure, Defender of Christian Wisdom," *Franciscan Studies* 3 (1943):159–179.

21. Latin text of the condemnations can be found in *Chartularium Universitatis Parisiensis*, ed. H. Denifle and E. Chatelain (Paris, 1889–91) I:543–561. English translations can be found in Wippel, "The Condemnations of 1270 and 1277," pp. 179–180; Weisheipl, *Friar Thomas d'Aquino*, pp. 276–301.

22. On Pomponazzi see Ernst Cassirer, *The Renaissance Philosophy of Man*, (Chicago: U. of Chicago Press, 1971), pp. 257–279. See also: Busson, *Le rationalisme*, 44ff.; Charles Trinkaus, *In Our Image and Likeness*, 2 vols. (Chicago: U. of Chicago Press, 1970) II:530ff.

23. P.O. Kristeller, "Ficino and Pomponazzi on the Place of Man in the Universe," *Journal of the History of Ideas* V (1944):220-242.

24. "On Immortality," tr. William Henry Hay II and J.H. Randall, Jr., in Cassirer, *The Renaissance Philosophy of Man*, p. 314.

25. Ibid., pp. 315, 323.

26. Ibid., p. 317.

27. Ibid., p. 322.

28. Ibid. Kristeller explains Pomponazzi's theory in the following: "Although the intellect is corporeal with regard to its objects, as a subject of thought it is immaterial, and in this sense it may be said that the human soul, though mortal in its essence, does at least participate in immortality." "Ficino and Pomponazzi on the Place of Man in the Universe," p. 223.

29. Hay and Randall, p. 379.

30. Cited by G.H. Williams, *The Radical Reformation* (Philadelphia: Westminster, 1962), p. 23. Latin text is printed in Mansi, *Concilia*, XXXII, col. 842.

31. Busson, *Le rationalisme*, 110ff., 157ff.; Bohatec, *Budé und Calvin*, 149ff. Many humanists, of course, argued for the immortality of the soul; see Trinkaus, *In Our Image and Likeness*.

32. In his treatise *Des Scandales* Calvin wrote: "It is çommon knowledge that Agrippa, Villanovanus, Dolet and their like have always proudly rejected the Gospel. . . . They have finally fallen into such a rage that not only did they spread execrable blasphemies against the Son of God and his doctrine, but they have imagined that in regard to their souls they were no different from dogs and pigs. Others like Rabelais, Deperius, and Goveanus and more than I can presently name, after having tasted the Gospel, have been struck with the same blindness. . . . They have no difficulty in saying that all religions have their origins in men's brains, that we believe in God because it pleases us to do so, that the hope of eternal life is only to deceive the simple, and that the fear of judgments is only to terrify little children." See *Des Scandales*, ed. Fatio, pp. 137-140.

33. Williams, *The Radical Reformation*, p. 24.

34. Christian Neff, "Sleep of the Soul," in *Mennonite Encyclopedia*, eds. Harold S. Bender and C. Henry Smith (Scottdale, PA: Herald, 1955-59) IV:543; Williams, *The Radical Reformation*, pp. 583, 597. Introduction to *Institution of the Christian Religion, 1536* tr., Ford Lewis Battles (Atlanta: John Knox, 1975), p. xxxiii. Battles also shows that in his correspondence with Sadoleto Calvin defended the belief in the continued life of the soul after death in order to distinguish himself from the "fanatics." Catholics saw the Reformers' rejection of purgatory and prayers for the dead as a denial of the continued existence of the soul. See Battles' introduction to *Institution of the Christian Religion, 1536*, pp. xxxiii-xxxiv, and Calvin, *Tracts and Treatises* tr., Benjamin Farley I:15. *Calvin, Treatises Against the Anabaptists and Against the Libertines* (Grand Rapids: Baker, 1982), pp. 19-21.

35. *Inst.* I.15.2. On Calvin's defense of the soul's immortality see also: Quistorp, *Calvin's Doctrine of the Last Things*, tr. Harold Knight (Richmond: John Knox, 1955), 55ff.

36. *Psychopannychia*, CO 5:177. The *Psychopannychia* was written in 1534 and published in 1541.

37. Williams, *The Radical Reformation*, pp. 24, 585, 611-614. It was in his effort to show how the divine spirit was communicated to all creatures that Servetus employed the medical analogy. As will be seen, Calvin was later to identify Servetus' error with pantheism, emanationism, or deification. The four charges brought against Servetus were Anabaptism, anti-Trinitarianism, pantheism, and psychopannychism. Calvin again pressed Servetus on psychopannychism at the trial but, as Williams stated, "it is clear from Calvin's summary of the interrogation that Servetus's deep eschatological convictions were misunderstood," p. 609. For references to the physiological discussions of the soul see: Busson, *Le rationalisme*, pp. 239-240.

38. *Psychopannychia*, CO 5:180-181.

39. Ibid., CO 5:196.

40. Ibid., CO 5:201. On p. 177 of the same treatise Calvin wrote: "But we insist that the soul is in itself a substance and that it continues truly to live after the dissolution of the body, gifted

with reason and perception. . . ." CO 5:177. I owe the citation to Quistorp, *Calvin's Doctrine of the Last Things*, p. 62.

41. *Psychopannychia*, CO 5:188.

42. Ibid., CO 5:190. Calvin discussed the presence of the soul with Christ after death in his comments on I Thess. 4:14 and I Cor. 13:12. For these discussions see Quistorp, *Calvin's Doctrine of the Last Things*, 81ff.

43. *Brieve instruction pour armer tous bons fideles contre les erreurs de la secte commune des Anabaptistes*, CO 7:111ff.

44. *Brieve instruction*, CO 7:112. Calvin cites the Book of Wisdom 2:23: "Man is immortal, seeing that he has been created in the image of God." Cf. *Inst*. III.25.6.

45. *Contre la secte phantastique et furieuse des Libertins*, CO 7:183ff.

46. Characterizing Loy Pruystinck, Williams argues that "Loy, adopting what looks like an Averroist view of the universal Intellect (*spiritus*), held that man's intellectual nature is a spiritual substance and that everyone who is reborn possesses the Holy Spirit. (In 1502, for comparison, the heretic Herman of Rijswijk, in or near The Hague, condemned by the Inquisition to life imprisonment, had denied God's creation out of nothing, had called Christ a 'fool and an innocent phantast,' and had specifically acknowledged his debt to Averroes, however much he oversimplified the philosophy of the latter.) Since man's flesh and spirit are thoroughly independent, and with no influence upon each other, the (renewed) spirit of man, according to Loy as interpreted by Luther and confirmed in part by the extant Loist *Summa doctrinae*, incurs no responsibility for the weakness of the flesh," *Radical Reformation*, p. 352. Farley points to the "remarkable affinity" between Loy's belief and the Quintinist doctrines described by Calvin: the belief in a universal *esprit* and the belief that the one who is reunited with this spirit transcends good and evil. Like the Loists, the Quintinists (whom Calvin opposed) also relied on I John 3:9 and I John 1:8,10. Farley concludes that "there is probably no direct tie between Calvin's Quintinists and Loy's group but Niesel's judgment that they shared a pantheistic spiritualism or mysticism appears to hold up." Calvin, *Treatises Against the Anabaptists and Against the Libertines*, p. 168. Cf. Wilhelm Niesel, "Calvin und die Libertiner," *Zeitschrift für Kirchengeschichte* 48 (1929):58–74; *Contre la secte phantastique et furieuse des Libertins*, CO 7:194ff.

47. *Contre la secte phantastique et furieuse des Libertins*, CO 7:221.

48. Ibid., CO 7:222.

49. Ibid., CO 7:221.

50. *Inst*. I.15.6. Calvin is most likely referring to Pomponazzi, *De immortalitate animae*.

51. *Inst*. I.5.5, I.15.2.

52. *Inst*. I.15.3.

53. Comm. on Gen. 2:7, CO 23:18–19.

54. Sermon on Job 3:11–19, CO 33:162; Quistorp, *Calvin's Doctrine of the Last Things*, pp. 62–63.

55. *Inst*. I.15.5.

56. Michael Servetus, *Christianismi Restitutio* (Vienna, 1553, repr. 1790). Describing the individual reborn through baptism Servetus wrote: "Constat itaque internus noster homo ex divina Christi, et humana spiritus nostri natura, ut ob id nos merito dicamur participes divinae naturae, et dicatur vita nostra cum Christo ibi abscondita. . . . Internus noster homo est vere caelestis, de caelo descendit, de substantia Dei, de substantia Christi divina. Non ex sanguinibus, nec ex voluntate carnis genitus, sed ex Deo. . . . Internus noster homo Deus est, sicut Christus est Deus, et spiritus sanctus est Deus," pp. 434, 557–558. See also: Roland Bainton, *Hunted Heretic* (Boston: Beacon, 1953), pp. 128–147; Jerome Friedman, *Michael Servetus, A Case Study in Total Heresy* (Geneva: Librairie Droz, 1978). Both authors deny that Servetus can be labeled a "pantheist." Bainton calls Servetus an emanationist and Friedman argues that he is a pan*en*theist. On Calvin and Servetus see Williams, *The Radical Reformation*, pp. 605–614.

Calvin also opposed Osiander's doctrine of essential righteousness, whereby Christ's divine nature becomes man's essential righteousness when the word is grasped in faith. On this subject see David C. Steinmetz, *Reformers in the Wings* (Philadelphia: Fortress, 1977), pp. 91–98. On Osiander's appropriation of Augustine's understanding of grace see Patricia Wilson-Kastner, "Andreas Osiander's Theology of Grace in Perspective of the Influence of Augustine of Hippo," *Sixteenth Century Journal* X (1979):73–92. Wilson-Kastner analyzes Osiander's emphasis on the indwelling Christ within the soul, through which believers are "made partakers of the divine nature." In order to counter the assertion that justification is merely an imputation, Osiander argued that a "seed of God" resides in the soul of the Christian, renewing and vivifying from within: "Porro hoc semen Dei, in credentibus et electis manet. Unde et filii Dei, ac divinae naturae consortes efficimur, qui enim Deo adhaeret, fit unus spiritus cum eo" (*De justificatione* f. 36; Wilson-Kastner, p. 83). For Melanchthon's attack on Osiander's "confusion" of justification and sanctification see *Iudicium de Osiando*, CR 8:579–584.

57. *Inst.* I.15.1.

58. Ibid.

59. Ibid., I.15.6. Calvin's earliest exposition on psychology can be found in his *Commentary on Seneca's "De clementia"* where he discussed the philosopher's idea of a threefold appetite: the natural, sensitive, and rational. The sensitive appetite is divided into the higher part containing the interior affections and the lower part consisting of bodily passions. The latter carry the human being off into various directions unless "mistress Reason" is in control. Barth, Niesel, and Battles argue that the reading of Themistius must be recognized as influential in the *Institutes*. Themistius' commentary on Aristotle's *De anima* was known in the Middle Ages through the translation of William of Moerbeke. On the reading of Themistius in the Renaissance see Edward P. Mahoney, "Neoplatonism, the Greek Commentators, and Renaissance Aristotelianism," in *Neoplatonism and Christian Thought*, ed. Dominic O'Meara (Albany: International Society for Neopl. Studies, 1982), pp. 169-177, 264-282. Calvin's reference to Plato in this citation is to *Theaetetus* 184D. For the history of such terms as *phantasm*, *ratio*, and *intellectus* see Edward P. Mahoney, "Sense, Intellect, and Imagination in Albert, Thomas, and Siger," in *The Cambridge History of Late Medieval and Renaissance Philosophy*, ed. Norman Kretzmann (Cambridge: Cambridge U. Press, 1982), pp. 602–622; Julian Peghaire, *"Intellectus" et "ratio" selon S. Thomas d'Aquin*, Publications de l'Institut de Études mediévals d'Ottawa, 6 (Paris: J. Vrin, 1936), pp. 85–210, 247–280.

60. *Inst.* I.15.6. Calvin added that "the philosophers" doubled this simple division: "They say the latter [understanding] is sometimes contemplative because content with knowledge alone, it has no active motion (a thing that Cicero thought to be designated by the term 'genius'), sometimes practical because by the apprehension of the good or evil it variously moves the will. In this division is included the knowledge of how to live well and justly. The former part (I mean the appetitive) they also divide into will and concupiscence; and as often as appetite, which they call βούλησις, obeys reason it is ὁρμή; but it becomes πα os when the appetite, having thrown off the yoke of reason, rushes off to intemperance. Thus they always imagine reason in man as that faculty whereby he may govern himself aright." Cf. *Calvin's Commentary on Seneca's "De clementia"* I.10, a passage which predates Calvin's reading of Themistius.

61. Ibid. Cf. Plato, *Phaedrus* 253D.

62. Ibid.

63. *Inst.* I.15.3. See also: Comm. on Gen. 1:26, CO 23:26–27.

64. *Inst.* I.15.3.

65. Ibid., I.15.4.

66. Ibid. See also: Comm. on Gen. 1:26, CO 23:26.

67. *Inst.* I.15.3.

68. Ibid., I.15.8.

69. Ibid., I.5.1, 6.1–2, 14.20; Argument to Genesis, CO 23:8; Comm. on Gen. 1:6, CO 23:18. The description of God's revelation in nature as a "book," "mirror," or the *vestigia Dei* was a traditional theme throughout the Middle Ages. Examples include Augustine's exegesis of Psalm 45:7

(PL 36:518) and the famous references to the book of nature also in Alan of Lille, *Rhythmus alter*: "Omnis mundi creatura/ quasi liber et pictura/ nobis est et speculum" (MPL CCX 579A). This theme found classic expression in Bonaventure, *Breviloquium* II.ii.12. St. Bonaventure also argued that we cannot read the book of nature unless the "mirror of the mind be cleaned and polished." This "cleaning" is obtained through prayer and the remorse of the conscience: *Itinerarium Mentis in Deum* I.2.4. For Bonaventure's use of this metaphor and his understanding of analogy and exemplars, see Etienne Gilson, *The Philosophy of St. Bonaventure*, tr. Dom Illtyd Trethowan and Frank J. Sheed (Paterson, NJ: St. Anthony Guild, 1965), pp. 185–214, and Sister Emma Jane Marie Spargo, *The Category of the Aesthetic in the Philosophy of St. Bonaventure* (St. Bonaventure, NY: The Franciscan Institute, 1975), pp. 130–148. For further examples and discussion of the "footprints" of God or the "book" or "mirror" of nature see: M.-D. Chenu, *Nature, Man, and Society in the Twelfth Century*, tr. Jerome Taylor and Lester K. Little (Chicago: U. of Chicago Press, 1968), pp. 114–119; Ernst Robert Curtius, *European Literature in the Latin Middle Ages*, tr. Willard R. Trask (Princeton: Princeton U. Press, 1953); Clarence J. Glacken, *Traces on the Rhodian Shore* (Berkeley: U. of California Press, 1967), 203ff.; H. Leisegang, "La connaissance de Dieu au miroir de l'âme et de la nature," *Revue d'histoire et de philosophie religieuses*, 17 (1937):145–171.

70. Comm. on Ps. 104:1, CO 32:85; *Inst.* I.6.1; sermon on Job 28:4–11, CO 35:374.

71. *Inst.* I.5.1.

72. Ibid., I.5.2–3; Cf. Cicero, *De natura deorum* II.lvi.133ff.

73. *Inst.* I.15.8. It should be noted that in *Inst.* II.2.3 Calvin conceded that "the philosophers" recognized the difficulty involved in maintaining internal order and the supremacy of reason. For an analysis of the view of human nature held by many Renaissance humanists see Trinkaus, *In Our Image and Likeness*.

74. *Inst.* II.2.22; Cf. Plato, *Protagoras* 357. In his attacks on Plato, Calvin ignored the discussion of the moral fall in the *Phaedrus* 246–255: "The soul in her totality has the care of inanimate being everywhere, and traverses the whole heaven in diverse forms appearing—when perfect and fully winged, she soars upward, and orders the whole world; whereas the imperfect soul, losing her wings, and drooping in her flight at last settles on solid ground—there, finding a home, she receives an earthly frame which appears to be self-moved, but is really moved by her power; and this composition of soul and body is called a living and mortal creature" (tr. Benjamin Jowett).

75. *Inst.* II.2.22.

76. Ibid., II.2.6. Calvin was referring to Lombard, *Sent.* II. dist. xxxvi.1 and Bernard, *De gratia* 14.46. The distinction is also found in Augustine, *De gratia et libero arbitrio* XVII.33, which Calvin cited with approval in *Inst.* II.3.11. It is not clear that Calvin attributed fairly to this "division" the idea that man "by his own nature seeks after the good." Bernard was claiming that there was one operating grace which effected consent and also stated that the good will itself was an effect of the preceding work of grace, Bernard *De gratia* 14:46. See also: Jill Raitt, "Calvin's Use of Bernard of Clairvaux," *A. für Reformations-geschichte* (1981):98–121. Lombard reads: "Haec est gratia operans et cooperans. Operans enim gratia praeparat hominis voluntatem ut velit bonum; gratia cooperans adiuvat ne frustra velit. Unde Augustinus '. . . cum autem volumus, et sic volumus ut perficiamus, nobis cooperatur. Tamen sine illo, vel operante ut velimus, vel cooperante cum volumus, ad bona pietatis opera nihil valemus.' Ecce his verbis satis aperitur quae sit operans gratia, et quae cooperans. Operans enim gratia est, quae praevenit voluntatem bonam: ea enim liberatur et praeparatur hominis voluntas ut sit bona, bonumque efficaciter velit; cooperans vero gratia voluntatem iam bonam sequitur adiuvando. . . . [Augustine] 'Non quia hoc sine voluntate nostra agatur, sed quia voluntas nostra nil boni agit, nisi divinitus adiuvetur.' . . . His testimoniis aperte insinuatur, quia voluntas hominis gratia Dei praevenitur atque praeparatur ut fiat bona, non ut fiat voluntas, quia et ante gratiam voluntas erat, sed non erat bona et recta voluntas" (*Sent.* II dist. xxvi.1).

77. *Inst.* II.2.6.

78. Ibid. II.2.4, II.2.12. Lombard, *Sententiae* II dist. xxv.8: "Haec sunt data optima et dona perfecta, quorum alia sunt corrupta per peccatum, id est naturalia, ut ingenium, memoria, intel-

lectus; alia subtracta, id est, gratuita, quanquam et naturalia ex gratia sint. Ad generalem quippe Dei gratiam pertinent; saepe tamen huiusmodi fit distinctio, cum gratiae vocabulum ad speciem, non ad genus refertur."

79. *Inst.* I.2.1, I.5.4.11.14.
80. Ibid., II.2.12.
81. Ibid., I.5.12.
82. Ibid., I.15.8.
83. Ibid., II.3.5.
84. Ibid.: "Manet nihilominus voluntas, quae propensissima affectione ad peccandum et propendeat et festinet; siquidem non voluntate privatus est homo, quum in hanc necessitatem se addixit, sed voluntatis sanitate." Cf. *Inst.* III.23.4-8.
85. Augustine, *De libero arbitrio* III.3.7.
86. Augustine, *De diversis quaestionibus ad Simplicianum* I.11.
87. Augustine, *De spiritu et littera* LIII.31.
88. Augustine, *De civitate Dei* XXII.30.
89. Luther, *De servo arbitrio* WA 18.709.11-19. Cf. WA 18.616. note 1.
90. WA 18.714.30-35.
91. Bohatec argues that since Luther does not "remain true" to the distinction between *coactio* and *necessitas*, Calvin's thought is closer to that of Bucer. See Bohatec, "Calvins Vorsehungslehre," pp. 372-373. Whether Luther remained true to this distinction, however, remains debatable.
92. Bernard, *On the Song of Songs IV*, 81, IV.7-V.9. See also: Raitt, "Calvin's Use of Bernard of Clairvaux," 102-111, and W. S. Reid, "Bernard of Clairvaux in the Thought of John Calvin," *Westminster Theological Journal*, 41 (1978) pp. 138-139.
93. *Inst.* II.3.5.
94. Ibid.
95. Barth, "No! Answer to Emil Brunner," p. 79.
96. Comm. on Ps. 24:1, CO 31:244. See also sermon on Job 10:7-15, CO 33:481. In his fifth sermon on Genesis, Calvin used the language of approaching God to describe man's status in creation: "Pourquoy . . . avons-nous ung degré si hault que nous aprochons de nostre Dieu . . . ? Don vient cela sinon qu'il a pleu à Dieu de nous discerner. Or ceste distinction nous est monstrée quand Dieu déclare qu'il veult faire ung chef doeuvre qui est plus que tout le reste qui avoyt précédé au paravant: combien que le soleil et la lune soyent des créatures si nobles qu'il semble qu'il y apparoisse quelque divinité, combien que le ciel aussy ayt ung regard qui estonne et ravit les hommes . . . tant y a que si nous faisons comparaison de cela avec l'homme, nous trouverons en l'homme des choses plus grandes et plus exquises beaucoup." Cited by Stauffer, *Dieu, la création et la Providence dans la prédication de Calvin*, p 237.
97. Comm. on Ps. 24:1, CO 31:244.
98. Comm. on Acts 14:17, CO 48:328.
99. *Inst.* I.5.3. For a history of the idea of the microcosm see Rudolf Allers, "Microcosmus from Anaximandros to Paracelsus," *Traditio* (1944):319-407, and G.P. Congar, *Theories of Macrocosms and Microcosms in the History of Philosophy* (New York, 1922).
100. Brunner, *Man in Revolt*, pp. 94-95.
101. *Inst.* II.2.12. See also Comm. on John 1:4-5, CO 47:78; sermon on Job 35:8-11, CO 35:237-239.
102. Comm. on Ps. 8:6, CO 31:92-93. Calvin refers David's praises to man as he was originally created.
103. Comm. on John 1:9, CO 47:9.
104. Sermon on Eph. 3:14-19, CO 51:497.
105. *Inst.* II.2.12.
106. Wendel, *Calvin, The Origins and Development of His Religious Thought*, p. 193.

IV. THEIR CONSCIENCE ALSO BEARS WITNESS:
NATURAL LAW AND SOCIETAL LIFE

1. On the history of natural law theory see A.P. d'Entreves, *Natural Law, an Historical Survey* (New York: Harper, 1965); idem, *Natural Law, an Introduction to Legal Philosophy* (London: Hutchison U. Library, 1970); Odon Lottin, *Le Droit naturel chez Saint Thomas d'Aquin et ses prédécesseurs*, 2nd ed. (Bruges: Charles Beyaert, 1931); D.E. Luscombe, "Natural Morality and Natural Law," in *The Cambridge History of Later Medieval Philosophy* (Cambridge: Cambridge U. Press, 1982), pp. 705–720.

2. Cicero, *De republica* III.xxii.33, preserved by Lactantius, *Divinae Institutiones* VI.viii (CSEL 19, p. 508).

3. *Digest* I.i.9.

4. Ibid., I.i.11.

5. Ibid., I.i.1.

6. *Etymologies* I.V.4 (PL 82, 199–200); Lottin, *Le Droit naturel*, pp. 9–11.

7. *Decretum Gratiani* I.1. Praef., I.V.1, I.VIII.2 (Leipzig, 1879); d'Entreves, *Natural Law, an Historical Survey*, p. 34; Lottin, *Le Droit naturel*, pp. 11–12.

8. S.T. IaIIae.90.1, 94.1.2.

9. S.T. IaIIae.91 art. 2: "Unde et in ipsa participatur ratio aeterna per quam habet naturalem inclinationem ad debitum actum et finem, et talis participatio legis aeternae in rationali creatura 'lex naturalis' dicitur."

10. S.T. IaIIae.94.2.

11. S.T. IaIIae.94.4.

12. S.T. IaIIae.94.4.1.

13. S.T. IaIIae.95.3. and IaIIae.95.4.

14. S.T. IaIae.94.4.2 (here Thomas echoes the traditional definition of natural law as that which includes both animals and humans); IaIIae.95.4.1; Cf. IIaIIae.57.3, 58.1.

15. Lottin, *Le Droit naturel*, p. 67.

16. Otto von Gierke, *Political Theories of the Middle Ages*, tr. F.W. Maitland (Cambridge: The University Press, 1922), pp. 172–173.

17. Francis Oakley, "Medieval Theories of Natural Law: William of Ockham and the Significance of the Voluntarist Tradition," *Natural Law Forum* 6 (1961):65–83; idem, *Omnipotence, Covenant, and Order, An Excursion in the History of Ideas from Abelard to Leibniz* (Ithaca, NY: Cornell U. Press, 1984), pp. 77–84. On the voluntarist tradition see also: A.P. d'Entreves, *Natural Law, an Historical Survey*, 36ff.

18. Oakley, "Medieval Theories of Natural Law," 65ff.

19. On the changing assessment of Nominalism see William J. Courtenay, "Nominalism and Late Medieval Religion," in *The Pursuit of Holiness in Late Medieval Religion*, ed. C. Trinkaus and H.A. Oberman (Leiden, 1974), pp. 26–59; H.A. Oberman, "Some Notes on the Theology of Nominalism with Attention to Its Relation to the Renaissance," pp. 46–76; idem, *The Harvest of Late Medieval Theology* (Cambridge, MA: Harvard U. Press, 1963); Leif Grane, "Gabriel Biels Lehre von der Allmacht Gottes," *Zeitschrift für Theologie und Kirche* 53 (1956):53–75; D.C. Steinmetz, "Scholasticism and Radical Reform: Nominalist Motifs in the Theology of Balthasar Hubmeier," *Mennonite Quarterly Review* 45 (1971):123–143.

20. Oakley, *Omnipotence, Covenant, and Order*, pp. 81–84.

21. John T. McNeill, "Natural Law in the Teaching of the Reformers," *Journal of Religion* 26 (1946):168–182. On Melanchton's view of natural law (which may have influenced Calvin) see Clemens Bauer, "Melanchthons Naturrechtslehre," *Archiv für Reformationsgeschichte* 42 (1951):64–100. On Luther's doctrine of natural law see John T. McNeill, "Natural Law in the Thought of Luther," *Church History* 10 (1941):211–227.

22. On Calvin's use of the concept "ius gentium" see Gloede, *Theologia naturalis bei Calvin*, pp. 182–187; Jürgen Baur, *Gott, Recht und weltliches Regiment im Werke Calvins* (Bonn: H. Bouvier, 1965), pp. 62–64, 214–215. This tradition stems from Ulpian and Gaius, although Calvin traces all law back to the will of God.

23. Joseph Bohatec, *Calvin und das Recht* (Feudingen: Buchdruck und Verlags-Anstalt, 1934), p. 4; idem, *Budé und Calvin*, p. 383.

24. Comm. on Rom. 2:14–15, *Commentarius*, pp. 45–46. See also: sermon on Job 31:1–4, CO 34:631; sermon on I Tim. 5:4, CO 53:456.

25. *Inst.* II.8.1. See also: sermon on Deut. 19:14–15, CO 27:568. "Ceste Loy a esté receuë des hommes, sans que iamais ils eussent entendu que Moyse eust parlé. Car ce faict nostre Seigneur ça imprimé aux coeurs des hommes ce qu'il a mis par escrit en son peuple. Il est vray que c'a esté une grace speciale, quand il a bien daigné prendre l'office de legislateur au peuple d'Israel: mais cependant si n'a-il point voulu que les hommes fussent si brutaux, qu'ils n'eussent ces principes d'equité, comme ils sont contenus en la Loy de Moyse. Voyant donc une telle conformité, notons que Dieu n'a iamais delaissé le genre humain, que tousiours il n'y ait demeuré quelque semence de droicture."

26. Calvin's commentary on the Ten Commandments can be found in *Inst* II.8.13–51 and Volume 24 of the *Calvini Opera*.

27. *Inst.* II.8.2. See also *Inst.* II.2.24.

28. In his Comm. on Rom. 2:15 Calvin argued that we cannot "conclude from this passage that there is in men a full knowledge of the Law, but that there are only some seeds of what is right implanted in their nature." On Calvin's combination of the Christian ethic with natural law see Bohatec, *Calvin und das Recht*, pp. 33–45; idem, *Budé und Calvin*, pp. 386–395.

29. *Inst.* II.2.13.

30. *Inst.* IV.20.16. See also Comm. on Gen. 29:17, CO 23:401; Comm. on Hab. 2:6, CO 43:540; Comm. on Matt. 10:21, CO 45:284. On Calvin's use of the ancient notion of "natural equity," see Bohatec, *Calvin und das Recht* p. 47, 97ff.; idem, *Budé und Calvin*, pp. 391–395.

31. Comm. on the Harmony of the Five Books of Moses, Ex. 3:20, CO 24:49, 131ff. Oakley links Calvin with the late medieval voluntarist position of Nominalism (*Omnipotence, Covenant, and Order*, p. 82). For a discussion of Calvin's belief that God transcends the "ius naturae," the importance of the principle "Deus legibus solutus est," and the inseparability of God's power and justice, see Gisbert Beyerhaus, *Studien zur Staatsanschauung Calvins, mit besonderer Berücksichtigung seines Souveränitätsbegriffs* (Berlin, 1910), pp. 71–77. For another analysis of Calvin's use of this Roman adage and a discussion of God's superiority over natural and Mosaic law see: Bohatec, *Calvin und das Recht*, pp. 91–93; idem, *Calvins Lehre von Staat und Kirche* (Breslau: Marcus, 1937), p. 25; Jürgen Baur, *Gott, Recht und weltliches Regiment im Werke Calvins* (Bonn: H. Bouvier, 1965), pp. 20–25. This theme is a constant one in the Job sermons.

32. A. Lang, *Die Reformation und das Naturrecht* (Gütersloh, 1909), p. 20.

33. Bohatec, *Calvin und das Recht*, pp. 98–99. Cf. Cicero, *De topica* II.9.

34. Beyerhaus, *Studien zur Staatsanschauung Calvins*, pp. 77–84; Bohatec, *Calvin und das Recht*, pp. 120–121.

35. Bohatec, *Calvin und das Recht*, pp. 103–129; J. McNeill, "Natural Law in the Teaching of the Reformers," pp. 168–182.

36. Emil Brunner, "Nature and Grace," p. 37; Gloede, *Theologia naturalis bei Calvin*, 78ff. See also Doumergue, *Jean Calvin – Les hommes et les choses de son temps*, V:469ff.

37. Bohatec, *Calvin und das Recht*, 133ff.; Beyerhaus, *Studien zur Staatsanschauung Calvins*, p. 97. See also: John T. McNeill, "John Calvin on Civil Government," in *Calvinism and the Political Order*, ed. George L. Hunt (Philadelphia: Westminster, 1965), pp. 22–45.

38. Comm. on Ps. 104:31, CO 32:96–97.

39. Comm. on John 5:17, CO 47:111.

40. Comm. on Ps. 96:10, CO 32:41; Comm. on Ps. 145:9,15–16, CO 32:415–417; Comm. on

Ps. 147:7-9, CO 32:428-429; Comm. on Is. 24:6, CO 36:402; sermon on Job 11:7-12, CO 33:540-541; Comm. on Gen. 8:22, CO 23:141; *Inst.* I.5.1-2,11.

41. Comm. on Ps. 8:7, CO 31:94; Comm. on Ps. 24:1, CO 31:244; Comm. on Ps. 115:16, CO 32:190; Comm. on Ps. 147-149, CO 32:428; Comm. on Acts 14:17, CO 48:327-328.

42. *Inst.* I.14.22.

43. Comm. on Gen. 9:6, CO 23:146; Comm. on Jonah 1:13-14, CO 43:226-227: "Et scimus etiam qua ratione Deus suscipiat vitam hominum tuendam, nemp quia creati sunt ad eius imaginem."

44. Comm. on Malachi 1:2-6, CO 44:395-409; Comm. on Ezekiel 3:18, CO 40:92.

45. *Congrégation sur la divinité de Jésus Christ*, C0 47:480-481, cited by Stauffer, *Dieu, la création et la Providence dans la prédication de Calvin*, p. 238. See Stauffer's discussion of the image of God on pp. 201-205, 244-245. See also sermon on Job 30:1-10, CO 34:595-596; sermon on Job 35:8-11, CO 35:240.

46. Comm. on Ezekiel 18:1-4, CO 40:424. See also: sermon on Job 23:13-17, CO 34:357ff.

47. Sermon on Deut. 13:1-2, 2-5, CO 27:234,244; sermon on Deut. 28:1-4, CO 27:488-489; sermon on Job 10:7-15, CO 33:483; sermon on Job 29:18-25, CO 34:571ff.; sermon on Job 35:8-11, CO 35:238-239.

48. Comm. on Is. 45:18, CO 37:144.

49. Herman Kuiper, *Calvin on Common Grace* (Grand Rapids: Smitter, 1928). Support for the doctrine of common grace began with Abraham Kuyper's three-volume work *De Gemeene Gratie* (Praetoria: Hoeker and Wormser, 1902-4) and was further supported by Bavinck's essay, "Calvin on Common Grace," in *Calvin and the Reformation*, ed. W.P. Armstrong (New York: Fleming H. Revell, 1909), pp. 99-131. For a history of the controversy over the doctrine of common grace see William Masselink, *General Revelation and Common Grace* (Grand Rapids: Eerdmans, 1953); H. Henry Meeter, *Calvinism: An Introduction to its Basic Ideas* (Grand Rapids: Zondervan, 1939), pp. 69-77; Cornelius van Til, *Common Grace* (Philadelphia: The Presbyterian and Reformed Publ. Co., 1947). Breen cites the following passages in Calvin's writings as referring to the term "common grace": Comm. on Amos 9:7, CO 43:164; Comm. on Col. 1:20, CO 52:89; Comm. on Heb. 1:5, CO 55:15; Comm. on Rom. 5:18, *Commentarius* pp. 116-117 (Breen, *John Calvin*, 165ff.).

50. Comm. on Ps. 145:9, CO 32:415.

51. Comm. on Ps. 74:16, CO 31:698; Comm. on Amos 3:1-2, CO 43:36-38; sermon on Deut. 28:9-14, CO 28:371-382.

52. Comm. on Ps. 31:19, CO 31:310; Comm. on Ps. 145:9, CO 32:415.

53. Comm. on Gen. 9:2, CO 23:143-144.

54. Sermon on Job 40:7-19, CO 35:462.

55. Comm. on Gen. 9:2, CO 23:143-144; Comm. on Isaiah 24:17, CO 36:408; Comm. on Hab. 2:5, CO 55:24.

56. Comm. on Gen. 9:2, CO 23:144.

57. Dowey writes, "It is legitimate to have shown briefly a relationship between conscience and the institutions of the church and state both, in so far as they are human institutions, have a continuing relation to this original endowment in man, and the state, at least, belongs to human society as God created it, apart from the Fall of man and his redemption" (*The Knowledge of God in Calvin's Theology*, p. 63). Troeltsch states that "a harsh expression of opinion about the State in the Augustinian and Lutheran sense we seek in vain. Everywhere and directly it is a Divine institution. . . . It belongs to the absolutely necessary means of human existence" (Ernst Troeltsch, *The Social Teaching of the Christian Churches*, tr. Olive Wyon [New York: Macmillan, 1949], II:898).

58. Comm. on Rom. 13:1, *Commentarius*, pp. 281-282.

59. *Inst.* IV.20.4.

60. Bohatec posited three causes for the origin of the state: (1) human sin, (2) divine goodness, and (3) maintenance of the human race (*Calvin und das Recht*, 57ff.). See also Bohatec, *Budé und Calvin*, pp. 439-464; idem., *Calvins Lehre von Staat und Kirche*, pp. 164-173. Bohatec

argues that Calvin's view of the origin of the state must be distinguished from Aristotle's. Calvin did not locate the reason for the state's origin in the natural communal drive of the human being but in God's ordinance.

61. On the Anabaptist understanding of the state see: Willem Balke, *Calvin and the Anabaptist Radicals*, tr. W.J. Heynen (Grand Rapids: Eerdmans, 1981), pp. 193–195, 260–265; Robert Friedmann, "The Doctrine of the Two Worlds," in *The Recovery of the Anabaptist Vision* (Scottsdale, PA: Herald, 1957):105–118; Robert Kreider, "The Anabaptist and the State," in *The Recovery of the Anabaptist Vision*, pp. 180–193.

62. Comm. on Rom. 13:1, *Commentarius*, pp. 281–282.

63. *Brieve instruction*, CO 7:49–142. For discussions of the radical differences between the views of the state held by the Anabaptists and Calvin, see Bohatec, *Calvins Lehre von Staat und Kirche*, and Balke, *Calvin and the Anabaptist Radicals*. At Neuchâtel in 1544 the *Confessio Schlattensis* or Schleitheim Confession was translated from the German (*Brüderliche Vereinigung*). Jean Chaponneau, pastor at Neuchâtel, gave a copy to Farel who in turn sent a copy to Calvin; see Balke, *Calvin and the Anabaptist Radicals*, pp. 174–175.

64. *Brieve instruction*, CO 7:84.

65. Bohatec criticized Troeltsch for identifying Calvin's perfectionism with that of the Anabaptists. According to Bohatec, Calvin developed a relative perfectionism in contrast to the absolute perfectionism of the Anabaptists (*Calvins Lehre von Staat und Kirche*, pp. 302–345). Several historians, however, have questioned the identification of all Anabaptists with the doctrine of perfectionism: Robert Friedmann, "The Essence of the Anabaptist Faith, an Essay in Interpretation," *Mennonite Quarterly Review*, 41 (April 1967):5–24; Hans J. Hillerbrand, "Anabaptism and the Reformation: Another Look," *Church History* 29 (Jan. 1960):404–424. These historians conclude that for the Anabaptists, perfection was the ultimate goal of the earthly life. Both point out, however, that although the Anabaptist texts speak of a perfection found in separation from the world, there are admissions by Anabaptists that they were not sinless. Hillerbrand concluded, "It can only be conjectured that, seen in the larger context of the Anabaptist view of justification, perfection was for the Anabaptist, unlike the Reformers, the potential goal, though not necessarily the empirical reality," p. 424. For an analysis of Calvin's attack on perfectionism see also Balke, *Calvin and the Anabaptist Radicals*, 228ff.

66. Michael Sattler, *Schleitheim Confession*, 1527, tr. John Yoder, *The Legacy of Michael Sattler* (Scottsdale, PA: Herald, 1973), pp. 37–38. See also: Clarence Baumer, "The Theology of the 'Two Kingdoms,' A Comparison of Luther and the Anabaptists," *Mennonite Quarterly Review* (Jan. 1964):37–49.

67. *Inst.* III.10.1–6.

68. Ibid., III.3.10–14, IV.1.17.

69. *Brieve instruction*, CO 7:66. *Treatise Against the Anabaptists and the Libertines*, pp. 58–59.

70. *Inst.* III.19.15. On Calvin's criticism of the Anabaptists for failing to distinguish between the civil and spiritual kingdoms see Balke, *Calvin and the Anabaptist Radicals*, p. 290. As Balke points out, "Calvin was convinced that it was not too long a step from the *ecclesiola* of the *perfecti* which existed defenselessly in the midst of a godless world and waited patiently for the coming of the kingdom, to the sect of the *fanatici*."

71. *Inst.* IV.20.1; *Inst.* (1536) VI.35.

72. Ibid., IV.20.2.

73. Ibid., II.8.35. For a discussion of this theme in Calvin's sermons see Erwin Mülhaupt, *Die Predigt Calvins: ihre Geschichte, ihre Form und ihre religiösen Grundgedanken* (Berlin: Walter de Gruyer, 1931), pp. 95–103.

74. Harmony of the Five Books of Moses, Lev. 19:3, CO 24:606–607.

75. Sermon on Eph. 5:28–30, CO 51:765. See also: sermon on Eph. 5:15–18, CO 51:716; sermon on Job 12:1–6, CO 33:566; sermon on Job 20:8–15, CO 34:161.

76. Sermon on Eph. 4:6–8, CO 51:529–30; Comm. on Is. 3:4, CO 36:82.

77. Calvin frequently referred to the idea that if people did not act morally or in accordance with "nature," they became bestial. Calvin may have been borrowing this theme from several classical sources popular in the sixteenth century. Human transformation into animals is a frequent theme in Ovid's *Metamorphoses*. Ovid's popularity reached its height in the twelfth to the fourteenth centuries; once established, Ovid continued to be one of the best-known classical authors. Translations of the *Metamorphoses* into more or less allegorized versions were produced in great numbers. In the sixteenth century there were versions in English, German, Italian, Spanish, and French. See Mary M. Innes, "Introduction" to Ovid, *Metamorphoses* (London: Penguin, 1955), pp. 18–24.

The notion that a human being is changed into an animal as an outward manifestation of the psychological condition of a person's soul is a dominant theme of Apuleius' *Transformations of Lucius*, or *The Golden Ass*. Apuleius doubtlessly derived his main inspiration from Plato's *Phaedo* 81D–82A. Apuleius was widely known among Christian writers including Augustine (*De civitate Dei* IX.18.18), Lactantius (*Inst*. II.15, V.3), Jerome (Psalm I:18), and Apollinaris Sidonius (Ep. II.10.5, VI.3.1). See: Carl Weyman, "Studien zu Apuleius und seinen Nachahmern," in *Sitzungsberichte Akademie der Wissenschaften zu Munichen*, II:321–392. Apuleius was enormously influential in the Middle Ages and the Renaissance. In the fourteenth to the nineteenth centuries, Apuleius enjoyed a wide audience in Italy, Spain, France, and Germany. See: Elizabeth H. Haight, *Apuleius and His Influence* (New York: Cooper Square, 1963), pp. 90–134.

It is noteworthy that the theme of man becoming bestial also appears in a Renaissance author such as Pietro Pomponazzi. Arguing from man's centrality in the universe and his twofold nature, Pomponazzi stated: "Therefore, the human soul also has some of the properties of the intelligences and some of the properties of material things. Hence it is that, when it performs functions through which it agrees with the intelligences, it is said to be divine and changed into gods; but when it performs functions of the beasts, it is said to be changed into a beast; for by reason of its malice it is called a serpent or fox by reason of its cruelty, a tiger, and so on." (Cited by Paul Oskar Kristeller, "Ficino and Pomponazzi on the Place of Man in the Universe," p. 241.)

78. Comm. on Is. 34:12, CO 36:586.

79. Comm. on Is. 24:2, CO 36:400; Comm. on I Cor. 11:3, CO 49:474.

80. *Inst*. III.10.6. The citation is from Cicero, *De senectute* XX.73. See also: Comm. on Ps. 131:1, CO 32:339; Comm. on I Cor. 7:20–21, CO 49:415–416.

81. Sermon on Eph. 5:28–30, CO 51:759–772; sermon on Eph. 6:1–4, CO 51:787; sermon on Eph. 6:5–9, CO 51:800; sermon on 2nd book of Samuel 4:11–12, *Supplementa Calviniana* I:95.

82. Sermon on Eph. 6:5–9, CO 51:800: "Il est vray que là notamment il parle des princes et magistrats: mais quoy qu'il en soit, cela s'estend à toute authorité, comme celle que les peres ont sur leurs enfans, celle des maris envers leurs femmes, et des maistres sur leurs serviteurs. Nous devons donc avoir ceci bien persuadé, que Dieu n'a point voulu que les hommes fussent pesle mesle, comme il en adviendroit sinon qu'il y eust quelque bride: mais que les uns dominent, et qu'ils ayent le credit de commander aux autres, et que ceux qui sont inferieurs leur obeissent." This appeal to order and fear of confusion also underlies Calvin's opinion that it is an abomination that women should rule. As Gloede points out, Calvin believed it was against "nature" or the "essence" of women to rule. To permit female rule, then, would reduce society to disorder (Gloede, *Theologia naturalis bei Calvin*, pp. 186–187).

83. Sermon on Deut. 19:14–15, CO 27:567. Calvin refused to grant the truth of this maxim, however, to the "papists."

84. *Inst*. IV.20.2.

85. Sermon on Job 1:9–12, CO 33:73.

86. *Inst*. IV.20.16. On the role of the conscience in Calvin's thought see M.E. Chenevière, *La Pensée politique de Calvin* (Genève: Ed. Labor, 1937), 46ff.; Bohatec, *Budé und Calvin*, pp. 384–385; David Lee Foxgrover, "John Calvin's Understanding of the Conscience," (Ph.D dissertation, Claremont Graduate School, 1978); Gloede, *Theologia naturalis bei Calvin*, pp. 103–134; Peter Pelkonen, "The Teaching of John Calvin on the Nature and Function of the Conscience,"

Lutheran Quarterly 21 (1969):77–88. Both Chenevière and Bohatec point out that Calvin differs from the Roman jurists and medieval theorists by arguing that the conscience, rather than reason, discerns natural law. On the role of conscience in discerning natural law see also Baur, *Gott, Recht und weltliches Regiment im Werke Calvins*, pp. 46–49. On the correspondence of the second table of the Law with the "order of nature" see Wallace, *Calvin's Doctrine of the Christian Life*, pp. 141–147.

87. *Inst*. IV.20.16.

88. Sermon on Job 10:7–15, CO 33:489 ". . . l'image de Dieu est imprimee en nous, d'autant que nous avons intelligence et raison, que nous discernons entre le bien et le mal, que les hommes sont nais pour avoir quelque ordre, quelque police entre eux: qu'un chacun a sa conscience qui lui rend tesmoignage que cela est mauvais que cela est bon." See also sermon on Job 35:8–11, CO 35:238–239.

89. Comm. on Gen. 4:15, CO 23:96–97; Harmony of the Five Books of Moses, Ex. 20:13, CO 24:611–612; sermon on 2nd book of Samuel 4:11–12, *Supplementa Calviniana* I:95ff.

90. Comm. on Gen. 38:8, CO 23:495.

91. Harmony of the Five Books of Moses, Ex. 22:25, CO 24:679.

92. *Inst*. II.2.13. Calvin may be relying on Aristotle, *Politics* I.2 (1252a.25–1253.18). Calvin, of course, attributed the origin of these "natural instincts" and "universal impressions" to God.

93. Comm. on Gen. 2:18, CO 23:46–47; Comm. on I Tim. 2:13, CO 52:277.

94. Comm. on Gen. 26:16, CO 23:362–363.

95. Sermon on Eph. 5:28–30, CO 51:759, 762.

96. Comm. on Deut. 22.22, CO 24:648. Calvin diverged from traditional discussions regarding natural law and polygamy. Augustine had defended the polygamy of the patriarchs on the basis of custom and the necessity for procreation. Medieval authors often distinguished between absolute and secondary precepts, noting that God could dispense with the latter in order to procure a greater good (St. Bernard, *Liber de praecepto et dispensatione*, ch. II–III; PL 182:863–865). (Cf. Thomas Aquinas, *In IV Sent*. d.33, q.1, art. 2, in Lottin, *Le Droit naturel*, pp. 31–93.) Calvin made no such exception: polygamy is always a sin and, therefore, Jacob departed from the law of God when he married Bilhah. God, Calvin added, may decide to bring good out of an adulterous union, but polygamy is not thereby condoned.

97. Comm. on Gen. 31:50, 38:24, CO 23:433,499.

98. Comm. on Gen. 38:26, CO 23:500; Harmony of the Five Books of Moses, Lev. 18:6, CO 24:661–662; sermon on 2nd Samuel 20:2–10, *Supplementa Calviniana* I:358,585–586.

99. Harmony of the Five Books of Moses, Lev. 18:6, CO 24:662; sermon on Deut. 22:25–30, CO 28:61,63.

100. Harmony of the Five Books of Moses, Lev. 18:6, CO 24:662–623.

101. Comm. on I Tim. 5:8, CO 52:309; Comm. on I Cor. 7:37, CO 49:425; Harmony of the Five Books of Moses 20:12, CO 24:602–603; sermon on Deut. 21:18–21, CO 27:686–687; sermon on Eph. 5:31,33, 6:1–4, CO 51:774,788.

102. *Inst*. II.2.15.

103. *Inst*. IV.20.8; Cf. Plato, *The Statesman* 291D; idem, *The Republic* VIII.

104. Comm. on Is. 3:4, CO 36:82. Calvin may have been referring to *Laws* XII where Plato stated that the guardian must have a knowledge of the gods. Plato also wrote in *Laws* VI.762–763 that the service of the law is the service of the gods. In *Laws* IV.709 he affirmed God's providence over human legislation. Nonetheless, in these texts Plato did not state that God "appointed" rulers.

105. *Inst*. IV.20.24. Cf. *Calvin's Commentary on Seneca's "De clementia"*, ed. Battles, I.XIV. Seneca used this phrase in *De clementia* I.XIV.2.

106. *Inst*. IV.20.14. Cf. Cicero, *Laws* II.IV, V.1; Plato, *Laws* IX.875. Most likely Calvin is relying here on Aristotle, *Nicomachean Ethics* V.4 (1132a, 20–22) which states that "the nature of the judge is to be a sort of animate justice. . . ."

107. *Inst*. IV.20.16. See also: Comm. on Gen. 29:17, CO 23:402; Comm. on Hab. 2:6, CO 43:540; Comm. on Matt. 10:21, CO 45:284.

108. *Brieve instruction*, CO 7:87ff.; *Contre la secte phantastique et furieuse des Libertins*, CO 7:103, 214–220. Comm. on Ps. 74:17, CO 31:698. On Hutterite communism see: Robert Friedmann, "The Christian Communism of the Hutterite Brethren," *Mennonite Quarterly Review* (April 1955):196–208; Williams, *The Radical Reformation*, pp. 429–436. For a discussion of the idea of property in the Middle Ages cf: A.J. Carlyle, "The Theory of Property in Medieval Theology," in *Property: Its Duties and Rights* (London: Macmillan, 1913), pp. 119–132.

109. Sermon on Deut. 19:14–15, CO 27:566.

110. Sermon on Deut. 19:14–15, CO 27:566–567: "Mais tant y a que nous voyons ce principe c'est que nature a tousiours enseigné, que si les bornes n'estoyent tenues et observees, il y auroit une horrible confusion entre les hommes, et que nulles loix ne seroyent plus gardees. . . . Car quand quelcun demande à s'eslargir, c'est autant comme s'il violoit l'ordre de nature. Voila Dieu qui a destingué les peuples: et c'est afin que tous vivent, communiquans les uns avec les autres, et qu'il n'y ait point une confusion desordonnee. Voila donc comme chacun se devroit contenter de ses limites." See also: Bohatec, *Calvin und das Recht*, pp. 61–65, 72ff.; Harmony of the Five Books of Moses, Ex. 16:17, CO 24:171. Calvin denied the traditional argument that private property came into being only after the Fall.

111. Sermon on Deut. 19:8–13, CO 27:563–564; sermon on Deut. 19:16–21, CO 27:588; sermon on Deut. 25:13–19, CO 28:236–237; Harmony of the Five Books of Moses, Lev. 19:35, CO 24:675.

112. Luther, *De servo arbitrio*, WA 18.720–21, 748–753; Brian Gerrish, *Grace and Reason* (Oxford: Clarendon, 1962), 25ff.

113. F. Edward Cranz, *An Essay on the Development of Luther's Thought on Justice, Law, and Society*, Harvard Theological Studies, No. 19 (Cambridge, MA: Harvard U. Press, 1959); Gerrish, *Grace and Reason*, 76ff.

114. WA 39–I.227.1, 230.4, 231.1; WA 40–I.370.23. See also: Gerrish, *Grace and Reason*, p. 73.

115. Gerrish, *Grace and Reason*, p. 76; Walter von Loewenich, *Luther's Theology of the Cross*, tr. Herbert A. Bouman (Minneapolis: Augsburg, 1976), pp. 58–76.

116. WA 40–I.365.15–30, 370.12.17.

117. WA 40–I.471.13.

118. Gerrish, *Grace and Reason*, 73ff.; Cranz, *An Essay on the Development of Luther's Thought on Justice, Law, and Society*, pp. 113–178.

119. Melanchthon, *Scholia in Epistulam Pauli ad Colossenses* MW IV.230–243.

120. Ibid., p. 235. Melanchthon defended philosophy as that which affirmed nothing except by certain reason or experience. For his concern with clear and certain knowledge obtained by natural philosophy, see *Initia doctrinae physicae* 13:179–189.

121. Melanchthon, *Scholia in Epistulam Pauli ad Colossenses* MW IV.230–234.

122. *Inst.* II.2.12–16.

123. On the issues of perfectionism and separatism, see Willem Balke, *Calvin and the Anabaptist Radicals*, pp. 248–252, 275–278; Bohatec, *Budé und Calvin*, pp. 298–299; idem, *Calvins Lehre von Staat und Kirche*, 302ff.; Walter Klassen, "The Anabaptist Critique of Constantinian Christendom," *Mennonite Quarterly Review* 55 (July 1987):218–231.

124. *Inst.* IV.20.2.

125. Ibid., IV.20.17; Comm. on I Cor. 6:7, CO 49:391–392; Harmony of the Five Books of Moses, Ex. 22:25, CO 24:680–683. See also: *Brieve instruction*, CO 7:93ff.; and John T. McNeill, "John Calvin on Civil Government." McNeill shows that Calvin was well informed about political matters and tried to influence the politics of France in a way beneficial to the Reformation. On this subject see Bohatec, *Calvin und das Recht*, 133ff. On Calvin's view of the active role that Christians are to play in the economic and political life of society see André Biéler, *Le Pensée économique et sociale de Calvin* (Geneva: Georg, 1959), pp. 281–292, 321ff., 378–478.

126. Comm. on Rom. 13:8–10, *Commentarius*, p. 287. Comm. on the Harmony of the Gospels, Matt. 7:12, CO 45:220.

127. Comm. on Is. 3:4, CO 36:82.

128. Comm. on Gen. 4:22, CO 23:100; *Inst.* II.2.14–16. See also Bohatec, *Budé und Calvin*, pp. 257–306.

129. Comm. on Is. 3:4, CO 36:82.

130. Comm. on Gen. 4:22, CO 23:100.

131. Ibid.

132. Comm. on I Cor. 1:17, CO 49:321–322.

133. Comm. on Titus 1:12, CO 52:414; Comm. on I Cor. 15:33, CO 49:554.

134. Sermon on Deut. 2:1–7, CO 26:9: ". . . mais si est-ce qu'il y a encores quelque communauté en general, que tous hommes doivent penser qu'ils sont formez à l'image de Dieu, qu'ils ont une nature commune entre eux. Et les Payens ont bien cognu cela. Ainsi donc quand nous n'aurons quelque discretion pour nous maintenir en paix et concorde, pour rendre le droit à un chacun, sans ravir le bien d'autruy, sans faire aucune extorsion ni excez: nous pervertissons l'ordre de nature, nous sommes pires que les bestes sauvages qui s'entrecognoissent quand elles sont d'une espece."

V. CREATION SET FREE

1. Standard works on Calvin's doctrine of sanctification include: A. Göhler, *Calvins Lehre von der Heiligung* (Munich: C. Kaiser, 1934); W. Kolfhaus, *Vom christlichen Leben nach Johannes Calvin*; R.S. Wallace, *Calvin's Doctrine of the Christian Life* (Edinburgh and London: Oliver & Boyd, 1959).

2. Heinrich Quistorp, *Calvin's Doctrine of the Last Things*, p. 185: "But although he [Calvin] speaks mostly of heaven only as the sphere of the perfected church and sees blessedness to consist in the purely spiritual vision and enjoyment of God, he turns aside from any mystical spiritualism which considers the visible things of creation to be wholly worthless in the final state of glory."

3. Milner, *Calvin's Doctrine of the Church*; Richard, *The Spirituality of John Calvin*; Wallace, *Calvin's Doctrine of the Christian Life*.

4. Comm. on Rom. 8:20, *Commentarius*, p. 174.

5. Comm. on Heb. 1:10, CO 55:18; Comm. on Ps. 102.26, CO 32:72–73.

6. Comm. on Ps. 102:26, CO 32:73.

7. Comm. on Rom. 8:20, *Commentarius*, p. 173.

8. Comm. on Heb. 1:10, CO 55:18.

9. On the eschatological interest among the Radical reformers see Williams, *The Radical Reformation*, esp. pp. 857–862.

10. Comm. on Rom. 8:21, *Commentarius*, pp. 174–175.

11. Comm. on II Peter 3:10, CO 55:476. See also Quistorp, *Calvin's Doctrine of the Last Things*, pp. 181–186. Richard argued that Luther believed creation would be fully destroyed at the end but that, in contrast, Calvin spoke of the renovation and renewal of the world, *The Spirituality of John Calvin*, p. 175. Luther's statements on eschatology and creation are both more dramatic and more confusing than those of Calvin. Unlike Calvin, Luther was convinced that the end of the world was imminent and referred frequently to signs of the coming judgment (Comm. on II Peter 3:10, WA 14.66; sermon on Matt. 24:32–33, WA 47:621,623). It is also true that Luther described the final conflagration which would fully dissolve and destroy the present creation (*Disputation on Justification*, WA 39,85; Comm. on II Peter 3:10, WA 14.66). Nevertheless, Luther also argued that creation would be transformed and renewed. Although he did not emphasize the concept of order in the way that Calvin did, he described the future creation as free from vanity, and the sun, moon, and stars as being renewed. At that time there will be neither mountains nor "noxious creatures" (Comm. on Rom 8:21, WA 56.373; Comm. on Is. 65:17, WA 312.562; Comm. on Ps. 8:3–4, WA 45.211–212). In the *Disputation Concerning Man* Luther stated that the "simple material" of the present creation will be the material for the future glorious form of creation. The most extensive treat-

ment of this subject in Luther's thought is found in Paul Althaus, *Die letzen Dinge* (Gütersloh: Bertelsmann, 1933), 351ff.

12. Comm. on I Cor. 15:28, CO 49:549–550. Against the spiritualized eschatology of the Libertines, Calvin wrote: "Et soyons certains selon le tesmoignage de l'Apostre (Heb. 11:40), que tous les sainctz Peres et Prophetes et autres fideles nous attendent, n'ayans point encor receu la couronne de gloire que Dieu leur a apprestée à fin que nous y pervenions tous ensemble. Et non seulement cela, mais aussi que toutes creatures nous tiennent compagnie, comme dict sainct Paul (Rom 8, 19ss), gemissans apres ie iour de nostre redemption, pour estre remises en leur premier estat, et estre retirées de la servitude où elles sont maintenant, à cause de noz pechez," CO 7:225. It is also important to note that Calvin refused to interpret Is. 65:17 and Matt. 24:35 as referring to a dissolution of the cosmos. Isaiah 65:17 teaches, Calvin thought, only that the "former times" are to be forgotten. Matt. 24:25 means only that we are not to judge Christ's words by the empirical evidence of change and instability in the world. Although Pilgram Marpeck was not Calvin's direct literary source in this controversy, the following passage illustrates the view Calvin opposed: "Time will cease to be. Sun, moon, stars, and everything that exists in time and for the sake of man (not created to remain eternally) must cease to be for the sake of that which is and must remain eternally (such as men and angels which are taken up into God and God into them). For there will no longer be any need for time nor the creatures of time such as animals, birds, fish, light, nor day. For in eternity time ceases and God himself is day and light. Darkness and night will [depart] from the light, the incarnate Word and Spirit, and go to its eternal place where no grace or creaturely light will ever again be seen. Only the hellish and eternally deadly fire is the revelation and illumination of everlasting torment. . . ." (From "Concerning the Love of God in Christ," cited in *The Writings of Pilgram Marpeck*, tr. William and Walter Klassen [Scottdale, PA: Herald, 1978], p. 536.)

13. Comm. on II Peter 3:10, CO 55:476. Cf. Comm. on Ps. 102:26, CO 32:72–73.

14. Comm. on Rom. 8:20, *Commentarius*, p. 174. See also: Comm. on Is. 65:17, CO 37:429; Comm. on Harmony of the Gospels, CO 45:245.

15. Margaret Miles, "Theology, Anthropology, and the Human Body in Calvin's *Institutes of the Christian Religion*," *Harvard Theological Review* 74 (July 1981):303–323.

16. *Inst.* III.25.6; *Psychopannychia*, CO 5:188.

17. Comm. on I Cor. 15:53, CO 49:563. See also: Quistorp, *Calvin's Doctrine of the Last Things*, pp. 133–142; James M. Stayer, *Anabaptists and the Sword* (Manhattan, KS: Coronado, 1976).

18. The argument in the *Institutes* is drawn from Calvin's correspondence with Socinus and can be found in CO 13:272–274, 307–311, 336–340. See also OS IV:443–444, a citation from the 1551 edition of the *Institutes*: "Ce qui est bien à noter contre la fantasie d'aucuns lesquelz imaginent que les hommes doyvent ressusciter prenans des corps tout noveaux, et non pas ceux qu'ilz ont maintenant vestuz. Or ce seul mot de Resurrection, singulierement quand il est attribué à la chair, est pour abbatre leur erreur. Car il n'est pas dit que Dieu créera d'autres corps à ses fideles apres que les premiers seront allez en pourriture, mais qu'ilz seront relevez en leur chair, en laquelle ilz estoyent decheuz."

19. Comm. on I Cor. 15:39, CO 49:547–548; *Inst.* III.25.8.

20. *Inst.* III.25.7.

21. Ibid.

22. Comm. on I Cor. 6:11, CO 49:395.

23. Comm. on II Cor. 7:1, CO 50:54.

24. Wallace, *Calvin's Doctrine of the Christian Life*, pp. 106–107; Richard, *The Spirituality of John Calvin*, pp. 111–116.

25. Richard Prins, "The Image of God in Adam and the Restoration of Man in Jesus Christ, A Study in John Calvin," *Scottish Theological Journal* 25 (1972):32–44. Prins argues that the contradiction in Calvin's reasoning regarding the development of man's restoration stems from his method in *Inst.* I.15.4. There he sought to derive the contents of the image from the renewal or a

restoration of the corrupted image. However, Calvin never rigorously followed that method because, as Prins shows, he never ascribed the life-giving Spirit to Adam. Consequently, in Calvin's interpretation of I Cor. 15:45, human renewal surpasses Adam's original creation.

26. Comm. on I Cor. 15:46, CO 49:559–560.

27. *Inst*. III.3.8–9. See also Comm. on Rom. 6:6, *Commentarius*, pp. 123–124.

28. *Inst*. II.3.9, cf. II.3.13.

29. Comm. on Phil. 2:13, CO 52:32.

30. *Inst*. II.5.14.

31. Ibid., II.5.15. The citation is from *De gratia et libero arbitrio* XX.41.

32. *Inst*. II.5.15.

33. Ibid., II.3.6: "Voluntatem dico aboleri, non quatenus est voluntas: quia in hominis conversione integrum manet quod primae est naturae: creari etiam novam dico, non ut voluntas esse incipiat, sed ut vertatur ex mala in bonam."

34. Ibid., II.7.13.

35. See also Richard, *The Spirituality of John Calvin*, 108ff.

36. *Inst*. III.6.3.

37. Ibid., III.6.5.

38. Ibid.

39. Ibid.

40. Ibid.

41. Comm. on John 1:13, CO 47:13.

42. *Inst*. II.1.9. See also: *Inst*. II.2.2; Comm. on Rom. 12:2, *Commentarius*, p. 266; Comm. on Col. 1:9, CO 52:81.

43. Comm. on Eph. 4:23, CO 51:208.

44. *Inst*. II.7.11–12, II.8.5–7. See also: Wallace, *Calvin's Doctrine of the Christian Life*, pp. 141–145.

45. Comm. on I Cor. 3:18, CO 49:359.

46. The definitions of implicit and unformed faith which Calvin attacked in III.2.2 and III.2.8 can be found in Lombard, *Sent*. III. dist. XXIII–XXV. Medieval theologians also distinguished between *fides quae creditur* which referred to the content of faith and *fides qua creditur* which designated the act of faith (dist. XXIII.3). The Christian was expected to believe implicitly on the basis of divine authority that which he did not yet fully understand. Lombard referred to this implicit faith in his chapter entitled *De fide simplicium* (dist. XXV.2).

In S.T. II.Iae.2.5–8. Thomas argued that Christians are required to believe explicitly in the articles of faith but that they may believe other matters implicitly. Moreover, just as angels have a fuller knowledge of the divine than do men, so too, those of a higher rank, whose office is to instruct others, must have a fuller and more explicit knowledge of those things which are to be believed. Therefore, explicit faith is not required of all equally (II.IIae.2.6.obj.1). See also: *De veritate* XIV.11. Aquinas insisted, however, that since grace has been revealed, all believers must have an explicit faith in the articles of the creed and the Incarnation, Passion, and Resurrection.

Calvin also attacked implicit faith in his letter to Sadoleto. Sadoleto assumed that when Calvin spoke of faith, he meant mere *credulitas*, or the assent of the mind without the infusion of love. For Sadoleto this faith was only the "first access" to God but was not sufficient for salvation. He argued further that Christians do not understand many things; judgments vary regarding true religion. In uncertain matters Christians are to follow the teaching of the church because the Spirit will preserve her in truth; since the church cannot fall into serious doctrinal error, one can implicitly trust her judgment. Calvin answered that such implicit submission was an "indolent theology" and that it left the believer unprepared for the spiritual warfare against the demons. Here again Calvin emphasized the activity of the Christian whose mind and will must be actively engaged in combat. These letters can be found in CO 5:365–416.

47. *Inst.* III.2.2. See also: Edward Dowey, *The Knowledge of God in Calvin's Theology* (New York: Columbia U. Press), pp. 167–172. Although Calvin attacked the notion of implicit faith, he did admit its existence. In *Inst.* III.2.4–5 he conceded that as long as we dwell as strangers in this world, "there is such a thing as implicit faith." He also was willing to admit the term as the proper description of the preparation for faith or the beginning of faith. He feared the suggestion of passivity and idleness implied by the term and emphasized that faith required a continual growth in knowledge or understanding. Rom. 10:10, according to Calvin, teaches that it is insufficient for one to believe implicitly what he does not understand; faith "requires explicit recognition of divine goodness upon which our righteous rests."

48. *Inst.* III.2.2.

49. Ibid., III.2.4.

50. Ibid., III.2.19.

51. Ibid., III.1.4. Calvin's statements about the necessity for the illumination of the mind by the Spirit reflects the hermeneutical crisis for certainty in the sixteenth century. Discussion of this crisis is beyond the scope of this study but needs further analysis by Reformation scholars. Briefly, the Catholic, Protestant, and Radicals all charged that the others could not interpret Scripture correctly. Theologians such as John Eck, then, shrewdly saw that this uncertainty about the final authority for interpretation was a major weakness of Luther's theology. Consequently, he opened his *Enchiridion Locorum Communium* with chapters about the authority of the Church, the councils, and the Apostolic See. Only then did he proceed to discuss Scripture. Calvin's emphasis on the work of the Spirit demonstrates his search for a locus of authority that would guarantee the certainty of interpretation. Some aspects of this crisis in authority and interpretation have been discussed by the following scholars: Karl Heim, *Das Gewissheitsproblem in der systematischen Theologie bis zu Schleiermacher* (Leipzig: J.C. Hinrichs, 1911), 220ff.; Richard Popkins, *The History of Skepticism from Erasmus to Descartes* (New York: Humanities, 1964), pp. 1–43. A brief discussion may also be found in Jeffrey Stout, *Flight from Authority* (Notre Dame: U. of Notre Dame Press, 1981), pp. 41–47.

52. On the third use of the Law as a means for a "well-ordered life" (*vitae bene compositae*), see also: John Hesselink, "Christ, the Law, and the Christian: An Unexplored Aspect of the Third Use of the Law in Calvin's Theology," in *Reformatio Perennis*, ed. B.A. Gerrish and Robert Benedetto (Pittsburg: Pickwick, 1981), pp. 11–26.

53. *Inst.* II.7.12.

54. Ibid., II.8.5.

55. Ibid., II.7.12.

56. Comm. on I Cor. 2:15, CO 49:345.

57. *Inst.* III.2.15; Comm. on John 1:13, CO 47:12. Cf. Peter Brunner, *Vom Glauben bei Calvin* (Tübingen: J.B.C. Mohr, 1925); Dowey, *The Knowledge of God in the Theology of John Calvin*, pp. 24–30; Walter E. Stuermann, *A Critical Study of Calvin's Concept of Faith* (Ann Arbor, MI: Edwards Brothers, 1952), pp. 62–123; Krusche, *Das Wirken des Heiligen Geistes nach Calvin*, 259ff.

58. *Inst.* III.2.14–15, III.2.38.

59. Ibid., III.2.16–23.

60. Ibid., III.2.17.

61. Ibid., III.2.17–20.

62. Ibid., III.2.23.

63. Ibid., III.2.21.

64. Ibid., I.VI.1–4, I.X.1–3; Dowey, *The Knowledge of God in Calvin's Theology*, 131ff. See also Paul Wernle, *Der evangelische Glaube nach Hauptschriften der Reformatoren* (Tübingen: Mohr, 1919), III:175; Brunner, *Nature and Grace*, in *Natural Theology*, p. 39.

65. *Inst.* I.6.1–4; Argument to Genesis, CO 23:10.

66. *Praefationes bibliis gallicis Petri Roberti Olivetani*, CO 9:791.

67. Comm. on Ps. 18:8, CO 31:174; sermon on Job 39:22–35.

68. Comm. on Ps. 75:3, 89:36, CO 31:701-702, 825; Comm. on Ps. 103:1, 136:4, 148:3, CO 32:75, 364, 433; sermon on Job 38:4-11, CO 35:366ff.; sermon on Eph. 2:11-13, CO 51:385ff.

69. Sermon on Job 5:8-10, CO 33:237: "Or il est vray que Dieu se declare à nous par sa parole, mais cependant si sommes nous inexcusables, quand nous ne l'aurons point consideré en ses oeuvres, comme là il ne se laisse point sans tesmoignage comme dit S. Paul au 14 des Actes parlant de l'ordre de nature qui est comme un miroir, auquel nous pouvons contempler que c'est de Dieu. Notamment donc S. Paul dit (Actes 14,17). que quand Dieu fait luire le soleil, qu'il envoye la pluye, qu'il envoye saisons diverses, qu'il fait fructifier la terre, en cela il ne se laisse point sans bon tesmoignage: c'est comme s'il plaidoit sa cause pour dire, Quand les hommes n'auront point cognu ma gloire et maiesté, n'auront point senti que i'ay tout en ma main pour gouverner les choses que i'ay creées, il ne faut point qu'ils alleguent ignorance: car en l'ordre de nature ils ont peu appercevoir qu'il y a un Createur qui dispose de tout. Ainsi donc ouvrons seulement les yeux, et nous aurons assez d'argumens pour nous monstrer quelle est la grandeur de Dieu, afin que nous apprenions de l'honorer comme il merite." See also: sermon on Job 12:7-16, CO 33:569; sermon on Job 18:1-11, CO 34:63-76; sermon on Job 31:5-8, CO 34:645; sermon on Job 39:22-35, CO 35:430; sermon on Job 40:7-19, CO 35:452.

70. Comm. on Ps. 104:3, CO 32:85-86.

71. On this dispute between Calvin and the Anabaptists see: Willem Balke, *Calvin and the Anabaptist Radicals*, pp. 309-313. As Balke points out, Stupperich has shown that not all Anabaptists were oriented predominately to the New Testament: R. Stupperich, *Die Schriften Bernhard Rothmanns* (Münster: Aschendorffsche Verlagsbuchhandlung, 1970). The Anabaptists of Münster, of course, were another exception. See also: Williams, *The Radical Reformation*, 304ff.; John C. Wenger, "The Biblicism of the Anabaptist," in *The Recovery of the Anabaptist Vision*, ed. G. F. Hershberger (Scottdale, PA: Herald, 1951), 167ff.

72. *Inst.* II.10.2. On Calvin's view of the relationship between the Old and New Testaments see: H.H. Wolf, *Die Einheit des Bundes. Das Verhältnis von Altem und Neuem Testament bei Calvin* (Neukirchen, Kreis Moers: Verlag der Buchhandlung des Erziehungsvereins, 1958); Wendel, *Calvin, The Origins and Development of His Religious Thought*, pp. 208-214; Milner, *Calvin's Doctrine of the Church*, pp. 71-98. See also: T.H.L. Parker, *Calvin's Old Testament Commentaries* (Edinburgh: T&T Clark, 1986), pp. 42-82.

73. *Inst.* II.9.1-II.10.23.

74. Ibid., II.10.7.

75. Comm. on Ezekiel 16:61, CO 40:395-396.

76. On the church as the agent of restoration of order in the world see also Milner, *Calvin's Doctrine of the Church*, pp. 46-70.

77. Comm. on Is. 65:25, CO 37:434.

78. Comm. on Eph. 1:10, CO 51:151; sermon on Eph. 3:9-12, CO 51:466.

79. Sermon on Eph. 3:9-16, CO 51:466.

80. Comm. on Acts 3:21, CO 48:72-73.

81. Comm. on John 12:31, CO 47:293; Richard, *The Spirituality of John Calvin*, p. 175.

82. Richard, *The Spirituality of John Calvin*, p. 114.

83. See also Wallace, *Calvin's Doctrine of the Christian Life*, 141ff. Wallace cites numerous passages which demonstrate Calvin's positive evaluation of the teaching and effectiveness of natural law. He tends, however, to overlook the "negative" function of natural law, i.e., that natural law causes shame and thereby keeps society from falling into chaos. One of Calvin's descriptions of the Christian life can be found in his exposition of the Sermon on the Mount.

84. Comm. on I Cor. 8:2, CO 49:429; *Inst.* II.2.4.

85. Comm. on I Cor. 8:2, CO 49:429.

86. See Wallace, *Calvin's Doctrine of the Christian Life*, 107ff. See also: André Biéler, *La pensée économique et sociale de Calvin*, pp. 246-269, 306ff., 436ff.

87. As Quistorp shows, Calvin believed that when Christ is victor over all his enemies, he

will restore the church to the government of God; see: Comm. on I Cor. 15:27, CO 49:549, and Quistorp, *Calvin's Doctrine of the Last Things*, pp. 165–171.

88. Comm. on I Cor. 15:24, CO 49:547. See also *Inst*. IV.21.1.

89. Comm. on I Cor. 15:24, CO 49:547. Calvin specifies, however, that angels will retain their distinctions.

90. Quistorp, *Calvin's Doctrine of the Last Things*, p. 193. Quistorp concludes: ". . . this spiritualizing tendency in the eschatology of Calvin was constantly interrupted and rectified by the influence on his teaching of Holy Scripture with its concrete hopes, especially in regard to the resurrection of the flesh as the resurrection of the body. The orientation of Calvin's eschatology (and of his theology) as a whole toward the general resurrection preserves its biblical character, even though that character is seriously threatened by the other aspect of his thought" (p. 193).

91. Comm. on I Thess. 5:23, CO 52:179.

92. *Inst*. I.16.9.

93. This theme runs throughout the sermons on Job. See, for example, sermon on Job 8:1–6, CO 33:373; sermon on Job 9:23–28, CO 33:447; sermon on Job 27:5–8, CO 34:462; sermon on Job 34:10–15, CO 35:146; sermon on Job 35:8–11, CO 35:231; sermon on Job 40:7–19, CO 35:458.

94. Sermon on Eph. 3:9–12, CO 51:462–463.

95. *Inst*. I.16.9, I.17.1–2. Charles Trinkaus, "Renaissance Problems in Calvin's Theology," *Studies in the Renaissance*, ed. W. Peery, I:65.

96. Martin Schulze, *Meditatio futurae vitae, Ihr Begriff und ihre herrschende Stellung im System Calvins* (Leipzig, 1901); idem, *Calvins Jenseitschristentum in seinem Verhältnis zu den religiösen Schriften des Erasmus* (Görlitz, 1902); Doumergue, *Jean Calvin—Les hommes et les choses de son temps* IV:309–314; Wallace, *Calvin's Doctrine of the Christian Life*, 130ff.; Richard, *The Spirituality of John Calvin*, 174ff.

VI. CONCLUSION

1. Luther, Lectures on Genesis 1:26, 3:17; WA 42.50.35, 153.5–35. For a discussion of this theme in previous commentaries see Arnold Williams, *The Common Expositor: An Account of the Commentaries on Genesis*.

2. Herbert Olsson, *Schöpfung, Vernunft und Gesetz in Luthers Theologie* (Uppsala: Appelbergs Boktryckeri, 1971), pp. 256–269.

3. Luther, Lectures on Genesis 3:1, WA 42.50.35ff. Cf. WA 42.90.10–30, 106.5–35.

4. Luther, Comm. on Romans, WA 56.372.3.

5. Luther, Lectures on Genesis 2:8, WA 42.68.35.

6. Marjorie Nicolson, *Mountain Gloom and Mountain Glory* (Ithaca: Cornell U. Press, 1959), pp. 100–104.

7. Luther, Lectures on Genesis 3:18, WA 42.156.5ff.

8. Nicolson, *Mountain Gloom and Mountain Glory*, pp. 96–104; George H. Williams, "Christian Attitudes Toward Nature," *Christian Scholars Review* 2/1 (Fall 1971):3–35 and 2/2 (Spring 1972):112–126. Both Nicolson and Williams mitigate Calvin's statements about the curse on creation. They argue that in comparison to Luther, Calvin held a more positive view of nature. While admitting that Calvin knew that the earth was not in its original form, Nicolson denies that Calvin thought nature reflected human sin. Williams contrasts the more positive views of Augustine and Calvin to the negative views of Chrysostom and Luther. Both Nicolson and Williams cite in support of their argument Calvin's comments on Gen 2:10: "Notwithstanding, I say that it is the same earth which was created in the beginning."

However, both authors take Calvin's statement out of context. In Genesis 2:10 Calvin was commenting on the topography of paradise and was confronted by the problem of the rivers. The entire passage reads as follows: "Yet it appears that the fountains of the Euphrates and the Tigris were far distant from each other. From this difficulty, some would free themselves by saying that the surface of the globe may have been changed by the destruction of the deluge; and therefore, they imagine it might have happened that the courses of the rivers were disturbed and changed, and their springs transferred elsewhere; a solution which seems to me by no means to be acceptable. For although I acknowledge that the earth, from the time that it was accursed, became reduced from its native beauty to a state of wretched defilement, and to a mournful state, and afterwards was further laid waste in many places by the deluge; notwithstanding, I say it was the same earth which had been created in the beginning." (CO 23:40) In the statement cited by Nicolson and Williams, Calvin was only referring to the topography of the earth, not to its nature or appearance after the Fall. Although it is true that the geography of the earth remained the same, nature itself reflected human sin.

As the first chapter of this study has shown, Calvin, like Luther, believed that the earth was infected by disorder brought on by sin. The beauty of the cosmos continued but the curse of sin was spread throughout nature. The beauty of the cosmos still reveals the nature of God, but the Fall is now reflected in this changed "theater of His glory." Moreover, Nicolson appears to contradict her own thesis about Calvin on p. 99 where she quotes Calvin's comments on Gen. 3:18. Here Calvin *agreed* that with the increasing wickedness of humanity, the remaining blessings of God are gradually diminished and impaired. He was only denying the theory of the earth's "exhaustion" by the succession of time.

9. Heinrich Bornkamm, *Luther and the Old Testament*, tr. Eric and Ruth Gritsch (Philadelphia: Fortress, 1969), pp. 57–64; idem, *Luther's World of Thought*, tr. H. Bertram (St. Louis: Concordia, 1965), pp. 431–462. Werner Elert, *The Structure of Lutheranism*, 2 vols., tr. Walter A. Hansen (St. Louis: Concordia, 1962), I:431–462.

10. Herbert Olsson, *Schöpfung, Vernunft und Gesetz in Luthers Theologie*, pp. 369–375, 393–397.

11. Bornkamm, *Luther and the Old Testament*, 60ff. See also WA 38.53.15ff., WA 31.1.407.28ff., WA 31.1.447.15ff.

12. Zwingli, *De providentia* CR 93 (*Huldreich Zwinglis sämtliche Werke*) VI:97–83. English translation: Zwingli, *On Providence and Other Essays*, tr., Samuel Macauley Jackson (Durham, NC: Labyrinth, 1983), pp. 146–147.

13. Zwingli, *De providentia*, CR 93:83: "Causas secundas iniuria causas vocari; quod methodus est ad providentiae cognitionem." See also CR 93:111. For a thorough treatment of Zwingli's treatise on providence and his geographical arguments see Manfred Büttner, *Die Geographia generalis vor Varenius* (Weisbaden: Franz Steiner, 1973), pp. 85–113; idem, *Regiert Gott die Welt?* (Stuttgart: Calwer Verlag, 1975), 23ff.

14. Zwingli, *De providentia* CR 93:112, Jackson transl., p. 156.

15. Zwingli, *De providentia*, CR 93:111–115. Zwingli argued that all things are preserved by the elements of food, air, sun, and water. Nonetheless, these things are "lifeless" by nature and used by God so that they are more properly called instruments than causes: "Porro cum natura sint inanima, attamen animatis omnibus divina liberalitas ex eis et per ea fomenta suppeditet, constat instrumenta rectius vocari quam causas. Causa enim nisi unica esse nequit; nam ut origo unica est rerum universarum, ita et causam unicam esse oportet," p. 113.

16. Zwingli, *De providentia*, CR 93:99.

17. Ibid. CR 93:224.

18. Ibid.

19. Ibid., Jackson transl. p. 229.

20. Rolf Bernard Huschke, *Melanchthons Lehre vom Ordo politicus* (Gütersloh: Gerd Mohn, 1960). Huschke lists the references to and the different meanings of the concept of order found throughout Melanchthon's writings. The idea of order is particularly important in the treatises *Initia doctrinae physicae* and *Loci praecipui theologici*, 1559.

21. Melanchthon, *Loci praecipui theologici*, 1559, MW II/I:220–221. On Melanchthon's doctrine of providence see also Büttner, *Regiert Gott die Welt?*, 50ff.; idem, *Die Geographia generalis vor Varenius*, 113ff.

22. *Loci praecipui theologici*, 1559, MW II/I:215–219, 222. The subject of creation became increasingly important in the successive editions of the *Loci*. In the 1521 edition, Melanchthon argued that he would follow St. Paul and refuse to speculate on issues such as "God," "unity and trinity of God," and the "mystery of creation." In the 1535 edition he treated these same topics which he formerly labeled "scholastic." He taught the doctrine of *creatio ex nihilo* and the perpetual sustenance and preservation of the world by God. He called the Epicureans atheists because they corrupted natural philosophy which should have led them to a study of the footprints of God in creation. From 1543 on, the sections entitled *De creatione* were constructed as a polemic against both the Stoics and Epicureans. Against the Stoics Melanchthon argued that God remained a free agent, independent of secondary causality. In opposition to the Epicureans, he emphasized the impossibility that order could arise from chance or matter.

23. Melanchthon, *Loci praecipui theologici*, 1559, MWII/1:238, 313ff.; *Liber de anima* CR 13:150; *Initia doctrinae physicae*, CR 13:181. See also, *Erotemata dialectica*, CR 13:649; *Scholia Epistulam Pauli ad Colossenses*, MW IV:230ff.

24. On Melanchthon's doctrine of natural law see Bauer, "Melanchthons Naturrechtslehre."

25. Robert Stupperich, "The Development of Melanchthon's Theological-Philosophical World-View," *Lutheran World* 7 (1960):168–180. See also *Loci praecipui theologici*, 1559, MW II/1:214ff.; *De astronomia et geographia*, CR 11:292,297; *Initia doctrinae physicae* CR 13:189.

26. Melanchthon, *Loci praecipui theologici*, 1559, MW II/I:221–223. See also: *Oratio de Aristotele*, MW III:133–134; *Initia doctrinae physicae*, CR 13:181,189,198.

27. Letter to Sadoleto, CO 5:368.

28. *Inst.* III.10.2. See also Comm. on Gen. 4:20, CO 23:99–100.

29. Brunner, *Nature and Grace*; Torrance, *Calvin's Doctrine of Man*; Gloede, *Theologia naturalis bei Calvin*; Dowey, *The Knowledge of God in Calvin's Theology*; Parker, *The Doctrine of the Knowledge of God in Calvin's Theology* (Grand Rapids: Eerdmans, 1959), p. 49.

30. Comm. on Gen. 3:17, CO 23:73.

Index